# Angel on a Freight Train

# Angel on a Freight Train

*A Story of Faith and Queer Desire in Nineteenth-Century America*

Peter C. Baldwin

Cover image: Samuel Edward Warren with unidentified young man, circa 1870. On back is written: "The Patience of Hope, or Showing Him His Mark," AC 18, Institute Archives and Special Collections, Rensselaer Polytechnic Institute, Troy, New York.

Published by State University of New York Press, Albany

© 2020 State University of New York

All rights reserved

No part of this book may be used or reproduced in any manner whatsoever without written permission. No part of this book may be stored in a retrieval system or transmitted in any form or by any means including electronic, electrostatic, magnetic tape, mechanical, photocopying, recording, or otherwise without the prior permission in writing of the publisher.

For information, contact State University of New York Press, Albany, NY
www.sunypress.edu

Library of Congress Cataloging-in-Publication Data

Name: Baldwin, Peter C., author.
Title: Angel on a freight train : a story of faith and queer desire in nineteenth-century America / Peter C. Baldwin, author.
Description: Albany : State University of New York Press, [2020] | Includes bibliographical references and index.
Identifiers: ISBN 9781438479958 (hardcover : alk. paper) | ISBN 9781438479941 (pbk. : alk. paper) | ISBN 9781438479965 (ebook)
Further information is available at the Library of Congress.

10 9 8 7 6 5 4 3 2 1

# Contents

| | |
|---|---|
| List of Illustrations | vii |
| Acknowledgments | ix |
| Introduction: Words, Flesh, and Spirit | 1 |
| Chapter 1. Friendship | 19 |
| Chapter 2. Teaching | 49 |
| Chapter 3. Evangelism | 75 |
| Chapter 4. Fatherhood | 101 |
| Epilogue: The Cross, the Grave, the Skies | 129 |
| Abbreviations in Notes | 139 |
| Notes | 141 |
| Index | 185 |

# Illustrations

Figure I.1.  Part of the entry for June 9, 1849, from Volume 2 of Warren's journal. Courtesy, Archives and Special Collections, Thomas Dodd Research Center, University of Connecticut, Storrs, Conn.  4

Figure 1.1.  Page from Volume 8 of the Journal. Courtesy, the Winterthur Library, Joseph Downs Collection of Manuscripts and Printed Ephemera.  29

Figure 2.1.  Charlton Schoolhouse No. 2, Charlton, Mass. (built 1848), where Warren taught in the fall of 1849. Photo by author, 2019.  61

Figure 2.2.  Warren as an RPI faculty member, ca. 1869 or 1870, AC 18, Institute Archives and Special Collections, Rensselaer Polytechnic Institute, Troy, New York.  69

Figure 3.1  Crude erasures in Warren's Journal, volume 7, 1994–6, Samuel Edward Warren papers, Institute Archives and Special Collections, Rensselaer Polytechnic Institute, Troy, New York.  89

Figure 4.1.  Erastus Dow Palmer, "Morning Star," (c. 1851–1855), marble, 20 in. diameter. Minneapolis Institute of Art, anonymous gift in memory of Mr. and Mrs. Palmer Jaffray, accession number 89.124.2. Photo: Minneapolis Museum of Art.  114

Figure 4.2. Digitally enhanced image of an erasure from Warren's Journal, Volume 2. Courtesy, Archives and Special Collections, Thomas Dodd Research Center, University of Connecticut, Storrs, Conn. Digital enhancement by Mark R. Smith of Macroscopic Solutions, LLC. 125

# Acknowledgments

In completing an academic book, there is no moment of achievement that seems to demand champagne. Every step is incremental and slow. You certainly wouldn't pop open the bubbly when you write the last word of the first draft, knowing that many drafts lie ahead. Nor does it seem worth celebrating when the manuscript goes to the publisher or when it passes peer review. Signing the contract is a formality, checking page proofs is a chore, and by the time the box of books arrives in the mail you've long since moved on to other projects. For me, *this* is the closest approximation to the finish line: writing the acknowledgments. During long years of working through this unexpectedly difficult project, I looked forward to the moment when I could thank the people who helped me along the way.

I started the project with modest ambitions. I built up more enthusiasm and new ideas as I talked about S. Edward Warren with my sister Sarah Baldwin Evangelista and my friend Randy Burgess, and when I shared a rough precis with my colleagues Alexis Boylan and Sylvia Schafer. Richard Brown, Howard Chudacoff, Patricia Cline Cohen, Timothy Gilfoyle, Robert Gross, and Peter Stearns all supported me in seeking funding for the project.

A year's fellowship at the University of Connecticut Humanities Institute gave me time for uninterrupted research and for initial formulation of the narrative. While there, I benefited from the helpful suggestions of Mohammed Albakry, Bob Gross, Sharon Harris, Jessica Linker, and Nicola McDonald. Jessica Linker deserves special thanks for volunteering many hours to helping me decipher the manuscripts; assisting me also in grant writing, she was invaluable in leading me rethink and refocus my interpretation of S. Edward Warren. Mark R. Smith took some amazing digitally enhanced photos of the manuscripts; financial support for this work came from the Felberbaum Family Foundation and the James L. and Shirley A. Draper Chair in American History.

I am grateful for the assistance of archivists and librarians at the American Antiquarian Society, Amherst College, the Charlton Historical Society, the Emma Willard School, the Harriet Beecher Stowe Center, Harvard University's Houghton Library, the Jackson Homestead and Museum in Newton, the Massachusetts Archives, the Massachusetts Historical Society, the Massachusetts Institute of Technology, the Newburyport Public Library, the New England Historic Genealogical Society, the New York State Library, Phillips Academy Andover, the Rensselaer County Historical Society, the Rensselaer Polytechnic Institute, Stevens Institute of Technology, the University of Delaware, the University of Connecticut, and the Winterthur Library. UConn Archivist Betsy Pittman and RPI Assistant Archivist Jenifer Monger were especially helpful and supportive. Frank Morrill of the Charlton Historical Society kindly showed me the places where Warren worked, lived, and walked.

Numerous people offered comments and suggestions in response to hearing my presentations or reading drafts of portions of the manuscript. Among the many helpful readers were Christopher Clark, Martha Cutter, Clare Eby, Kathryn Lofton, Vicki Magley, Susan Matt, Shawn Salvant, Nancy Shoemaker, and Chris Vials. I am particularly grateful to Dick Brown for reading and extensively commenting on the first completed draft. Thanks also to the editors at the State University of New York Press, Rebecca Colesworthy and Amanda Lanne-Camilli, and senior production editor Diane Ganeles; the copyeditor, Alan Hewat; and the peer reviewers (William Benemann, Janet Moore Lindman, and John Corrigan).

Throughout the long travail of writing and publishing the book, I was fortunate to have the encouragement and advice of wonderful colleagues, including Dick Brown, Pat Cohen, Frank Costigliola, Cornelia Dayton, Bob Gross, Micki McElya, Nancy Shoemaker, and Manisha Sinha. As always, I relied on the support of the efficacious Vicki Magley.

There are no doubt others I have neglected to thank. I may remember them later, with embarrassment and a slap to the forehead. (My apologies in advance.) But by then the book will be out and this project will have finally come to an end.

# Introduction

## *Words, Flesh, and Spirit*

> When I was a child, I spake as a child, I understood as a child, I thought as a child: but when I became a man, I put away childish things.
>
> —1 Corinthians 13:11

Professor Samuel Edward Warren loved to save boys and young men from sin, especially boys who struck him as pretty and young men who seemed sensitive or confused. An opportunity arose one day in 1860 as he walked the unpaved streets of Troy, New York: a loose ball from a boys' game bounced into his path. Deep in thought as he tended to be on his walks, the grave young professor may have been too slow to stoop and make the catch, or perhaps he was disinclined to touch the grubby toy with his fingers. He simply turned his foot to stop the ball and watched as the pursuing boy ran up to him. The child had been cursing, much to Warren's chagrin, but his profanity stopped and his frown cleared when he saw what the bearded gentleman had done. He flashed a brilliant smile before recovering the ball. As the boy ran back to his friends the professor walked on alone, pondering what had just happened.

Two lives, two very different consciousnesses, had briefly crackled into contact, and the encounter had seemed blessed. Warren had succeeded, he wrote, in performing God's work on this "providential occasion of putting an end to another's sin."[1] But the human connection was weak and fleeting, a pale ghost of the full-blooded engagement with young sinners that Warren had once enjoyed. In his adolescence, Warren had cultivated intense friendships with slightly younger boys. He would draw, read, and sing with them, and when the time felt right he would engage them in conversation on the state of their souls. With a few, he became intimate, sealing their Christian brotherhood with kisses and loving embraces in bed.

There, then, and among Warren's sort of people—affluent Northeasterners in the years before the Civil War—such behavior was understood very differently from how it would be today. Emotionally intense and physically affectionate pairings were commonplace among "youths": males and females in the transitional phase of life between young childhood and mature adulthood. These "romantic friendships," as scholars have called them, were not seen as signs of a homosexual orientation in either partner. Friends held hands and hugged, and shared beds for affection as well as convenience. "Physical contact was an incidental part of sharing a bed, but it happened—and in the context of a very affectionate relationship, this contact could express warmth or intimacy. It could even express erotic desire," observed one of the early scholars of male romantic friendship, Anthony Rotundo. "A wide spectrum of possible meanings, from casual accident to passion, could be felt in the touch of a bedmate. In the absence of a deep cultural anxiety about homosexuality, men did not have to worry about the meaning of those moments of contact." As the evidence is thin, scholars such as Richard Godbeer have been cautious in discussing the extent of erotic behavior between men in such circumstances, thus seeming to imply asexuality. William Benemann has leaned in the other direction, emphasizing that "a romantic friendship might indeed have included a sexual component. . . . A fluidity to male intimacy admitted a wide repertoire of physical expression." The frequency of sexual behavior is impossible to determine, but the point is that romantic friendship (and the practice of bed sharing with which it often overlapped) afforded opportunities for two males to ease comfortably into erotic relations.[2]

Americans had not yet come to see sexual preferences as distinguishing markers of personal identity, symptoms of an inherent nature as heterosexual or homosexual. The antebellum Northeast, in which Warren grew up and developed his relationships, was generally accepting of male love before full adulthood. Expressions of affection might be unusually strong, but love between youths was accepted and admired, understood to be rooted in emotions even if it was expressed physically. Such feelings could be problematic only if love turned to unrestrained lust and led to sinful actions—notably sodomy, considered an egregious crime far different from mere caressing. The erotic side of intimate friendships was winked at among male youths, but was expected to be left behind with the start of careers, marriages, and full adulthood. The friendships, as they receded into fond memories, suggested to most observers no lasting alternative to marrying a woman.[3] Gradually, in their twenties, friends and bedmates moved off into marriages, leaving behind a shrinking minority of bachelors. Many men whose strongest erotic desires were for women remained bachelors by choice. Having experienced same-sex intimacies as precursors to adult intercourse with women, they embraced a bachelor subculture and a mature sexuality focused on the brothel. It was a very different matter for bachelors to seek same-sex encounters with youths, or to habitually engage in full sexual relations with other men—though the bachelor subculture in big cities such as New York did provide such opportunities.[4]

Men who preferred males to females must have faced the end of youth as a time of anxious transition or painful loss, as their field of potential lovers contracted drastically. This suspicion seems unavoidable, but historians have uncovered limited documentary evidence through which we can explore such an experience. That is what this book will do, using the previously unexamined journals of that introspective professor, Samuel Edward Warren, who lived in Massachusetts and upstate New York from 1831 to 1909. These journals provide a glimpse into profound desires for, and relationships with, other males. They reveal first the freedom and sensuality of youthful romantic friendships, then an attempt to join with younger men in a spirit of loving mentorship, and then the tortured introspection of an adult whose age seemed to shut him out from an idyllic lost world.

Warren's deepest sense of identity throughout the period covered by the journals was as a Christian—first a Congregationalist and then an Episcopalian. He had seen no conflict in his teenage years and early twenties between his love of God and his love of youths. In mature adulthood, though, as his friends and peers drifted off into relationships with women, Warren's encounters with other males began to feel odder and more shameful. Protestant religious communities offered some of his contemporaries the chance to build loving relationships with those of the same sex, but Warren proved unsuccessful in this respect. By the spring of 1860, when he ruminated in his journal about the incident with the ball, the twenty-eight-year-old Warren had become painfully aware of a struggle between his higher spiritual nature—which aspired to the purity of angels—and what he called "the freight train of animal life below."[5] He was trying to redirect his affections into a dignified fatherly role, but he missed the freedoms and pleasures of youth. When the smiling boy ran back to his ballgame, Warren must have resumed his solitary walk with a heavy heart and a grim determination to trust in God.

†

My sense of Warren's life began (as all things are said to begin) with words: neatly inked words in a graceful running hand. I came across his words as I was rummaging through a box of old, poorly catalogued diaries in the University of Connecticut's special collections. Skimming through his school news and notes of sermons, I was startled to find a page that had been carefully edited. In a passage that began, "Last night my dear John slept with me . . . ," the words immediately following had been scraped from the page and "we enjoyed ourselves" had been written to partially fill the gap. The passage went on to reveal that the two enjoyed themselves "beyond even my expectations. We had the . . . best time that ever could be, before going to sleep. We woke up and frolicked a little then went off a little after five as he had to be at home early."[6] If the author was willing to say this much, I wondered, what had he chosen to conceal, and why?

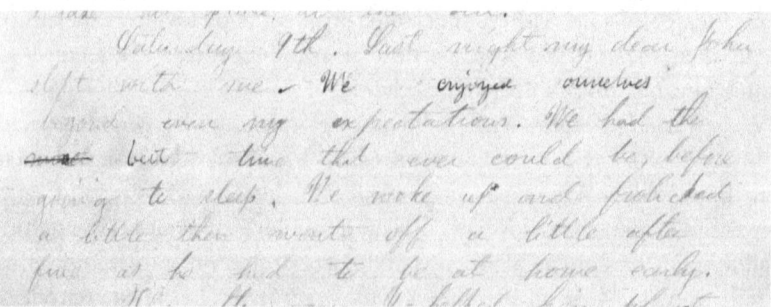

Figure I.1. Part of the entry for June 9, 1849, from Volume 2 of Warren's journal. Courtesy, Archives and Special Collections, Thomas Dodd Research Center, University of Connecticut, Storrs, Conn.

People's lives are much more complicated than the stories they tell about themselves, even if they try to be candid, which Warren certainly did not. Amid all the simplifying and clarifying needed for a story to make sense and to satisfy the author, the written record leaves out a lot. What remains is often like a fiction—a rather bloodless fiction that presents the diarist or autobiographer as the protagonist of a drama, meeting and overcoming challenges. The crafting of one's life story allows opportunities for reinventing the self, as the literary scholars Sidonie Smith and Julia Watson observe, following the insights of the feminist philosopher Judith Butler. Although individuals feel the pressure of many cultural norms in their daily life, Smith and Watson argue, the very multiplicity of these norms offers some freedom of choice both in behavior and identity. The individual can choose different behaviors and identities for different contexts of self-presentation, including in written words. "Both the unified story and the coherent self are myths of identity," they write. "We are always fragmented in time, taking a particular or provisional perspective on the moving target of our pasts, addressing multiple and disparate audiences. Perhaps, then, it is more helpful to approach autobiographical telling as a performative act."[7] Thus, the calculated, semifictional life story bears only a partial resemblance to a real life—a squalling human mess conceived and birthed in a chaos of raw emotions and moaning physicality. The emotions and physicality of lived experience are only dimly glimpsed in the written record.

I have spent nearly a decade with Warren now, struggling to know him through his words. I have read all of the journals and letters I can find, most of his published articles on education and religion, parts of his textbooks on mechanical drafting, and a short autobiographical essay.[8] The journals are the richest but trickiest sources. Warren kept a journal in various forms from shortly before his fifteenth birthday until a few months before his thirty-first. At first he tried to make entries every day, typically in the evening or on Sunday afternoons, but he allowed gaps of several months when he neglected the habit, and by the end he was making only occasional entries.[9] Interrupted by missing volumes and numerous excisions of text, the journals tell an incomplete story of his experiences and thoughts from the mid-1840s through the early 1860s. Four of a numbered series of eight volumes have inexplicably come to rest at four different archives, in Connecticut, New York, and Delaware.[10] The remaining four numbered volumes cannot now be located and may have been destroyed. Two diaries of "thoughts" followed the numbered journals, filled with decreasingly frequent ruminations on religion, slavery, youth, and other topics that interested him. Within these surviving six volumes are references to at least three more missing volumes: a volume of "heart reveries," a "journal" of his friendship with a group of boys he called the Dry River Brotherhood, and at least one "diary of daily items." Warren also alluded to drawing books, an account book, and a scrapbook. He mentioned plans to keep an additional daily diary of the Dry River Brotherhood, a collection of notes on sermons, a book of good stories to use in social settings, and a book of sentiments that he could inscribe in autograph volumes. Much has been lost, but the amount that remains is impressive. The six surviving volumes, richly introspective but unused by previous scholars, contain a total of more than 850 pages and well over one hundred thousand words. Warren's journals and letters, on top of his early textbooks, added up to a staggering heap of literary production during the 1850s and early 1860s. He kept publishing throughout the 1860s, 1870s, and beyond, but his surviving personal writings became scarce. The second thought diary ended in the summer of 1862 with gloomy anticipations of a companion's death, realized a few weeks later when his first lover, Dicky Derby, was shot through the head at the battle of Antietam. After that, only brief personal references appeared in Warren's publications and surviving letters.

The basic outline of his life is easily reconstructed. Samuel Edward Warren (1831–1909) was born in Newton, Massachusetts, near Boston, and grew up as the only child of deeply religious Congregational parents, Dr. Samuel Edward Warren and Ann Catherine Reed Warren. He attended an innovative model school in Newton, and then private schools at Andover and Newburyport. He studied engineering at RPI in the early 1850s. He stayed on after graduation as an instructor and then a professor of drawing and descriptive geometry. Called Edward by his friends and family, he appears as S. Edward Warren on the title pages of his many textbooks, in all of his correspondence, and in every professional context, evidently to distinguish him from the father whose full name he shared. He was a socially awkward man who took a conservative outlook on life. Slight in build, his thin face muffled in a heavy beard, he watched the world through wary eyes. Although generally uninterested in marrying a woman, he placed a high value on his moral reputation, career, social status, and faith. As he gained prominence with the publication of his textbooks in the 1860s he looked for more lucrative positions and was hired in 1872 by the Massachusetts Institute of Technology, located then in Boston's Back Bay, which allowed him to move back to his hometown. He lasted only three academic years at MIT. He was fired in 1875 for reasons that are not fully explained in surviving Institute records, and his teaching career came to an end around the time of forty-fourth birthday. Warren continued to live in Newton with his mother and an immigrant housemaid, whom he eventually married in 1884. Little further information survives about his reclusive final years. He died in 1909 at the age of seventy-seven.[11] There remain large questions, probably unanswerable. What was the extent of Warren's sexual involvement with other males? What was the real reason for his dismissal from MIT? Why didn't he find a new permanent teaching position? Did he form new friendships with other men and boys after his early retirement? Why did he marry? Why didn't he destroy all the journals or ensure that his widow would do so?

Warren revised the journals after he wrote them. In the 1850s and 1860s, he tried to remove evidence of passionate emotions and intense personal relations. He ripped out pages; he blacked out words; he scraped the ink from portions of numerous pages and wrote new, shorter entries in the space. Warren wrote and revised his journals with a growing awareness of potential readers, whom he hoped could profit from his example. He sensed that his contemporaries would find his revised story persuasive because it conformed to their expectations of what human relationships were like: intimacy with others could grow from a sincere and open expression of one's inner self. The problem as Warren came to understand it was that his inner self was flawed by unruly passions that he should have outgrown. He could no longer risk fully unveiling his heart to the people he knew. Resigned to loneliness in this life, he imagined that his journal would provide a posthumous link with loving companions, if some judicious revisions could turn him into a lovable character. The final document reveals his idea of a resolution: it is the story of a Christian serving God by mentoring younger males. Yet the later entries suggest he doubted his success.

Few journals exploring sexuality survive from the American nineteenth century. Antebellum New Englanders left copious letters and diaries that document their friendships, but they say little about their physical desires and couplings. As a result, historians trying to understand sexuality before the end of the nineteenth century confront discouraging limitations in the source material. One can find discussion of sex in legislation, judicial records, racy newspapers, novels, and reform literature, but few surviving personal papers show how typical heterosexuals experienced sexuality in their daily lives. Such potentially embarrassing documents, probably rare to begin with, must have been destroyed later by their writers, recipients, or heirs.[12] Scholars of sexuality between men, too, have found sparse first-person evidence. With the exception of literary works, much of the available nineteenth-century material originated directly or indirectly from efforts at condemning and prosecuting sodomy. This may have skewed historical interpretation by exaggerating the influence of persecution on the nineteenth-century experience of same-sex desire. Further, despite the recent emergence of archives and counterarchives of sexuality, scholarship in queer history has been complicated by longstanding archival practices that had the effect of concealing material from view. "Even when references to same-sex attractions, affairs and relationships can be found in historical sources," writes the scholar Craig Loftin, "such references are scattered, institutionally unnoted, and difficult to recover."[13]

Warren's journals and letters (themselves scattered and unclearly catalogued) can help us better understand erotic relationships that had not yet become menaced by modern anxieties about homosexuality, were only partially addressed by Christian tradition, and were incompletely restricted by law. Here it is important to briefly note the prevailing scholarly consensus that the modern Western idea of homosexuality did not emerge until the late nineteenth century, long after the years covered by Warren's diary. Certainly there is nothing new about men lusting for each other and having sex with each other (or women doing the same thing), but same-sex desire has been expressed, experienced, and understood differently in different historical eras. One familiar version of this argument, put forth by Michel Foucault and other scholars, is that the very words *homosexual* and *homosexuality* didn't exist until the late 1860s, after which the concept spread through medical literature in the 1880s and 1890s; this pseudo-scientific idea constructed the homosexual as a distinct "species," whereas previously same-sex intercourse was merely an act that did not define one's identity. The social and cultural construction of homosexuality produced what Eve Kosofsky Sedgwick called our society's "radically disrupted continuum . . . between sexual and nonsexual male bonds." The homo/heterosexual definition would mark and calcify many other binary categories, including masculine/feminine and public/private.[14]

Following much scholarly debate over whether homosexuality is socially constructed as Foucault would have us believe, or whether it is rooted in the "essential" and timeless inclinations of individuals, the classicist David Halperin offered a reformulation of the question. Halperin posits that before the late nineteenth century there were four distinct, long-standing "traditions of discourse pertaining to aspects of what we now define as homosexuality." These included first, the idea of effeminacy, which was a style of behavior that did not necessarily mean the man was sexually attracted to other males; second, pederasty or "active" sodomy, which characterized a man whose behavior was masculine; third, passivity or inversion, associated with a man who was obviously womanly and subordinate in sexual behavior; and fourth, friendship or male love, which was not necessarily sexual. Halperin suggests that these traditions all contributed to the development of the modern concept of homosexuality, which helps explain its persisting internal contradictions. One appealing aspect of Halperin's formulation is that it conforms nicely to the insight in queer theory that identity is multivalent and mutable; each individual can draw on multiple codes of behavior and multiple identities in choosing his self-presentation at any moment.[15] Warren's own tendency was toward Halperin's category of male love, edging into sexual territory.

Male love in antebellum America was not yet haunted by the specter of homosexuality, nor was it understood to be biblically condemned, contrary to what we might assume in a twenty-first-century moment when some evangelicals try to "pray away the gay." Heather White, a scholar in religion and queer studies, observes that not until the mid-twentieth century did Americans read the word *homosexual* in the Bible. That neologism, which had been coined in 1868, was inserted into the first edition of the Revised Standard Version in 1946. Only then, White writes, were the Bible's references to sexual sin "retroactively sorted into the binary of the therapeutic grid," which sharply distinguished homosexual from heterosexual acts and ascribed each to deep-seated personal inclinations.[16]

That is not to say that sex between men in nineteenth-century America was considered morally benign. Since the colonial period, as Richard Godbeer has observed, Americans were physically demonstrative in their friendships, but "were taught to believe that all sex outside marriage—whether masturbation, casual fornication, premarital sex, adultery, or sodomy—was driven by innate moral corruption inherited from Adam and Eve." Nineteenth-century religious writers were intensely hostile to sodomy. The Andover theologian Moses Stuart, in an 1832 commentary on the Apostle Paul's letter to the Romans, interpreted *Romans* 1:27 as specifically condemning the "horrible vice" of sodomy. "What else could be expected from those who sunk themselves far below the brute creation, but that their moral sense would be degraded, their conscience 'seared with a hot iron,' and all the finer feelings and delicate sensibility of life utterly extinguished?" Such behavior would undoubtedly destroy the sinner's physical and mental health. But Americans in practice allowed some latitude for other erotic actions. Spilling of semen was frowned upon, both for moral and health reasons, but mutual gratification was apparently no worse than indulgence in the "solitary vice," which moral reformers considered a dangerous plague that threatened the manhood of America. Solitary masturbation might even be more dangerous, as it lacked any mitigating social element and relied entirely on the fevered imagination. Nineteenth-century Americans would have seen non-penetrative eroticism as sinful excess at worst—or, more generously, as the misguided high spirits of healthy young males. It fell into the category of what the scholar Anna Clark has called "twilight moments," defined as "sexual practices and desires that societies prohibit by law or by custom, but that people pursue anyhow, whether in secret or as an open secret."[17]

Laws condemned certain sexual acts, but not until the very late nineteenth century were the laws specifically aimed at suppressing same-sex relations. In New York State, where Warren lived as a young adult, state statutes forbade rape (involving penile penetration of a vagina) and sodomy—"the detestable and abominable crime against nature"—too vile to be clearly defined in statute but understood by courts to involve any penile penetration of an anus, carrying a penalty of up to ten years in prison. Acts of sodomy were illegal regardless of the age or sex of the partners; if an adult man sodomized a child, both were culpable if the child had consented. Though broadly framed, the sodomy law was enforced usually in the context of sexual assault. Fellatio was disreputable, like other forms of non-procreative sex, but was not illegal in New York until 1886. Statutory rape laws were lax. Until 1886, when New York raised the age of consent to sixteen, vaginal sex between a man and a girl was punishable only if the girl was under ten years of age, or if the man had coerced her. Sexual activity between men and boys was not illegal in mid-nineteenth-century New York as long as no sodomy was involved. In 1855, when Warren slept with and "carressed" a fifteen-year-old, no law prohibited him from doing so.[18]

Warren and his contemporaries would have been puzzled by the idea that physical sexuality should be the central reference point for understanding intimacy. They would have placed emotion at the center, and would have seen this emotion as originating from the spirit or the heart, not from the body. Romantic feelings were not assumed to be linked to sexuality.[19] Well into his adult years, Warren understood even his physical expressions of affection as signs of his heart's strong feelings. If his actions were excessive, then perhaps they reflected immoderate feelings that were inappropriate for a grown man. Instead of gaining a mature discipline over his youthful sentiments, he had allowed them to grow into undisciplined passions that overpowered his judgment. The problem was not a sexual orientation rooted in a queer body—such an idea was alien—but what he called "an outbreak of the constitutional excess of the emotional over the rational."[20]

Warren believed his feelings were not wrong in themselves, and his contemporaries would have agreed. The experience of strong emotion was celebrated in antebellum America as never before. Deep feeling and sincere expression were the marks of greatness in art, music, and literature, as they had begun to be with the emergence of European Romanticism in the eighteenth century. People with aspirations to cultural sophistication cultivated a keen "sensibility," and felt themselves lacking if their feelings were insufficiently intense. Changes in American Protestantism legitimized and reinforced this new culture of emotionality, as the historians Peter Stearns and John Corrigan have argued. Powerful sensations and feelings might have the sublime power to lift one's consciousness closer to the divine presence. Even Unitarians, known for their emphasis on rationality, saw deep feeling (if properly channeled) as one component of a balanced character.[21]

People in Warren's educated, affluent milieu expected and even celebrated the intense emotional bonds that could develop in all forms of human interaction. Nineteenth-century Americans were not as fastidious as we are in policing the boundaries of friendship, teaching, evangelism, and courtship. As the religious historian Shelby Balik observes in considering the social network of the lovers Charity Bryant and Sylvia Drake, nineteenth-century lives were built on "layers of intimacy connected through different kinds of social ties." Romantic relationships, friendship networks, and spiritual communities fit together seamlessly.[22] A sincere connection between two minds or two souls might easily edge into territory that we would now call the erotic. While later generations would draw a sharp line between friendship and eroticism—placing many physical expressions of affection on the same side of the line as romantic love, sensual pleasure, and sexual intercourse—Warren's contemporaries saw subtle shading. A wide range of emotional and physical intimacy was acceptable within the twilight edge of the erotic, especially between youths of the same sex.

In contrast to the Enlightenment tendency to consider friendship as a rational, masculine quality—a belief rooted in classical antiquity—antebellum Americans believed friendship flourished best among women (considered the more emotional sex) and sensitive men. Writers of fiction and philosophy placed emotional bonds at the core of friendship, disparaging rational considerations as selfish and peripheral.[23] As the following chapters will describe, New England educational reformers argued for new approaches to pedagogy, downplaying rote learning and striving to unlock the potential of the ordinary individual. They hoped that caring, inspirational teachers would inspire a love of learning, and would produce citizens better suited to life in a republic. American Protestantism was marked by a rising belief in an individual's power to create a personal relationship with God, and with a shift in emphasis from fear of damnation to love of Christ. Nineteenth-century religious devotion became more emotional, and the ideal relationship with God more intimate: a style of faith that some called "heart religion." Practices and theories of parenting too were becoming less authoritarian and more attuned to cultivating the sensibilities of the child. Teachers, parents, and God were all discussed less as dominating, punitive figures and more as caring friends.[24]

Changes in these various areas of life reinforced each other, partly because some writers offered advice on multiple topics, and partly because changing outlooks transferred easily to different contexts. Antebellum Americans were still just beginning the long, modern project of compartmentalizing the functions of daily life. Work was beginning to be separated from leisure both temporally and spatially, and employers were giving up direct control over the lives of workers who had once lived under their roofs.[25] Parental authority remained the model of power in workplaces, schoolhouses, and churches, but in all these places parents were being reimagined in less authoritarian ways. The cultural trend toward "heart religion" and sensitivity offered Americans the opportunity to reimagine manliness in ways that countered the aggressive hypermasculinity that emerged as the dominant model in the Jacksonian era. Warren consistently identified himself as masculine in his diary, appears to have presented himself as such in personal interactions, and directed his desires toward similar males (with the possible exception of Dicky).[26] But his was a masculinity with an evangelical inflection. As early as the Revolutionary era and lasting at least through the late nineteenth century, evangelical manliness distinguished itself by its firm insistence on righteous behavior, its acceptance of emotionality, its rejection of the rough sports and pleasures of normative masculinity, and its persistent expression of physical affection between men. As religious Americans were encouraged to act in ways that seemed feminized or at least gender neutral, men who followed this distinctive style of performing manhood were sometimes demeaned by those who did not share their faith. Yet with the expansion and growing influence of evangelical culture in the early to mid-nineteenth century, religious men such as Warren could find sufficient personal and societal acceptance.[27]

Warren could see legitimate reasons to develop emotional bonds in all his interpersonal relations, as he talked with friends, taught his students, and struggled to bring souls to Christ. When the sincere outpourings of his heart met those of a youth, he believed, intense friendships might develop and physical affection might ensue. He believed discussion of faith and the soul were the basis for building what William Benemann has termed "romantic mentorship"—an affectionate relationship between an older and a younger male, possibly including sexual contact. Antebellum Americans had yet to develop a strong taboo against sexual contact between adults and teenaged children. There was still no clear idea of adolescence as a distinct biological and psychological life phase, only a sense of a lingering period of immaturity known as youth, roughly corresponding to the teenage years, in which the pubescent or newly postpubescent individual was not yet living independently.[28]

The friendships described in his journals were emotional and spiritual. They were also unquestionably erotic. The journals explore not the bright hot center of male sexuality—penetrative intercourse—but the margins. Here in the soft glow of eroticism, a man such as Edward Warren could feel a shiver in meeting the gaze of a new friend. Here, in encounters framed by friendship, teaching, and evangelism, he saw a romantic aura that might or might not just be his imagination. Here, where glances and touches flickered with meaning, were the moments when he and a friend drew uncertainly nearer. And here are the nights when Warren kissed and caressed a friend in bed, and perhaps enjoyed other bodily pleasures for which he left no written record.[29] Laws were irrelevant to Warren's relationships as long as he avoided sodomy. Only moral concerns were involved, and Warren felt those were manageable. Refusing to see a fundamental conflict between his faith and his desires, he hoped for a communion of soul mates, a merging of personal intimacy and Christian love. Such friendships proved easy to develop within the free-spirited culture of mid-century youth, where Warren enjoyed affectionate bonds with three boys slightly younger than himself.

As he moved into adulthood, the social milieu of evangelical Protestantism seemed to offer a fertile field in which to cultivate relationships. Richard Godbeer, Bruce Dorsey, Rachel Hope Cleves, Janet Moore Lindman, and Jessica Warner have documented close same-sex friendships between devout Protestants in the early Republic, friendships that blended spirituality, tender feelings, and physical love. Unlike the intense but short-lived romantic friendships of youths, writes Warner, "the typical evangelical friendship would appear to have grown richer and stronger over time." Some of these friendships continued to be emotionally and physically demonstrative throughout adulthood, though Warner finds such behavior came into conflict with evangelical codes of restraint and self-control. Dorsey writes that evangelicals in the 1830s and 1840s rejected a tolerant vernacular sexuality and, amid conflict and scandal, imposed new restraints on behavior. Warner identifies a somewhat later transition, as a sense of formality chilled evangelical friendships in the 1850s and 1860s.[30]

Warren remained hopeful as he reached adulthood in the 1850s that his relationships would serve God if they were premised on Christian love, even when expressed physically. He continued to believe that emotional intensity was a good thing, but as he matured he became more wary of the dangers of excess. Whether because of his own limited social skills, or the sparse network of potential companions in a small city, or his aversion to the disreputable bachelor subculture, or evangelicals' shrinking tolerance for exuberant physicality, Warren found it difficult in adulthood to develop satisfying relationships. He came to believe that his character was flawed by a shamefully immature weakness for sensuality, making it difficult to control himself when interacting with what he called "a warm hearted friend."[31] Excessive feeling could contaminate his conversation and letters, alienating friends instead of drawing them closer. Excessive feelings could also lead him to caress a friend immoderately, with similar effects. Embarrassed by physical desires that exceeded those of his closest friends, he learned to be wary of adult sensuality, eventually to the point of distrusting the body below his chest as a necessary evil. Yet he believed that desire for other males was not the problem except when it became so extreme that bodily sensuality took priority over God. Since he thought his basic problem was excess rather than a distinctive sexual orientation, he considered his example to be relevant to the religious experience of other Christians.

And so in the late 1850s and 1860s, Warren expected that the toned-down story of his life would be acceptable and helpful to his readers. His journals, as revised, were intended to be persuasive to Warren's contemporaries, and particularly to his imagined readers, who eventually resolved into his parents and a few close friends. The early journals openly described his affectionate relationship with other boys, and the later ones guardedly defended "the peculiar affection and relationship of benevolent manhood for genial youth."[32] Warren hoped readers would find in his life story a plausible and inspirational tale of Christian moral progress. Thus, the journals can be read not just to understand Warren but to understand his world, as he saw it. He saw correctly that the culture in which he lived gave him the latitude to pursue loving friendships with other males in every important aspect of his life.

The chapters that follow will explore four different modes of social interaction that were salient in his Edward Warren's mind at particular phases of his life. The first three chapters consider in turn his early friendships, his teaching, and his efforts at evangelism (defined here as spreading the word of Christ in order to produce religious conversions). There is a rough chronological order to these thematic chapters, but inevitably some overlap, topically as well as chronologically; indeed, part of my argument is that these aspects of human experience could not be neatly separated in antebellum America. The fourth chapter considers the importance of "Fatherhood" in Warren's mature conceptualization of himself and his relationships with younger males. The idea of fatherhood provided Warren with an alternative way of understanding his role, allowing him to show manly affection without indulging the erotic feelings that had become too difficult to manage. Still single and childless in his forties, Warren told his cousin that he hoped to serve as "a universal father" to those who needed it. The Epilogue briefly sketches Edward Warren's life after 1862, when Warren's introspective writing ceased. The Epilogue traces what can be known about the abrupt termination of his career and his marriage to an immigrant housekeeper nineteen years his junior.[33]

This book is a study of how Warren experienced personal intimacy in youth and young adulthood, and how he reinterpreted his experiences to meet the approval of others. I argue that the journals reveal, sometimes unintentionally, Warren's beliefs about what degrees of intimacy were socially acceptable for a male at each life stage. These beliefs, I argue, can be placed in a larger American context of emotionally intense bonds in overlapping social relationships: friendship, teaching, evangelism, and courtship. Same-sex eroticism was accepted up to a point as an extension of youthful friendship. Pedagogy and religious conversion were said to be made more effective by sincere personal connections at any age. This context of expectations allowed intimacies of all sorts to flourish, and it allowed Warren to follow to some degree his sexual inclinations.

The book will examine a moment in the past to see what it can tell us about the larger context.[34] I certainly would not claim that Edward Warren represents the men of the United States, a diverse nation with regional differences further complicated by subcultures linked to class, religion, and ancestry (and in the antebellum South by the enormous burden of slavery). Still, Warren, like each of us, was both his own person and the creature of the world in which he lived. His personality developed in interaction with the people and the broader culture around him, and it bears the marks of those connections. His extraordinarily thoughtful journals allow us to explore how emotions, desires, and behaviors evolved as a youth and then a man reached out for fellowship in antebellum America. Ultimately, I seek to root the specialized study of same-sex desire in the deeper historical context of American emotional culture. In creating a valued role for the emotions in interpersonal relations, nineteenth-century Americans made room for intimacy between youths and—in different ways—between men. Youths desiring other males did not have to choose between strictly asexual forms of romantic friendship and covert participation in urban subcultures where sexual fulfillment carried the risk of arrest. S. Edward Warren's revised journals reveal an attempt to follow same-sex desires within a mainstream, Christian life.

The book is subtitled "A Story of Faith and Queer Desire in Antebellum America," but really there are two such stories here: the one Warren told in the pages of his journal, and the one I assemble using the journal and additional evidence. Both are incomplete stories, each one selecting certain pieces of information and omitting others that seem insignificant or are unavailable. Warren and I have both struggled to make sense of the overly abundant, disorderly details of his life. He struggled to do so day by day, sometimes in anguish, and then manipulated his journals to better reflect the resolution that seemed most satisfactory. Hoping that his experience might prove beneficial to his readers, he concealed and distorted his most troubling challenges. In writing my own story of his life, I have had to rely in large part on Warren's words, respecting the man for his moral seriousness but aware that his story is not to be fully trusted. Warren did not imagine that there might be such a skeptical reader of his story. The very survival and public availability of the journals is an improbable accident, one that he may have wished to prevent. In the pages that follow, I will examine both the solutions he tried to craft and the doubts and desires he tried to suppress as he sought intimacy with warmhearted friends.

# 1

# Friendship

> Very pleasant hast thou been unto me: thy love to me was wonderful, passing the love of women."
>
> —2 Samuel 1:26

"A youth leaving home! There is something not a little melancholy in the idea." So begins an advice book that Edward Warren may well have carried with him as he left his parents' home to attend boarding school in Andover, Massachusetts, in 1846.[1] Warren was a diligent reader of religious tracts who strove to follow their advice about faithfulness in prayer, regularity in habits, and resistance to temptation. He would have learned from his reading that youth was a perilous time in a male Christian's lifelong struggle against sin. "Character for life, and for eternity too, is usually formed in youth," warned the English clergyman John Angell James, in *The Young Man from Home* (1839). Warren, having departed "the sweet fellowship of domestic bliss," had like so many other nineteenth-century youths embarked "on life's stormy and dangerous ocean." His future on earth and in the afterlife could be determined during the next year or two.[2]

If Warren pored over one of the American Tract Society's inexpensive editions of James's book during a quiet moment at Andover, he would have been reminded that friends posed the greatest danger during this chapter of his life. "Man is a social being, and the propensity is peculiarly strong in youth," James explained. Once away from parental supervision, a youth might fall in with wicked companions who would gradually destroy his morals. A charming co-worker or fellow boarder might give sin a cheerful face, leading the once pious youth into new social vices: the conviviality of the drinking party, or the pleasures of lewd women. "Set a strict guard upon your senses, your imagination, your passions," James implored. "Once yield to temptation and you are undone: purity is then lost, and, sunk from self-esteem, you may give yourself up to commit all uncleanness with greediness."[3]

Warren was fourteen years old when he left his childhood home in the little village of West Newton, Massachusetts, for the uncertain company of strangers. He went first to Andover, a small town near the border with New Hampshire, and then to the growing commercial and industrial cities of Newburyport and Troy. Every year during the mid-nineteenth century thousands of teenagers and young men were making similar journeys throughout United States, England, and Western Europe, drawn by expanding opportunities for education and especially for work. These journeys, like Warren's, often led to towns and cities. America's older seaports grew quickly between 1820 and 1860 while new towns sprang up along canals and navigable waterways in the interior. Ambitious young men flocked to these places to find work in the factories, shops, waterfronts, and construction sites. In 1830, only three-quarters of a million Americans lived in cities and towns of at least ten thousand people. By 1860, 4.6 million did so. Many a young man arriving in one of America's sudden metropolises or raw settlements found himself in a world of strangers. Young workers in antebellum cities were no longer likely to be brought under the surrogate family governance of their employer. As work units expanded with industrialization, and as affluent men and women sought greater privacy for their nuclear families, employees were left to find their own lodgings.[4]

How could personal morality survive without traditional structures of personal influence? Some evangelicals placed their faith in the written word. "Words produce actions," declared a speaker at the 1856 convention of the American Baptist Publication Society. "The public mind, and consequently public and private transactions, are pre-eminently the product of the Press. From books men derive thoughts. Those thoughts become motives; and those motives action. . . . The printed page, then, is a thing of power." Evangelical publishing societies put this philosophy into action in the antebellum decades by distributing free religious pamphlets and inexpensive books. The largest of these organizations was the American Tract Society, created by the merger of New England and New

York groups in 1825 and lavishly funded by wealthy Presbyterians and Congregationalists. High-speed steam presses at its New York headquarters cranked out five million tracts and volumes a year by 1850, ranging from short, sentimental narratives to older and more challenging works such as Bunyan's *The Pilgrim's Progress*. Despite their interest in exerting power, producers of evangelical literature strove for an egalitarian, intimate tone on paper. Authors directly addressed the reader as a "friend" and declared a personal interest in the reader's well-being. Whether issued by the tract societies or by commercial presses, antebellum advice for solitary young men conjured a caring companion to fill the place of parental authority.[5]

The friends who spoke from the pages of evangelical literature sympathized with the torment of a youth who feared sin but lived "in a state, so far as any real affection or friendship is concerned, of complete orphanage." No matter how badly he needed companionship he must keep his distance from those who were not truly Christians, for they would lead him to value pleasure over piety. Better fellowship might be found through the church. Since Biblical times, writes the historian Janet Moore Lindman, devout Christians had celebrated a style of friendship rooted in religious faith and in concern for the spiritual state of fellow believers. Such friendships encouraged emotional intimacies. Still, even a congenial Christian friend might lack the power to be the moral protector that a young person needed, observed Jacob Abbott, another advice author that Warren is likely to have read. Abbott was an educator who had trained for the Congregational ministry at Andover Theological Seminary, a few hundred yards east of Warren's room in the English Commons dormitories at Phillips Academy. Abbott explained in *The Young Christian*, published in multiple editions beginning in 1832, that the best friend of all would combine power and sympathy, and could through diligent effort be welcomed into one's life as an inseparable partner and guardian. This was the Friend, of course, who could be encountered through prayer and devotional reading. Abbott's idea of Christ was widely shared. Even before a Canadian school teacher penned the words in 1855 that would become the famous hymn, many nineteenth-century evangelical writers were fervently expressing the general sentiment: "What a friend we have in Jesus!"[6]

Youths were sensitive to the benefits of earthly friendship, too, antebellum American writers believed. From classical antiquity through the eighteenth century, secular European writers had suggested that true friendship required qualities they ascribed to men: rationality in place of emotionality, and virtue instead of self-interest. In its highest form, friendship rested on mutual esteem, shared ethical values, and reciprocal devotion, not on considerations of personal advantage or pleasure. Women could not experience this, since they were capable only of passion and love, while boys had not reached the age of reason. The friendship of Damon and Pythias was cited by Cicero and other writers as representing the ideal. The story goes that when one of the friends was condemned to death by the tyrant of Syracuse, the other offered himself as collateral so that the prisoner might have a brief furlough to visit his family before his execution. When the condemned man honorably returned to face death, the tyrant was so impressed that he freed both men and asked to be their friend so that he too could learn virtue. Into the early nineteenth century, a dramatic version of the Damon and Pythias tale portrayed feminine emotion as the antithesis of virtuous male friendship, as the two men spurned the weak tears of their women in order to act with integrity.[7]

The value of emotion was reconsidered by Romantic writers in the late eighteenth and early nineteenth centuries, and by affluent and cultured gentlemen. "Male friends often characterized the feelings that bound them to one another in terms of *sensibility* and *sympathy*, associating themselves with a culture of emotional awareness and expression that was highly influential in eighteenth-century polite society," writes Richard Godbeer. "According to those who wrote about sentimental friendship, whether in general terms or as a personal experience, developing an intense capacity for emotion and a loving intimacy with the feelings of others constituted an important part of becoming a worthy and refined man." Sympathetic bonds between men took on tremendous cultural and political importance in the era of the early Republic, as they were seen as an essential glue holding the Republic together in the absence of monarchy's patriarchal power.[8]

By Warren's time, the dominant view was that friendship thrived among women and sensitive youths who had not yet learned to suppress their feelings. Indeed, as Caleb Crain has observed in his study of early-nineteenth-century literature, "[M]en and women shared their styles of same-sex intimacy, even when intimacy itself did not cross the line of gender."[9] The qualities of selflessness, like-mindedness, and mutual concern that had been idealized in earlier writing were now reimagined to emphasize their emotional qualities. "Friendship, in virtuous minds, is but the concentration of benevolent emotions, heightened by respect and affection," begins one 1847 article in a Boston publication. "A generous, disinterested, affectionate spirit, elevation of character, and firmness of principle, are among its essential elements. It comprises sympathy in sorrow, council in doubt, encouragement in virtue, that blending the strength of two minds, which nothing but death can part, and which, cemented by piety, looks to a consummation in that purer clime, where 'affection's cup hath lost the taste of tears.'" As implied by the marital overtones here, the line between romance and friendship was blurry.[10]

Both men and women were said to be most inclined toward meaningful friendships in their early years. A poetess writing for the *Lowell Offering* in 1843 sighed about the exquisite "friendships of childhood and youth,/ Before the heart loses its freshness and truth,/ When its best, kindest feelings gush joyously forth." A male poet in 1850 recalled his college friendships, when "the unquenched stars of Passion trembled o'er us,/ Luring and lovely to our tearless eyes." Such feelings faded as the sorrows of passing years chilled the heart, leaving only the afterglow of memory. Other writers warned that passions, understood as intense feelings surpassing rational control, took uglier forms in later years. Envy, hatred, and greed—as well as cold calculation—often choked out purer sentiments. An essay on college friendships saw only a passing phase between the undiscriminating love felt by children and the sober reserve and grasping self-interest of adulthood. "Friendship," claimed this essayist, "is only experienced when the mind of its possessor is partially matured."[11]

A fortunate youth might form loving friendships to last throughout life. Arising from innocent affections, such friendships might survive whatever misfortunes befell one of the partners. While fickle acquaintances, like most self-interested friends encountered in adulthood, would fall away at the approach of adversity, kindred spirits could share misfortunes and solace each other. "Sickness only draws such friends the closer, and afflictions causes [sic] their love to burn the brighter," wrote one essayist. Friends of a forgiving nature could overcome their inevitable moments of conflict, knowing "how much of sin and ingratitude there is in every thought of our mind, and every act of our life." Even physical distance was no barrier.[12] Warren believed he had a true friend like this back in his hometown. This was "my long loved Dickey," whom he kept, with Jesus, ever present through the love in his heart and through the power of the written word.[13]

## Sweet Tones of Innocence

Warren had grown up as an only child, experiencing a quieter, more isolated, early childhood than was typical for the time. Families in antebellum America were large by today's standards. Multiple siblings crowded the rooms and beds of small homes, and competed for the attention of parents. Warren's parents each had at least eight siblings, all born in quick succession; his paternal grandmother finally died in childbirth when Warren's father was a toddler.[14] Families of that size were not quite so common by the time Warren was born, on October 29, 1831. Married women's fertility rates had begun to fall in New England around 1800, partly because of a pattern of somewhat later marriage, while premarital pregnancy rates dropped even faster. New England couples successfully spaced pregnancies out during women's years of peak fertility so that fewer children were born and nuclear families shrank. Still, it was considered a misfortune for a couple to be childless and it was unusual to stop at one child.[15] The absence of any births after Warren suggests that one of his parents might have experienced an event that impaired their fertility; possibly Catherine Warren suffered lasting damage while birthing her only child. Lacking brothers or sisters to play with, the young Warren was left to amuse himself in the family's large, Georgian home in West Newton.[16]

His father, the elder Samuel Edward Warren, came from an affluent farming family in nearby Weston. He had received the best education New England had to offer: after attending Phillips Andover Academy, he had continued his studies at Yale University and Harvard Medical College. Though trained as a physician, he lost interest in the profession and devoted most of his time to studying the Bible, aided by his self-taught knowledge of Hebrew. He also took an interest in botany and amassed a collection of rare plants.[17] Samuel Warren tried to live the easy life of a leisured gentleman without quite enough wealth to make it easy. His son later estimated his net worth in 1857 at $10,600, half of it in his house and land. Samuel Warren's income from interest and dividends came to a paltry $410 at that time, Edward Warren estimated (an amount that roughly corresponds to the purchasing power of $12,200 in 2018 dollars).[18]

Newton, which included the village of West Newton, was a rural township during Warren's early childhood. The U.S. census had counted a total of only 2,377 inhabitants in all of Newton in 1830, a number that doubled during the next two decades. Before Edward Warren's third birthday in 1834, the Boston and Worcester Railroad began service to

West Newton from Boston. A hotel opened near the depot shortly before the railroad arrived; over the next fifteen or twenty years West Newton developed into a thriving railroad suburb. By 1850 about sixty houses stood in the village, along with a blacksmith and a cluster of small shops along Washington Street, abutting what is now the Massachusetts Turnpike. The local educator Nathaniel T. Allen, who arrived in West Newton in 1848, recalled it as a "pleasant and healthful village." Allen's younger brother James gushed about the views of the Charles River valley and the verdant countryside that could be enjoyed from the nearby hills. But Julian Hawthorne, the son of novelist Nathaniel Hawthorne, who lived briefly in a house near the village, recalled it differently: "A more dismal and unlovely little suburb than West Newton was in the winter of 1851 could not exist outside of New England. It stood upon a low rise of land, shelving down to a railway, along which smoky trains screeched and rumbled from morning till night."[19]

Warren took the positive view of his surroundings. Trains fascinated him. In early childhood he enjoyed "playing cars" in imitation of the ones that ran near his home. Otherwise, he enjoyed "in-door or home pleasures," especially drawing. He retained through adolescence an interest in examining and drawing locomotives. Rather than perspective drawings he sketched two-dimensional front elevations, and later cross-sections—a method he would eventually teach to engineering students and readers of his textbooks. Warren thought West Newton and its surroundings were beautiful. As a teenager returning home from boarding school in the summer of 1847, he likened the journey to the Pilgrim's passage in John Bunyan's *The Pilgrim's Progress* from the "slough of despond" to the "land of Beulah." Far from being dismal and unlovely, in Warren's view, his hometown was like what Bunyan had described as a haven close to paradise, "whose air was very sweet and pleasant," and where "they heard continually the singing of birds, and saw every day the flowers appear in the earth."[20] Warren received some schooling in this idyllic village by the tracks in the early 1840s. In 1844 he was enrolled in the new West Newton Model School, taught by teachers in training at the State Normal School. It was there, he recalled, that he gained his love of learning.[21]

At the Model School, Warren developed the most important friendship of his life, with "a delicate, fatherless school-mate, of whom, till his death as a captain at Antietam, I was very fond." Richard C. Derby—whom Warren interchangeably called "Dickey" or "Dicky"—was indeed fatherless but came from a moneyed family. Dicky's dead father,

Elias Hasket Derby, had been named for a grandfather who was among the wealthiest merchants in the early United States. The merchant Elias Hasket Derby achieved such prominence in Salem's East India trade that Nathaniel Hawthorne later referred to Salem's heyday as "the days of old King Derby" in the introduction to *The Scarlet Letter*. The younger Elias Derby did not add to the family's luster. His stepsister recalled him as an eccentric troublemaker, "always lasy [*sic*]—good looking but not very bright." Elias settled down eventually, managed to graduate from Harvard, and served as a selectman and town clerk in Medfield, Massachusetts. He hanged himself in 1840 at the age of forty-four, leaving his wife Mary Ann to raise three young children on her own. Dicky was six years old at the time of his father's suicide, with an older sister Sarah Ellen and a younger brother Benjamin. Benjamin died of cholera two years later, so Dicky grew up brotherless as well as fatherless. Still, his mother had enough money to live on, and she maintained ties with the more fortunate Derby relatives. Settling in a small house in West Newton, she sent the "feeble little boy" to spend summers with the Salem cousins. Dicky stood to inherit a chunk of the Derby wealth himself.[22]

Dicky was a quiet, serious, bashful child. A memorial biography written after his death described him in terms usually applied to girls, praising his gentle manners, his "obedience and docility," his "sweet tones of innocence," and his "little guileless heart." His character was said to have been shaped by his natural godliness and his sensitivity to the influence of nature. He loved sketching in his early childhood, and later playing the flute. Somewhat incongruously, he also enjoyed taxidermy; he meticulously preserved and mounted small birds that he shot. This was the boy whom Warren met in 1845. The eleven-year-old Dicky had a job, perhaps as a delivery boy or news carrier, that brought him to the door of the Warren home every day. Warren and Dicky became friends and Warren came to love him as "my brother."[23]

The two boys had a lot in common despite their three-year age difference. Each had opted out of the rough, defiant "boy culture" that prevailed among their peers in the mid-nineteenth-century North. Each had a shy, quiet personality and an affinity for nature, music, and drawing. They enjoyed examining, discussing, and reading about the function of machines. They were obedient students and wanted to serve God. Warren wanted to keep Dicky close to him in West Newton or in Andover, both to maintain their friendship and to protect the impressionable boy from the bad influences he might encounter if he were sent to school in Boston as his mother contemplated. "I fear that the influence of his aristocratic foolish companions some of which there will be in such a school together with other city Influences will be bad for him unless he is very firm in the path of right. It is my prayer that he may be a learned a good man and that when he visits me I shall see him in all his innocence and desire for knowledge, for which I love him." Coming from truncated families, Warren and Dicky filled for each other the place of an absent brother. When Warren went off to boarding school at Andover he wrote, "I still love to imagine myself comfortably off with a snug little home of my own, and Father, Mother and Dickey living in it, if perchance he was [poor?] or friendless." It was a fantasy of a family made whole.[24]

## A Little Record of the Events

Warren was homesick for much of his year at Andover, 1846–47, though he made some new friends. He began his first journal, which, he observed upon reviewing it thirty years later, "is interesting as preserving the seeds of settled principles afterward." The first volume is by far the least sophisticated and least guarded of his journals, documenting daily experiences with few later alterations. It describes Warren's social encounters, his studies, and his efforts to encourage morality and piety among the other students. Warren "always warmly took sides against rum, tobacco and slavery," he noted later, and the journal also describes his disapproval of reading novels on the Sabbath and drinking coffee.[25]

Warren began the journal with a hazy set of intentions he shared with many of his contemporaries. "It has been so quiet here to day that I have had more time to think of home than on week days, and I resolved to make a little record of the events of the day," he wrote on September 6, 1846.[26] It was Sunday, traditionally a day of rest and reflection for devout New England Congregationalists, and Warren was living in a place where traditional Congregational devotion was valued: Phillips Academy at Andover, a boarding school adjacent to Andover Theological Seminary, the bastion of New England orthodoxy.[27] Keeping a journal was a widely respected method of reflection at this time. New Englanders of all ages and walks of life kept diaries wherein they recorded daily events, emotional states, and ideas, or commonplace books where they saved valuable excerpts from their readings. Eastern Massachusetts was an exceptionally literate region in the antebellum decades, thanks in part to improvements in public education and to the rising affluence that allowed time for reading and writing. The raw materials were affordable and readily available: mass-produced paper, blank books, pens, ink, and improved lamps. As individuals, especially young people, moved away from their families for jobs and schooling, their social support networks had to be sustained through writing if at all. Correspondence kept the sojourner connected to loved ones, while the diary built greater self-awareness to fill the absence of daily social guidance.[28]

Warren's handwriting is unusually clear and regular, each character leaning forward at an angle of about 30 degrees. Nineteenth-century Americans, observes the historian Tamara Plakins Thornton, understood the mastery of handwriting to represent self-mastery and self-improvement—"the triumph of the student's will over the body." Only through painstaking hours of practice could one produce a fluid script that appeared effortless. According to handwriting experts in the second third of the century, Thornton writes, "the achievement of a beautiful hand was no longer represented as a passive process of mental imitation. Instead, it was regarded as an active process in which the soul was uplifted and the body disciplined. Victorians were to form their letters as they formed themselves, through moral self-elevation and physical self-control." Warren carried this quest for perfection a step forward: the errors in the journal are so few that it appears he drafted each entry before inscribing it in the volume.[29]

Journals were an important technology in a larger cultural project of rethinking the self. "The period between the Revolution and the Civil War marked an explosion and transformation in discussions of selfhood and identity," observes the historian Louis Masur. "Some words, such as self-government, self-culture, and self-reliance, emerged for the first time in this period. Older words, such as self-denial and self-improvement, became vested with new meanings." Self-denial became less a virtuous suppression of selfishness for the greater good of the American republic, and more a matter of controlling the appetites while improving individual character.[30] In one widely read book on character building, *The Young Christian* (1832), the clergyman/educator Jacob Abbott assured his readers "that the power of the pen for such a purpose is not overrated." Abbott urged keeping a personal journal in which daily events and ideas could be systematically recorded. The diarist would gain the greatest rewards if he reflected on the moral implications of everything he read or heard, as well as on his behavior and his thoughts. Though

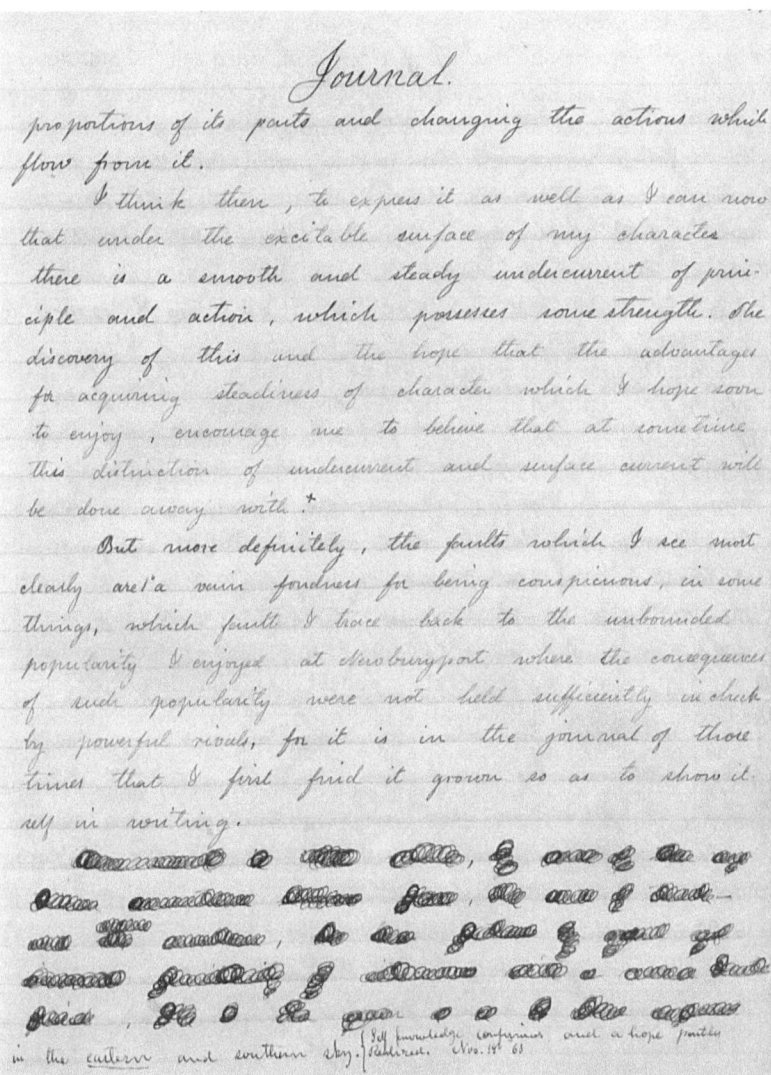

Figure 1.1. Page from Volume 8 of the Journal. Courtesy, the Winterthur Library, Joseph Downs Collection of Manuscripts and Printed Ephemera.

Abbott offered advice on the proper use of the journal in self-education, he emphasized that the intellect "is only *the avenue* by which the heart is to be reached." Thus, Abbott combined the new interest in self-culture with an older Protestant concern for searching the soul.[31]

As Abbott suggested, Warren's journals included notes on the books he read and sermons he heard. His reading included sentimental fiction, Christian allegories, and advice literature—all of which left an imprint on the way he wrote and the roles he imagined for himself in the pages of the journals. Passing references in the journals indicate that he read Charles Dickens's *Oliver Twist*, Henry Wadsworth Longfellow's *Evangeline*, and Charlotte Elizabeth Tonna's *The Siege of Derry*. All these dramatic tales contained clear-cut distinctions between good and evil. Their Romantic heroes could be read as models of Christian virtue; beleaguered, suffering, and swept by strong emotions, they held steadfastly to their morals or faith. Similar short stories, serialized novels, and poetry appeared in the magazines Warren read at least occasionally in young adulthood: *Atlantic Monthly*, *Harper's Monthly*, and *The Knickerbocker*. Sentimental poems were published as well in *Scientific American*, to which he began subscribing at the age of seventeen.[32]

His journals describe his constant reading of the Bible, mainly the New Testament, and mention allegorical and didactic fiction such as John Bunyan's *The Pilgrim's Progress*, Bunyan's *Holy War*, Legh Richmond's *The Young Cottager*, and Frederic Adolphus Krummacher's *Parables*. The hero of any Christian narrative was the troubled soul. Like Bunyan's Pilgrim, the Christian struggled through his sojourn on Earth, confronting obstacles before reaching his destination in Heaven or Hell. Successful passage through life demanded not merely the development of an admirable character, but also a sincere effort to help others on the road to redemption. The Christian could not shirk this duty, though many dangerous temptations came from personal relationships where his character was put to the test. People in Warren's social world often expressed concern for the inner lives of friends and relatives through gifts of such inspirational literature, and of even more overt religious exhortations. Warren mentions giving or receiving many such gifts; he once presented "12 of my best tracts" to a sick friend. Warren also read and gave literature offering advice on the proper conduct of life, including Henry Ward Beecher's popular *Lectures to Young Men*. He had enough familiarity with the essays of Ralph Waldo Emerson to quote from "Spiritual Laws," refer to thoughts on consistency from "Self Reliance," and allude to both the "beauties" and the "fog" of Transcendentalism.[33] The strongest common theme in Warren's reading was the internal struggle of the individual. It was an appropriate theme for any devout young man to explore in his diary, and a particularly appropriate one for Warren as he grew anguished in later years about his own moral challenges. Warren expanded on the ideas he encountered, writing increasingly long, abstract musings in later volumes on religious and philosophical questions. The journals from his adult years would evolve toward deeper self-examination.

From the beginning, Warren's journal was not just a personal record for private remembrance or meditation. Antebellum diaries "were generally conceived of as public forms of literature," write the scholars Ronald J. Zboray and Mary Saracino Zboray. Diarists knew that it was almost impossible to keep their little books safe from prying eyes. Some writers felt inhibited by the lack of privacy, while others welcomed the opportunity to communicate their thoughts to family members or to future generations.[34] Warren didn't think at first that his parents would read his words, or he would have been more cautious about what he wrote from the outset. Nevertheless he approached his task as an author communicating to a reader. His imagined readers had yet to be determined: they were hypothetical observers who would follow his story with sympathy.

Warren's friendship with Dicky had grown emotionally intense by the time he went to Andover in 1846. Warren brought along a miniature portrait of his friend, upon which he would gaze in solitary moments, savoring his homesickness and daydreaming about afternoons together at the Model School. Painted miniature portraits were used by many affluent Americans for precisely this purpose: private evocation of an absent beloved. Even after the invention of photography made cheaper alternatives available in the 1840s, colorful miniatures were often given or exchanged as tokens of affection between family members or between a betrothed man and woman.[35]

Warren expressed affections for his faraway friend in diary entries referring to "my little Dickey," "my pet," "Darling Dickey," "sweet Dickey," "the little dear," and "my beloved friend." Such endearments were common in nineteenth-century romantic friendships.[36] Warren very much wanted an intense, loving friendship with Dicky, but it is uncertain whether Dicky's feelings were as strong. Indeed, descriptions of Dicky in the memorial biography and in Warren's journal suggest passivity rather than intensity. He was said to be unusually silent, and "constitutionally reticent in the expression of religious emotion."[37] Contemplating this bland absence, as he mooned over the sentimentalized features of a miniature, Warren could give free play to imagination.

Luckily for Warren, his boarding school days coincided with a revolution in American communications that helped him sustain a sense of intimacy with those he left behind. Just one year before, in 1845, Congress had enacted a change in the postal code that transformed the experience of correspondence. Mail in the United States until then was slow, irregular, and expensive. Mailing a letter from New York City to Troy in 1843, for instance, cost considerably more than shipping a barrel of flour. Merchants used the U.S. Post Office to exchange important business information but ordinary people did not use it for casual social purposes. The 1845 legislation established the modest price of five cents for sending a half-ounce letter to any address within three hundred miles; an 1851 revision lowered the prepaid postage rate to three cents and applied it to more distant addresses as well. The number of letters mailed in the United States tripled from 1845 to 1855, with the greatest growth occurring in Northeastern cities. The change created what the historian David Henkin has described as a new culture of interconnectedness, simultaneously reinforced by the telegraph, railroad, high-speed newspaper presses, and the spread of mass literacy. Cheap postage allowed citizens of a frenetically mobile nation to maintain personal ties across long distances.[38]

Letter writers liked to imagine that the magic of the mail brought them "into some sort of instantaneous communion" with people far away, Henkin observes, but were frustrated by the obvious deficiencies of the medium. They struggled to achieve on paper the complex meanings and emotionally rich connections that can be conveyed through nonverbal cues in face-to-face conversation. Stock expressions served as clumsily as emoticons do today to reassure recipients of the writer's intentions. Yet when communication was reduced to writing, correspondents found new tools for presenting and subtly redefining the self. Middle-class Americans who aspired in the mid-nineteenth century to the refined qualities of gentility were simultaneously urged to express sincere sentiments and to do so in modulated ways that today seem stylized and artificial. Epistolary advice literature, like etiquette manuals, advised the uncertain to "act naturally" while speaking from the heart.[39] Meeting this challenge on paper required a different set of skills than were demanded by conversation—skills that some socially awkward people such as Warren may have found easier to acquire. It took years to develop the ability to compose a graceful letter and write it in a beautiful hand, and still each new letter demonstrated the time and care that the writer had devoted to the absent friend. Personal letters allowed the writer to develop an idea at length without fear of interruption, and to craft elegant sentences without anxiously attending to their effects on his conversational partner. Writing in solitude, to the ideal of the friend evoked by his memory and the miniature, Warren had the courage to say what he might have hesitated to say in person. The slower pace of written communication, and the unequal skills of correspondents, also treacherously gave misunderstandings time to grow and metastasize.

Warren did not record the contents of his early correspondence in any detail, but the letters seem to have relayed news of daily events along with expressions of affection. "Got the bad news that Father lost a cow which took a destructive fancy to a pot of paint," he wrote one day. Warren had no scruples about letting his parents read much of his correspondence with Dicky. He often folded a note to Dicky inside a letter home, trusting his parents to pass it on, and received notes from Dicky inside letters from his parents. Correspondence with his cousin Henry Allen traveled by the same route. Some of Warren's letters to and from Dicky were sent separately, though Warren's journal provides no hint of why the boys sometimes found this worth the extra postage.[40]

## In Each Other's Arms

It is unclear when, and to what extent, Warren and Dicky became physically intimate. Warren's admiration of Dicky's appearance both in person and in the miniature suggests that he had felt a romantic attraction even before leaving for Andover, but the only physical contact before 1849 is described ambiguously. When Warren was back in West Newton for Thanksgiving 1846, the boys "slept in each others arms, a most pleasant winding up." In February 1847, Dicky rode the train to Andover for an overnight visit; "After sleeping in each others arms all night Dicky and I rose and went to breakfast then passed away the time pleasantly . . ." It was an ordinary experience in antebellum America for two people of the same sex to share a bed and it did not necessarily mean sexuality. Children in a large family were often expected to double up in bed and would have grown accustomed to whispered conversations before sleep, welcome warmth on a cold night, a comforting presence on waking from nightmares. Warren and Dicky might occasionally have shared beds with cousins during family visits, but doing so with each other would still have held the tingle of novelty. Warren was delighted by the February visit, though afterward he felt lonelier than ever; Dicky enjoyed it enough that he returned for two nights in June. When Warren went home for Independence Day, the boys slept together again though there was no practical reason for it when their two homes stood in the same tiny village. Doing so was a choice, stirred by an affection that was growing warmer. Unhappy with Andover, Warren stayed in West Newton in the fall and winter of 1847–48, reading Thucydides and doing farm work while waiting for a promising new academy to open in Newburyport. What happened in his relationship with Dicky during those months is not written in the journal. Not until an 1849 entry did Warren mention that he and Dicky had gotten into the habit of kissing. After a lovely day with his new friend John Bagley, he wrote, "to crown all, we had a genuine Dicky parting of two good smacks."[41]

Warren was troubled by the state of Dicky's soul, for Dicky's family were not orthodox Congregationalists. Back in Dicky's original hometown of Medfield, orthodoxy had suffered a grievous blow in 1815; the First Congregational Parish installed a pastor whose liberal views alienated traditionalists. Fed up with the growing Unitarian tone, the remaining orthodox members broke away in 1828 and formed their own church. Dicky's father, Elias Derby, remained a Unitarian, becoming what his Bible student Nathaniel Allen recalled as a very effective Sunday school teacher. Dicky was baptized in Boston at King's Chapel, a formerly Episcopalian church that had become America's first Unitarian congregation in 1785; the pastor performing the baptism was his uncle, the Rev. Ephraim Peabody. Religion appears to have been less important to Dicky's mother. By choosing West Newton as a place of residence after the death of her husband, she placed her little family far from the nearest Unitarian meeting house. Unitarians in Newton in the early 1840s had to travel to worship in the adjacent town of Watertown. A Unitarian society briefly met at the hotel in West Newton in 1844, then came back to life in 1847 with regular meetings at the village hall. It is uncertain whether the Derby family attended, but Dicky did profess specifically Unitarian views in the late 1840s.[42]

Warren worried about Dicky's lukewarm religious faith. Believing that Dicky "delights to receive advice," he provided plenty of it to counteract his friend's Unitarian background. The boys had what Warren considered a loving and harmonious talk about religion on Dicky's first visit to Andover. "The happiest part of the day to both of us, no [doubt], was the hour between seven and eight in the evening in which I talked as plainly and gently as possible with my brother about religion, and from the five things he said I believe he is one of the dear lambs of Christ's flock. He said he read his Bible every day because he loved to, that he prayed every night, [and] that he loved God." Warren began making fruitless plans to have Dicky join him the following term at Andover or to have the two of them attend the new academy in Newburyport. He devoted part of his 1847–48 interlude in Newton composing what he called a "doctrinal epistle with practical remarks to Dicky."[43] They separated again in the spring of 1848 when Warren entered the Putnam Free School in Newburyport at the age of sixteen.

## Shuffled About

Newburyport, like Salem, was a seaport on the north shore of Massachusetts where merchants had accumulated great wealth during the earliest years of the American republic. It stagnated in the early nineteenth century, losing much of its trading hinterland to Boston with the completion of the Middlesex Canal in 1802, suffering a devastating fire in 1811, and enduring a prolonged disruption of trade caused by the Embargo and the War of 1812. Population declined in the 1810s and 1820s and the town took on a shabby appearance. Newburyport saw prosperity and growth return in the 1840s. The small city at the mouth of the Merrimack River still maintained a sea trade. It imported molasses from the West Indies, shipped out the grain from surrounding farms, and harvested cod and mackerel from the Newfoundland Banks. Ropewalks, wharves, warehouses, and shipyards remained active within the Newburyport boundaries and the adjoining Newbury neighborhoods of Belleville and Joppa, encouraging development in a long thin strip along the waterfront. Shipping and shipbuilding were in decline, though, hampered by a bar across the river mouth that resisted all efforts at removal. Newburyport's rebirth depended on industrialization, particularly the manufacture of textiles and shoes. The first cotton factory had opened in 1834; it was soon joined by three others, as well as woolen mills in Newburyport and Newbury, by the time the arrival of the railroad in 1840 gave a further boost to industrialization.[44]

Industrial Newburyport was a compact city of tree-lined streets and tidy sidewalks, with ornamental front gardens in the better neighborhoods. Only about 9,500 people lived within the narrow municipal limits at the time Warren arrived, and another three thousand lived in Joppa and

Belleville, which Newburyport annexed in 1851. The town remained small enough that it could be easily traversed on foot. From High Street, the southwestern boundary until annexation, streets sloped gently down past about five blocks of clapboard houses and brick commercial buildings to the waterfront. Gazing out from the wharves—between masts, hulls, and bowsprits—one could see the stone piers and wooden arches of the bridge just upriver, the low shore of Salisbury across the harbor, and a glimpse of the channel to the Atlantic where distant breakers crashed on Plum Island's beach.[45]

Newburyport in the late 1840s experienced some of the social problems that could be found in any growing city. Impoverished laborers struggled to support their families on intermittent employment. Many of the poorer families, especially in the growing Irish immigrant population, did not send their children to school. Despite the efforts of abstinence and temperance societies, Newburyport contained "a large number of Grog shops and Tippling Houses," many of them unlicensed, that were blamed for public disorder and drunkenness. In an 1848 letter to the Newburyport *Daily Herald*, a correspondent with the pseudonym "Merrimac" suggested that the public morals were deteriorating. Newly planted trees were vandalized, fences daubed with paint, and flowers and fruit stolen from private yards by "our overgrown boys, and rowdy young men." Juveniles clustered idly on street corners or wandered the streets smoking foul cigars. Still, the town was tame enough in 1848 that it employed only four constables, three nighttime police officers, and one daytime police officer.[46]

The Putnam Free School was the long-delayed fruit of Newburyport's earlier mercantile heyday. The merchant Oliver Putnam, who had made a small fortune in the Atlantic trade, left a bequest on his death in 1826 for a "free English school" to instruct youths in "reading, writing, and arithmetic and particularly in the English language and in those branches of knowledge necessary to the correct management of the ordinary affairs of life, whether public or private, but not in the dead languages." Twenty years later, the school trustees finally constructed a two-story brick building at the corner of Green and High streets, opposite a small park known as Bartlet Mall where there were some shade trees, a promenade, and a "Frog Pond" that served as the city's reservoir. After some controversy over whether to admit only boys, they opened the school in April 1848, with a student body of forty girls and forty boys, most of them drawn from Newburyport and Newbury.[47]

Warren's first year at the school was difficult. A barrage of grim news that spring and summer heightened his fears that the thirteen-year-old Dicky might die before experiencing a Christian conversion. Warren's grandmother died of cancer in June. In July came the death from puerperal fever of William Wells's wife, a woman whom Warren had personally lobbied for Dicky's admission, and on the same day a classmate went home to Vermont so ill that there was little hope of recovery. Warren worried that delicate Dicky was next and sent him notes with copious advice. "Thoughts of Dicky weigh me down," he recorded in the journal. "I do hope that the sad day dreams which I sometimes have about him will not be realized when I go home. I hope to be able to do him considerable good while I am there." Still fretting about Dicky's health, Warren attended an art exhibit before heading home for a five-week summer vacation, noting two potent paintings by Benjamin West: "Christ Healing the Sick in the Temple," and a copy of the nightmarish "Death on a Pale Horse."[48]

Dicky turned out to be healthy when Warren found him, able to go hiking and attend church with his friend, but he fell ill near the end of the visit. Warren "gave him 12 of my best tracts" before he had to catch the train back to school. It was a sickly summer in Newton, where cholera, dysentery, and fevers carried off about twenty young children, and in Newburyport it was just as bad. In Warren's absence a plague of dysentery had swept through the northern end of the city where the Putnam Free School was located. A classmate, Mary Andrews, was among the dead. By the time it subsided in mid-October, the epidemic claimed thirty-four or thirty-five lives in Newburyport, including those of thirty-one children under eight years old. Sickness struck the home where Warren was boarding, and then came the news that Dicky had suffered a relapse and was near death. Warren rushed home for an anxious week of waiting, forbidden to enter the sick room for the first five days. "I saw him both Sunday and this morning," he wrote on his return to Newburyport. "He is now able to be dressed and I suppose he will soon be quite well, but I do hope it will benefit his soul to think how near to death he has been, I trust it will."[49]

Dicky's 1848 brush with death had more effect on Warren than on Dicky. "Dicky's welfare is the great thing which lies upon my heart for this I daily pray, and I do trust he will be led along into truth gradually perhaps as I have been," Warren wrote a month later. He did not trust this religious growth to occur unaided, though. He bombarded his friend with advice and exhortations, as well as recommendations for reading, "believing that the more earnestly I try to benefit him the better and sooner I shall see the reward of my care for him." He scrutinized Dicky's intermittent letters for evidence of progress, and seized the opportunity of a long Thanksgiving vacation for frequent companionship. "Have seen my dear Dicky about 60 hours or about 4¼ hours a day or 5 times at about 12 hours average at a time which is nearly double as much as I saw him last [vacation]," Warren wrote, evidently counting both sleeping and waking hours. By the end of the year he was optimistic. "I trust the Lord has begun a good work in his tender soul that he will perfect. Oh what is gold or even learning compared with such a friend. I feel that the time has come when the full reward of all my care for that dear child is received, and that now we can go hand in hand and heart in heart to heaven."[50]

Yet the boys could not go together to school, as Warren had hoped. After pulling Dicky out of the declining Model School, Mary Ann Derby had placed him with a teacher at Newton Corner and then enrolled him in the Lawrence Academy at Groton in January 1849, when Dicky was fourteen and Warren seventeen. Dicky took a long time to write after reaching Groton. Warren struggled to put a good face on the situation. Ever since leaving West Newton for Andover, Warren had felt his moods rise and fall with the irregular rhythm of correspondence. He exulted when letters arrived and suffered through silences. Now his doubts grew. What did it mean that there was no note from Dicky? Was it just that Dicky's note was being relayed through West Newton? Did Dicky not really care about him? In the prolonged separation, Warren jotted notes about Bible verses he wished to discuss in his next letter. Warren was "ready to cry" as he endured a fourth week of silence. "He never neglected me so before," he told his journal. A week later, Warren was "almost in despair I feel so miserable about his unkindness" and fired off a letter he would soon regret. Dicky's response arrived at the beginning of February, containing "stronger proof of the sincerity of his love than any thing he ever did to me before." Giddy with relief, Warren sent an effusive answer in which he tried to "undo my unkindness to him."[51]

If Warren had been more attentive to his friend's feelings, perhaps he would have taken that gap as a warning. But he continued to ply Dicky with advice. He came back happy from a two-week spring vacation in 1849, having spent sixty-three hours with Dicky and having "having prayed with my brother and talked to him and asked him not to listen to false teachers."[52] Correspondence seemed to slacken after that. Warren made fewer mentions of Dicky in his journal. He began to lose confidence that Dicky was "to be a Christian," and he began to doubt his own ability to make a difference. Dicky now openly resisted Warren's proselytizing, telling him that the Bible supported Unitarianism. After sending unanswered letters, Warren received on June 21 "two notes from Dicky and one from his mother, finding fault with my writing on religion." He discovered on his summer vacation "a great falling off in the friendship between Dicky and I. . . . We have not slept together at all and have not had one loving time. Still I do not give him up."[53] Warren backed off on his religious advice. The friendship had its ups and downs over the ensuing years, but never fully recovered. "Where else can I better say Poor Richard," Warren wrote in February 1858. "His last letter to me was received a year ago this month. I postponed answering till last fall, for no conscious reason, and if involuntarily it may have been from a dimly felt sense of the fact that I would avail nothing." Still, Warren insisted in 1865, "I was true to him to the last."[54]

For many antebellum youths who experienced a romantic friendship, such an experience would be a passing interlude that would fade into memory once the mature man married a woman.[55] This was not what happened with Warren. His romantic friendship with Dicky provided the template for all the close relationships he described in his surviving journals. He developed romantic friendships with two slightly younger boys in Newburyport that were at least as physically expressive as the one with Dicky. Then and in his adult years he directed his attention to youths of similar social standing who had absent or inattentive fathers. He also kept an eye out for "pretty" young boys who reminded him of Dicky.[56] He remained single until the advanced age of fifty-three.

Warren continually compared the boys he met at Andover and Newburyport to his little "brother." At Andover, he was impressed by the speaking skills of a twelve-year-old prodigy but insisted that Dicky's "gentle ways and minute knowledge of mechanical philosophy" fully balanced out the boy's facility in Greek and Latin. He was disappointed that other boys did not share Dicky's enthusiasm for Jacob Bigelow's *The Useful Arts*, an overview of technological development. Laboring to persuade a "rowdyish" younger boy to give up smoking and other minor sins, "I took Jeffords on my knee and spoke to him of the pleasure arising from a consciousness of doing right, and then of the bad influence of novels and the theatre and although I think he can be made better by kindness yet I thought of the difference between him and my gentle brother."

That spring, he wrote, "I have at last found one really beautiful little fellow in Andover. I mean Lamson he looks and appears very much like Dicky and this is the secret of my liking him." Warren enjoyed spending time with twelve-year-old Sammy Lamson, going on two excursions to pick berries with him, and buying him a gift before they parted ways.[57]

Dicky remained Warren's standard of comparison at the Putnam Free School from 1848 to 1850. Warren's eye was drawn to Isaac Denny Balch, the twelve-year-old son of a local mill agent.[58] "At Andover I began to like Lamson on account of his resemblance to Dicky and for the same reason I like Balch," he wrote two weeks into his first term. "He will be emphatically my boy among the small boys as Whipple is among the large ones but if Dicky were jealousy itself he could not keep a stronger look out that [sic] I do, lest he should have one particle less thought on account of my absence." The more he saw Denny Balch the more Warren liked him, and the attraction seemed mutual. In early May 1848, "I moved my seat into the back row and I sit side of Balch which pleases him. I see plainly that the feeling in him is that he likes to have me side of him, but I am so jealous of myself that I will say that I shall never become any more attached to any new friend than I am to Dickey." Warren's journal does not indicate that the two boys became intimate in any way. They attended church together at least three times. On one occasion Warren and his older friend J. Francis Whipple "talked to Denny about morals and so on." Warren later mentioned a fleeting classroom flirtation in 1849: "As I smiled to little Denny this afternoon . . . he threw me a kiss with his hand which I returned and intend to pay more <u>closely</u> the first chance I have." But there is no surviving mention of whether Warren ever followed through, or of any physical contact between the two.[59]

Warren's friendship with "Whipple," as he called him, was the closest friendship with an older male that is mentioned in the surviving journals. Jonathan Francis Whipple, a native of Grafton, Massachusetts, was older than the other students at Putnam Free School. He was twenty when the school opened in 1848 and would turn twenty-one that fall; one of the instructors was only twenty-two. One of Whipple's friends there was John Ellsworth Blunt of Georgia, who was at least nineteen when the school opened. Warren was sixteen at the time. Whipple and Blunt had previously attended Phillips Andover with Warren, and had likewise followed the instructor William Wells when he left for Newburyport. In Newburyport, Warren accompanied one or both of them frequently as they attended church, visited local mills, hiked through the countryside, and paid social visits to classmates.[60] Warren was never as fond of Blunt and turned quite critical of him after Whipple left the school in the spring of 1849. Warren tried to maintain his relationship with the absent Whipple through correspondence.[61]

Warren's comparison of his relationships with Denny and Whipple suggests that he hoped Whipple would be an affectionate older brother or mentor. The existence of such mentorship in an American boarding school may seem comparable to the custom in nineteenth-century British boarding schools known as "fagging." There, younger boys known as "fags" were expected to serve as personal assistants to older students known as "masters" or "prefects," who were supposed to supervise the studies and behavior of the younger ones. The master had the power to administer corporal punishment to a misbehaving fag, and there were cases of cruel abuse, but the relationship was often amicable and sometimes led to lasting friendships. This arrangement was sanctioned by school authorities as a way to preserve order within an otherwise poorly supervised student body.[62]

There is no evidence that such a system existed at the Putnam Free School, though the school did try to create a "Monitorial System of Instruction," in which selected students had some supervisory duties. The Putnam school had opened less than two weeks before Warren's observations, far too early to have developed a student culture as complex as that in the English schools. Furthermore, though it was like the English "public schools" in enrolling children from elite backgrounds, the Putnam school did not house its students together in dormitories. Most students lived with their families; others boarded in scattered homes near the school. Warren, for instance, boarded with the family of Baptist pastor Nicholas Medbery at Brown's Square, two blocks from the school.[63] Except in his own case, Warren's journal does not describe close mentorships, friendships, or supervision between Putnam boys of significantly different ages. Moreover, as the Putnam school enrolled both girls and boys, it reduced the danger of a rowdy boy culture where fagging might be seen as a necessary form of governance.

Girls and boys at the Putnam Free School socialized together and sometimes formed romantic attachments. Whipple developed a close connection with a Newburyport girl the same age as Warren: Augusta E. Wood, an affluent merchant's daughter who attended the school along with her younger sister Clarina ("Cattie").[64] Warren began spending time with Augusta as soon as Whipple left town in the spring of 1849. This is the only example in all of his surviving papers in which he discusses a close friendship with a female, and he appears to have had mixed motives for pursuing the relationship. Augusta is barely mentioned in the journals before Whipple left, although Warren had been to her house for a choir practice. Starting on May 1, 1849, he began to see her frequently, accompanying her to church and social events. He paired up with her one day while walking through the woods with a group of students, and after a momentary interruption "I willingly grabbed a chance to seize my old place." The problem was that this was still Whipple's place, as Warren well knew, having mused just the week before that Whipple must be spending a Newburyport visit having "a beautiful time with his dear." Perhaps for that very reason, Warren pressed on. "I had a splendid cozy time with Augusta," he wrote after an evening choir meeting at the Wood house, "but I shall not get deep till I know Whipple's mind more." When Whipple wrote, suggesting that Warren should back off, Warren made a point of sulking and acting cold toward her—a display that years later he called "absolutely appalling." Augusta felt compelled to have a conversation with him in which she revealed her locket with Whipple's miniature, but the intimacy of their talk emboldened Warren to resume his attentions until a letter arrived from Whipple on June 19 implying that he and Augusta were engaged. "I am glad to know it for I don't want any temptation to get into a difficulty in love matters and I have no such temptation now, I am sure," Warren sniffed. He still escorted her home from a lecture the next week "as usual."[65]

This awkward love triangle produced one clear effect, possibly the one Warren was aiming for: by forcing Whipple to consider him as a rival, it provoked an animated exchange of letters. Warren created the sort of erotic rivalry that, as Eve Kosofsky Sedgwick and other scholars have observed, can build bonds between two males at least as potent as the bonds between either of them and the female. Warren relished a continued correspondence with Whipple and Augusta that autumn through his months of absence at his teaching job, amid signs that the couple was falling apart. Warren enjoyed the excitement of being at the center of a drama whose cast he imagined expanding to include other friends. "No one can say how Augusta, Jenny, Cattie, John, Micajah, Whipple and I may be shuffled about," he wrote upon returning to Newburyport in January 1850, now at eighteen years of age. Warren then brought the farce to a conclusion by showing Augusta unpleasant passages from one of Whipple's letters, in an apparently malicious effort to destroy that relationship. "She is decided never to trust herself to him again and I am glad," Warren wrote. Augusta and Whipple separated. She married Whipple's friend Blunt in 1853.⁶⁶

## Frolicking

Amid his flirtation with Whipple and Augusta in 1849, Warren was engaged in simultaneous romantic friendships with John A. Bagley and Micajah Lunt Jr. Warren spent more time with John and Micajah during his months in Newburyport than with anyone else. He and John cut wood together to earn money and worked on the school garden. He and Micajah went sailing. With both boys—sometimes together—Warren sang, swam, went for long walks in and around Newburyport, went for a sleighride, and attended church, lectures, and Sunday school. He spoke with each about religious matters, getting vaguely positive responses that filled him with hope.⁶⁷

"My new friend Bagley I became intimate with" one evening in February 1849. The boys had been playing with John's "electrical machine" and Warren felt a "shock . . . through my chest"—perhaps metaphorical as well as literal. After spending subsequent evenings together, Warren reported that they were "getting to be quite loving," and that they were kissing. He suddenly decided to stay at Newburyport for another two terms instead of following his original plan of going to the Bridgewater Normal School, a counterpart to the teacher training school at West Newton. When he received a letter containing his parents' consent for the change in plans, "I rushed up to my friends house to tell him, and we had a grand kissing time over it." Warren began describing John as if he were on par with Dicky himself: "I wish most earnestly to have my two little friends united with me through life and to have us all love God."⁶⁸

John Bagley was not quite two years younger than Warren. He, like Dicky, was of modest height, but Warren's habit of calling them "little" had more to do with the protective role he wished to assume. Like Dicky, John was "well worth looking after," Warren wrote. Warren tried to provide guidance on matters of physical health as well as spirituality, believing the two to be interconnected. He read medical advice literature and passed on important information to Dicky and to John, whom he considered out of shape. Warren was developing a regimen of bathing and chest exercises for himself that he tried unsuccessfully to have John adopt. "Poor John! Every spark of interest in having a handsome chest all gone," he lamented. "How thankful should I be that long years of dreadfully injurious habits have not made me as unfortunate as he is. I do most sincerely desire patience and wisdom to guide him so that he may be an industrious and healthy man for Laziness and blind satisfaction with an injured constitution are his great faults." Warren was proud to have succeeded at least in persuading John to quit smoking.[69]

Another problem was John Bagley's perplexing interest in a classmate named Jenny Andrews, a few months his junior. A shy, nervous, and "most laughably innocent" girl whose sister Mary had died in the 1848 epidemic, Jenny began accompanying John on walks and socializing with him at her house in the spring of 1849, shortly after Warren developed his own crush on John. Warren teased them and expressed mild annoyance at John's distraction, but John didn't care. He adored Jenny and was "in perfect ecstacy" as he held her hand, Warren reported. "They are an innocent couple," he wrote, implying that he was less innocent himself. By the middle of June the Putnam school was buzzing with romantic energy. Warren's triangle with Whipple and Augusta was reaching a crisis, Denny Balch was blowing kisses at Warren, and John and Jenny were kissing. "I thrill at the thought of what John did last night," reported Warren, who had witnessed their first kisses. With John's permission, he told their mutual friend Micajah the next day and "he almost dropped down at the thought of it."[70] This astonishment at the kissing of Jenny seems surprisingly strong, given that Warren was already kissing both of the boys. Evidently, Warren and his friends saw kissing a girl as much hotter than kissing a boy.

Just a few days previously, Warren had managed to get the lovestruck John into bed for an experience that he later decided to partly conceal in the pages of his journal. "Last night my dear John slept with me," Warren began, in his entry for June 9, 1849, in Volume II of the journal. The rest of the line was later scraped away so meticulously that the words cannot be recovered even at extremely high resolution with a digitally enhanced imaging process. In the gap, Warren inserted the words "we enjoyed ourselves." The original text continues: "beyond even my expectations. We had the most . . ." Here Warren later crossed out the word "most" and scraped away the following word, an adjective. The word "most" is replaced with "best," and then the abbreviated passage concludes: "time that ever could be, before going to sleep. We woke up and frolicked a little then went off a little after five as he had to be at home early."[71]

John Bagley, of New York City, was away from parental supervision while attending school in Newburyport. But his aunt, with whom he lived, appears to have taken seriously her duty to supervise him, keeping him at his homework while his friends were out having fun. For a time she tried to stop John from socializing either with Warren or with Jenny. Warren strongly disliked "the old woman," referred to her by insulting names, and made matters worse by badmouthing her around town. The boys tried various subterfuges to evade her restrictions; when John had to leave Warren's bed "a little after five," he may have been trying to sneak back home before his aunt awoke to discover his absence. Warren and John planned strategies by which they could correspond secretly after he left Newburyport.[72] The journal records only one other night when Warren and John slept together, and no further record of their kissing. They remained close friends into 1850, when the second volume of the journal ends; in 1850 they both moved to Troy to attend the Rensselaer Polytechnic Institute.

Micajah Lunt Jr. became Warren's favorite of the two, partly because he was more frequently available than John and undistracted by any girlfriend. "Cajah" was not so strictly controlled by his family. He was the son of Captain Micajah Lunt, one of the Newburyport area's leading merchants, who served simultaneously as president of the Newburyport Marine Society, president of the Bartlet Steam Mills, and president of the Institution for Savings. The Lunt family—the captain, his wife, four surviving children, and brother-in-law—lived at this time in a three-story house on High Street, a short walk south of the school. The family's wealth allowed Cajah to take his friends riding in a chaise.[73]

Warren began spending more time with Cajah as John's aunt grew strict and as John devoted much of his limited free time to Jenny. He clearly would have preferred John's company at first, but Cajah grew on him. "I really have some hope of Lunt. He is a most excellent fellow to work upon," he wrote rather arrogantly. He drew a picture (of the Charles River) as a present for Cajah, as he often did for boys he admired. "This evening I have had a beautiful time with 'Cajah for about an hour and a half," he wrote on June 12, 1849, three days after sleeping with John. "I told him of all the doings in the school and at last kissed the dear fellow and came off." Ten days later, "I had the great pleasure of sleeping with my dear 'Cajah' after waiting on Augusta home." The journal entries from this period reveal none of Warren's previous scruples about fidelity to Dicky or to anyone else. If anything, as implied by the juxtaposition of Cajah and Augusta in the preceding quotation, the energy he drew from each relationship seems to have fueled his enthusiasm for the others.[74]

Warren saw no reason to conceal his relationships. John's aunt may have objected to such sleepovers, but Cajah's family either didn't notice or didn't care. When Warren slept with John or Cajah, he did so in his bedroom in the home of Rev. Medbery and his family, who apparently allowed it. The only time Warren mentions interference from the Medbery family is when, after his return from a short-lived teaching job, he was expected to share his bed with eleven-year-old Jimmy Medbery, which precluded having Cajah sleep with him. On one of those frustrating evenings, Warren and Cajah had to make do with a "walk home hand in hand," and an affectionate parting at Cajah's gate.[75] Warren's affection for Cajah was so obvious that students at the Putnam school began to refer to him as Warren's "wife." The students used the nickname "playfully," Warren later added, yet Warren himself embraced the term and used it repeatedly in his journal, usually as "my dear wife" or "my dear 'wife.'" This joking adoption of alternate gender roles had a long history in Western friendship, one that would be disrupted later in the nineteenth century by the construction of the modern category of the homosexual, and its connection with a stigmatized effeminacy. The openness of Warren's relationship with Cajah, and the acceptance by their peers, suggests that the boys felt under no pressure to be "closeted," as males who identified as homosexual would be a century later.[76]

It is unlikely that Cajah was ignorant of the sexual possibilities of romantic friendship. He had grown up in an active seaport and helped outfit his father's ships while in port, though there is no record of whether he had gone on an ocean voyage before he developed his friendship with Warren at the age of sixteen. Only a year younger than Warren, he must have been aware that nautical subculture involved sexual relations between males, especially between older and younger males. Sexual habits among antebellum sailors are described in detail in a diary by Philip Van Buskirk, a Marine Corps drummer on board U.S. Navy ships in the 1840s and 1850s. Van Buskirk, three years younger than Warren, was similar to him in his piety and his desire to encourage morality among his shipmates. He was disturbed by sailors' common practice of "going chaw for chaw," as they called mutual masturbation. Sailors considered this a relatively innocent practice no worse than solitary masturbation. Sodomy was also common, often between an older and a younger partner in a relationship known as "chickenship." The younger partner, the "chicken," would receive gifts, cash, and other favors from the older one. "Certainly ninety per cent of the white boys in the Navy at this day . . . are, to an extent that would make you shudder, blasphemers and sodomites," Van Buskirk wrote. The historian B. R. Burg, in a book on Van Buskirk's diaries, adds that sharing a bed with a friend "implied more than convenience or friendship," and that same-sex intercourse was not stigmatized among sailors. "Being known as a sodomite or as a sailor who would masturbate or be masturbated by a friend did not imply physical weakness, fear, effeminacy, or a dependent character." Philip Van Buskirk had more scruples than his shipmates, believing that any sensuality that produced ejaculation was sinful and unhealthy. Nonetheless, he had first masturbated a man when he was ten years old and had become a compulsive masturbator at the age of fourteen when he was instructed in the art by another boy. Like Warren, he tried repeatedly in his young adulthood to develop amorous relations with attractive younger boys while also trying to improve their moral character.[77]

What Warren and Cajah did in bed is not recorded in Volume Two of the journal, and the subsequent four volumes are missing. At the time Volume Two ended in January 1850, it was uncertain whether Cajah would sail out on one of his father's ships, or whether he would finish the term at school with Warren. Newburyport remained his home. He married Augusta's younger sister Clarina Wood in 1857, and became a "master mariner." Later volumes of the journal do not record whether the friends kept in touch after Warren moved to Troy, but Warren wrote a mysterious footnote in Volume II, probably in October 1865, that "Lunt's natural character was vastly better than mine." Micajah Lunt had died that January of unexplained causes in Dansville, New York, about 250 miles west of Troy.[78]

The volume's final entry records Warren's receipt of an acceptance letter from RPI. He was bound for college, for life in a larger city, for new friendships, and eventually for a career in teaching.[79] The educational experience that he had shared with his friends would guide his work and his interpersonal relationships in the years ahead.

# 2

# Teaching

Thou therefore which teachest another, teachest thou not thyself?

—Romans 2: 21

Edward Warren was sure he was "a born teacher." He clung to that certainty throughout his career and beyond, despite early failure in a one-room schoolhouse, years of disappointing results in the college classroom, and public ridicule in student newspapers.[1] His belief was not anchored in delusions about his pedagogical skill, though he certainly had those. His trust in his calling came from a conviction that students needed his moral guidance. Even as he taught technical classes in geometry and drafting at the Rensselaer Polytechnic Institute, he preached sermons to mold the character of America's next generation of engineers. His heartfelt concern for students' well-being extended outside of class as he sought social interactions with students and spoke to them about their personal weaknesses.

Warren shared the widespread belief that teachers should promote the balanced development of each student's "faculties"—the collection of personal characteristics that included the moral sense. Based in part on nineteenth-century Scottish Common Sense philosophy, the theory of faculty psychology continued to be espoused by antebellum educational reformers, who referred to it in their more controversial effort to motivate students by stimulating their natural love of learning and their self-discipline instead of by imposing rigid authority. From the primary schools to the universities, both conservative and reformist educators remained committed to strengthening students' morality.² Where Warren differed from his peers was that he approached the task without detachment or moderation. He developed a style of personal intimacy in which his ethical stewardship was muddled with his own emotional needs. He insisted that his intense engagement made him a better teacher, regardless of the conflicts he provoked and the personal turmoil he suffered.

## Harmony and Affection

Warren's early education had introduced him to sharply contrasting styles of teaching. Controversy raged in Massachusetts in the 1840s over the newer pedagogical philosophy of reformers such as Horace Mann. After experiencing a range of different classroom atmospheres, Warren firmly committed himself to the "kindly parent" model of a teacher.

Until he entered the West Newton Model School in 1844, at the age of twelve, Warren later recalled, he "went to school because I was sent, and with no special study preferences." Warren had attended private school from about the age of five. Private schools in Newton in the late 1830s included the Fuller Academy, in a two-story, "elegant and commodious building" on Washington Street near the West Newton railway depot. The academy offered college preparatory instruction for boys and later instruction for girls as well. Warren was probably enrolled there for at least part of his childhood; his journal records that he had studied with "Davis," evidently Seth Davis, who had run his own private school in Newton before taking over as principal of the Fuller Academy. The academy building was put up for sale in 1842, and presumably had been closed at some earlier date, but a smaller boys' school in West Newton was opened in 1840 by the Rev. George C. Beckwith, a Congregational clergyman; it is uncertain whether Warren went here or elsewhere after the Fuller Academy closed. Relatives in Boston persuaded Warren's parents in 1842 to send Warren to live with them in a house overlooking the Common and to attend public school for the 1842–43 winter term. The Adams School on Mason Street provided Warren with a very different educational experience than was available in the elegant Fuller Academy or in the Rev. Beckwith's classroom: a harsh regimentation that he later understood as the opposite of good teaching. As one of Boston's fifteen Grammar and Writing Schools at the time, the Adams School enrolled more than three hundred boys between the ages of seven and fourteen.

Half the students spent the morning in the dimly lit hall of the grammar department, learning spelling, reading, geography, and natural history, while the other half was instructed in the writing department, which also taught arithmetic and bookkeeping; at midday, the two groups switched. Students at the Adams School later recalled the discipline as "so severe as to almost amount to tyranny," with Grammar Master Samuel Barrett alert for opportunities to beat naughty boys. Barrett and Writing Master Josiah Fairbank were among the thirty-one Boston schoolmasters who would vehemently rebut the criticisms of traditional teaching methods leveled by State Board of Education secretary Horace Mann in his 1844 annual report.[3]

Mann was the most prominent of the antebellum educational reformers who challenged older notions of the mind as a passive "storehouse of knowledge." He and like-minded educators throughout the Northeast and Midwest, influenced by the work of European theorists John Locke, Jean-Jacques Rousseau, and Johann Pestalozzi, believed learning happened as each child developed at an individually appropriate pace. Like Mann, educational reformers followed Locke in believing that affectionate leadership would get better results than rigid authority, by instilling self-control, kindliness, and a desire for lifelong learning.[4]

Mann's 1844 report unfavorably compared Massachusetts common schools to those in Saxony and Prussia, drawing on his own observations and those in a report by Calvin E. Stowe. Mann admired the German practice of dividing students into different levels, of encouraging quantitative reasoning, and of teaching phonics, drawing, and music. Germans promoted understanding instead of memorization, he wrote. Most of all, Mann was impressed by "the beautiful relation of harmony and affection which subsisted between teacher and pupils" in Germany. Unlike in Massachusetts, he never saw teachers hitting or humiliating students. Mann quoted a German teacher as saying that corporal punishment was falling into disuse and that "when we teachers become fully competent to our work, it will cease altogether."[5] Despite the fact that Prussia was no democracy, Mann believed its classroom practices were ideally suited for the United States. Order should be based on each student's self-control instead of servility to despotic power, and the student should learn to "think with his own mind." Mann's praise of the affection between teacher and student echoed the emerging sentiment that bonds of sympathy provided a foundation for a republican society. The common schools, he believed, could educate all ranks of American children together in a "truly republican manner" that would break down artificial distinctions between citizens.[6]

Boston schoolmasters, including Warren's former teachers, accused Mann of being ignorant of teaching both in Boston and Germany. Germans had put on a show for him that he had gullibly accepted, they suggested. The schoolmasters charged that Mann and Cyrus Peirce, superintendent of the teacher training school at Lexington, were promoting radical and impractical theories. Teachers who were too engaging would dangerously inflame the emotions of their students and lead them to appreciate learning only for its entertainment value. The Bostonians warned against imposing on American children a foreign educational system that threatened to "enfeeble rather than to invigorate, their mental faculties; and . . . render them the weak subjects of passion, rather than rational freemen." This countered one of Mann's major arguments for educational reform, which was that common schools would prepare children for republican citizenship. The Boston teachers defended traditional practices of memorization and reliance on textbooks, and disputed the value of phonics in early reading. They insisted on preserving order through authority. In Mann's theories, they scoffed, "The child's pleasure [is] to be consulted at the expense of order! at a sacrifice of first principles, the only *basis* of a thorough education!" The teachers were incensed by the comments of Mann and Peirce on corporal punishment. It might be wise to be kind to young students and judicious in punishing older ones, they acknowledged, but beatings must continue as long as children misbehaved.[7]

Educational controversies were also shaped by religious disputes. Mann's educational writings echoed his Unitarian faith in a benevolent God and his postmillennialist optimism about human progress. Mann's religious mentor, the leading Unitarian preacher William Ellery Channing, held similar pedagogical views. In his 1819 exposition of the Unitarian creed, Channing had spoken of God as a fatherly teacher who made the world as "a place of education, in which he is training men . . . by a various discipline suited to free and moral beings, for union with himself, and for a sublime and ever-growing virtue in heaven." Mann reversed the metaphor in his report for 1845, comparing the affection between a teacher and his students to that between Christ and his disciples, a comparison that Warren would later make as well.[8]

There were plenty of non-Unitarian educational reformers who supported Mann. As Mann noted, the majority of the reform-minded state Board of Education in 1844 were orthodox Calvinists, including three clergymen. Among the leading school reformers in other states were John D. Pierce of Michigan and Calvin Stowe of Ohio, both former Congregational clergy. Mann reproduced sympathetic letters from Catharine Beecher and Jacob Abbott in his *Eleventh Annual Report*, emphasizing that their Calvinist belief in innate human depravity did not preclude optimism in children's moral potential. Mann did not dwell on the point, but his friend Channing had observed that even orthodox Congregationalists were retreating from the harsh implications of Calvinist doctrine.[9]

But some of the more conservative Congregationalists in Massachusetts feared that Unitarians were trying to fill a vacuum in the moral supervision of schools, a weakness created by the 1833 disestablishment of the Congregational church in Massachusetts that diminished the local power of Congregational pastors. Controversy flared over whether Mann was preventing the proper teaching of Christianity. The charge was made by a disgruntled former member of the state Board of Education (a Congregationalist), was published by an Episcopal journal, and was kept in the public eye throughout the first half of 1844. Criticism focused on whether Mann had revealed his bias by excluding sectarian works from a list of recommendations for school libraries and by his influence over Normal School curricula. Mann's critics charged that schools failing to emphasize the redeeming power of Christ's sacrifice were in effect pushing Unitarianism, which differed from other major sects by denying Christ's divinity. Worse, avoidance of controversial religious doctrines was a slippery slope that might lead to Catholics' preventing the reading of the Protestant Bible in the schools.[10]

Further, Mann faced resistance from local officials who resented state government's growing role in education. The newly created Massachusetts Board of Education had limited powers, as had similar agencies in Connecticut, New York, Michigan, and other states. Schools in most towns remained under neighborhood control, governed by district boards that provided a one-room schoolhouse, determined the curriculum, and hired the teacher using mainly local tax money. Nonetheless, state education officials used their public pulpit to spread reform beliefs. They organized teacher institutes that functioned as revival meetings for the new pedagogical creed. They issued reports with town-by-town data about school spending per child, shaming the stingier towns. They lobbied for state laws that chipped away at local autonomy—most potently, forming state "normal schools" to train future teachers.[11]

Massachusetts established the first state normal school at Lexington in July 1839, followed by ones at Barre and Bridgewater. Mann hired Cyrus Peirce, a former Unitarian pastor, to be principal of the Lexington school, having been impressed by Peirce's skills when he saw him teaching private school on Nantucket. The Lexington school enrolled only teenage girls and young women as its students, while the other two schools accepted male students as well. Mann believed that women were the ideal teachers, especially of younger children. "Their manners are more mild and gentle, and hence more in consonance with the tenderness of childhood. They are endowed by nature with stronger parental impulses, and this makes the society of children delightful, and turns duty into pleasure," he wrote. Women could create in the classroom the homelike atmosphere that would nurture children's moral character, now understood to be the most important goal of education. They would govern by instilling self-discipline instead of relying on violence that might produce resentment, malice, and hatred. Plus, women could be paid a lot less than men for the same work, and they would not be tempted away by more lucrative opportunities, as men constantly were. The Lexington Normal School enrolled twenty-five aspiring teachers by the end of the first academic year. Mann and Peirce established an experimental "model school," attended by thirty boys and girls from throughout Lexington, where the Normal School students could develop teaching skills under Peirce's direction. Occasionally, Peirce would teach the model school himself as a demonstration for the Normal School students.[12]

The growing Normal School relocated in 1844 to a larger building, the former Fuller Academy in Warren's hometown of West Newton. Mann and Peirce arranged with Newton school officials to establish a new model school as a laboratory for their student teachers, as they had in Lexington. The West Newton Model School, in a classroom in the Normal School building, enrolled district school students and those who had formerly attended a small private school. It offered free education for the boys and girls from the village and adjoining Auburndale. This was the school that Warren and his friend Dicky would attend.[13]

The arrival of the Normal School and the Model School made local religious and cultural conflicts inevitable. West Newton was a conservative, Calvinist enclave in the largely Unitarian region of eastern Massachusetts. The Congregational pastor, Lyman Gilbert, persisted in combating the liberal theology that he felt had unfortunately overwhelmed the Boston area earlier in the century. The arrival of the Model School helped draw new Bostonian families, including Unitarians, into what would become a bedroom community of railroad commuters. Mann was part of this Unitarian influx; he moved with his family to a house on the edge of West Newton in late 1846 with the intention of keeping his eye on the schools and eventually sending his children there.[14]

Congregationalists in West Newton, led by the Rev. Gilbert, watched the new Normal School suspiciously. Local school officials complained that student teachers (who were mostly Unitarians) profaned the Sabbath by failing to attend Gilbert's church. The tension exploded into public conflict in 1847 when the Rev. Matthew Hale Smith, a Boston clergyman, denounced a public performance of "tableaux vivants" by Normal School teachers and students. The Rev. Gilbert had witnessed this scandalous event himself, seeing a young woman dressed in man's clothing in violation of Biblical injunctions, and another woman dressed as an Indian with "naked arms and neck" and a skirt that revealed calves covered only in flesh-colored tights. Smith linked such lax morality to Mann and Peirce's educational theories, including their disavowal of corporal punishment and Mann's supposed belief that "nothing above the lowest form of Deism can be taught in any common school." By 1848, a frustrated Peirce was denouncing West Newton as a "region of bigotry, narrow-mindedness, and intolerance."[15]

## Ardor in the Cause of Learning

Edward Warren's father, though an orthodox Congregationalist, evidently trusted the Model School enough to keep his son there for two years. Edward Warren flourished under the gentle guidance of his young women teachers. "I learned to love study and showed fondness for arithmetic, geometry, physiology, and natural philosophy," he later recalled. His friend Dicky Derby also loved the school and the Normal School principal Cyrus Peirce—"better known to his loving pupils everywhere as 'Father Pierce,'" according to Dicky's memorial biography. "Here was a mind he could but respect, a heart he could but love; and, under his tuition, Richard not only grew in earthly wisdom, but in spiritual stature." Warren, Dicky, and the other model school students had limited contact with Mann himself, other than greeting him as a neighbor and hearing an occasional speech.[16]

As Edward Warren approached his fifteenth birthday, Dr. Warren decided to have his son follow his footsteps into the Phillips Academy in Andover. Possibly this had been his plan all along, or perhaps he had come to share his neighbors' skepticism about the Model School. The Model School was in decline in 1846 as parents withdrew their children, Edward Warren reported on a visit back home later that autumn: "It is sad to see how dull it is, only six boys and a few little girls besides two or three large ones." Warren attended the Model School examinations and found they "lacked brilliancy."[17]

At Andover, Dr. Warren could at least be confident that his son would encounter impeccably orthodox religion. Adjacent to Phillips Academy was the Andover Theological Seminary, established by Calvinist diehards in 1808 to train ministers after Harvard College was captured by Unitarians. The educational complex on Andover Hill expanded in 1830 as the Academy added a teaching program. The Teachers' Seminary initially served a double purpose: to provide a nonclassical counterpart to the pre-college preparatory classes at Phillips Academy as well as to train young men to be schoolteachers. By the time of Warren's arrival in 1846, the Teachers' Seminary had devolved into a less prestigious "English" division of Phillips Academy but remained appealing for other reasons. Unlike the "Classical" department, it offered instruction in the sciences. Warren enjoyed "excellent advantages in botany, chemistry and surveying." He and the other Phillips students worshipped together with the Andover Seminary students at their chapel, attended prayer meetings with them, and heard special lectures there.[18]

Warren's entrance into the English division of Phillips Academy, instead of the Latin division, suggests that even before he turned fifteen years old he was considering a career as a schoolteacher. Shortly after his arrival, he listened with interest to a discussion among teachers about "what constitutes an orderly school." He also learned by example. Warren was disgusted by the dictatorial manner of Phillips principal Samuel H. Taylor, who beat boys in what Warren considered an inappropriate rage. "Of course it makes the scholar mad and utterly destroys the dignity of the master," Warren wrote in his journal. Some of Taylor's students came to respect the high standards he set for them and his air of aloof authority. Many others were terrified both of "Uncle Sam's" violence and his habit of relentlessly interrogating students to expose their ignorance. In contrast, English division head William H. Wells was beloved for his affable manner. "He encouraged intimacy, and responded with advice and sympathy," recalled another of his students.[19]

In the spring of 1847, Wells told Warren and other students that he was looking into a position as head of a new academy to be opened in Newburyport. Warren decided to follow him there in the next term.[20] The Putnam Free School of Newburyport declared as its purpose "to lead Pupils through a thorough and extended course of English study, embracing the higher branches of Mathematics, with their application to Mechanics, Surveying, Navigation, etc.; Natural, Mental, and Moral Philosophy; Chemistry, Geology, Astronomy, Rhetoric, History, etc." Unlike Phillips Academy, it was coeducational. The school belatedly opened in the spring of 1848 with eighty students, selected from a much larger pool of applicants after competitive examinations. The average age of the boys was fifteen and the girls seventeen. Boys and girls studied in separate classes most of the time, though recitations were held in common. Wells was assisted by two instructors.[21]

"Mr. Wells loved to speak of that first class as one of shining talents," recalled one of Warren's schoolmates. "It was the darling of his early enthusiasm, and thoroughly magnetized by his zeal; into the life of each member he projected his high ideals and fervent aims." Wells inspired "mutual ardor . . . in the cause of learning and character." He ran his classroom without resort to harsh discipline, gently reproving any disruption with a glance and a cough. Though he maintained a degree of formality in interactions with students, he nonetheless was friendly and kind, and invited students to his home for social events and stargazing through a telescope. Nearly half of his early students went on to work as teachers.[22]

Phillips Academy and the Putnam school stimulated Warren's interest in science, mathematics, and technology as well as in teaching. In 1848, he sketched out a plan for himself that included studying at the state normal school at Bridgewater, and then at the Rensselaer Institute in Troy. It is likely that this plan was suggested or influenced by a new neighbor in West Newton, Nathaniel T. Allen, who took over as principal of the West Newton Model School on the same day that the Putnam school opened, April 12, 1848. Allen had attended Bridgewater and Rensselaer himself, though he left Rensselaer without graduating. His cousin, Edward A. H. Allen, and his brother, James T. Allen, followed the same path, both staying on to graduate from Rensselaer and later serving with Warren on the faculty for a few years each. Warren had great respect for Nathaniel Allen and drew on him for advice when he began his first teaching job.²³ Warren changed his mind about Bridgewater once he "became intimate with [John] Bagley" in February 1849. He decided to remain at the Putnam school for two more terms before going directly to Troy, and he hoped that John would follow in another year when he completed his own studies at Putnam. Warren's parents were not as delighted with the idea as John was, but Warren succeeded in persuading them.²⁴

## Forlorn Lack of Mutual Adaptation

Oliver Putnam's will stipulated that the Putnam school would try "the Monitorial System of Instruction," in which older students would assist with the instruction and control of the younger ones. This was a reference to the theories of English educational reformer Joseph Lancaster, in vogue among American educators at the time of Putnam's death in 1826. The Lancasterian style of teaching had fallen into disrepute by the 1840s, having gained a reputation for lockstep acquisition of knowledge and rigid discipline; reformers now preferred the gentler, individualistic approach of Pestalozzi. Nonetheless, the Putnam school at least made attempts in its early years to involve older students in teaching. Warren enjoyed the opportunity, "being one of a few older boys and fond of befriending the younger ones in matters of morals and physiology and mathematics (being so far a born teacher)." When Wells was out sick, and his assistant Mary Ann Shaw was away because of a death in the family, Warren filled in as a substitute; "I heard the second class in Arithmetic and a class in Grammar and in History, which was pleasant to me." He also took a leading role in the students' garden committee and edited the newspaper. "I have seen no happier days since," he recalled many years later.²⁵

In preparation for teaching, Warren began in the autumn of 1848 to read *The School and Schoolmaster*, a two-part manual of advice for educators published in 1842 by Alonzo Potter and George B. Emerson. Potter praised Mann and echoed much of what he had to say both in criticizing conditions in the common schools and in outlining an appropriate pedagogy. Quoting Locke, Potter argued that education has the power to "turn the minds of children as easily this way or that, as water itself." Teaching therefore required skilled practitioners and "an active exercise of the *moral* sentiments and affections." Teachers should help students develop their own intellectual, moral, and physical faculties in a balanced manner. A properly educated child would gain the self-discipline to control his lower appetites and the reason to be a virtuous citizen of the republic. Emerson, a Boston private school teacher who sided with Mann during the 1844 controversy, wrote that children learned as much by example as by precept. "The appeal to the generous qualities of children can be safely made only by one who has entire confidence in their existence and strength, and who has a sympathy and affection for children. A teacher, therefore, should be a *lover of children*. This is one of the most essential qualifications. He who has it will spontaneously feel such an interest in children as will enable him to bear with their faults, to encourage their efforts, to feel for their griefs, and do what he can to make plain their difficulties." Order must be maintained in the classroom, but the teacher should strive to govern his students in a loving, patient way that provided them with a worthy model.[26]

As he began the Autumn 1849 term at Putnam, Warren decided he was ready to teach school himself in the remaining months before going to Rensselaer. On Wells's advice, he tried to apply for jobs in person, walking from town to town throughout northeastern Massachusetts. He also wrote letters and left his name with a teaching agency. Common schools in Massachusetts suffered from high turnover in teachers, partly because of the miserable pay and lack of year-round employment, but apparently the towns that Warren contacted were not eager to fill a vacancy with an inexperienced seventeen-year-old boy. Finally, he received a response from Charlton, west of Worcester. They wanted him to start almost immediately.[27]

Warren packed his bags, said goodbye to friends and teachers in Newburyport, and boarded the train to begin his journey to the new job. Although he had excelled in his studies, he approached the challenge of teaching with trepidation. Public speaking had not come easy for him, and keeping a district school was a tough job for anyone. Classrooms often held fifty or more students, with attendance varying unpredictably and the ages ranging from under four to over sixteen. The schoolmaster typically divided the class into five or ten groups, hearing the recitations of each group in turn while the rest sat quietly on benches and occupied themselves at their books and slates. Interruptions, whispering, and minor disturbances were constant. Despite frequent whippings, discipline was so tenuous that many rural schools were broken up by student rebellion, particularly in the winter when older boys were present. If the schoolmaster was physically unable to quell the violent resistance of the older boys, Mann wrote, the term would end with the "teacher going forth from the door of the schoolhouse . . . in mortification and dishonor, instead of respect and affection; and followed by insurgent and tumultuous scholars, proclaiming their own infamy, by shouts of triumph and language of insult." Other teachers quit before trouble reached that extreme, or were fired by district boards who discovered belatedly that the teacher lacked knowledge, skill, or disciplinary ability. In the 1844–45 academic year, a total of ninety-one school terms were broken up in Massachusetts by teachers quitting, being fired for incompetence, or being forced out by rebellions.[28]

Charlton was not immune to these problems. Its schools followed the common practice of having less expensive women teach the summer term and physically stronger men teach in winter when classroom control was more demanding. Nonetheless, three of the thirteen district schoolmasters failed to finish the winter term prior to Warren's arrival, one quitting because of insubordinate students, one fired for failing to keep order, and another quitting because of a dispute about his board. The town's school committee reported serious complaints about three other schoolmasters, mostly on disciplinary matters. Warren's North Side school had reportedly succeeded in the hands of an experienced teacher. It also differed in that it was housed in a beautiful new building created by the generosity of families in the surrounding District No. 2; the school committee praised this as a model for what other districts should build in place of their drafty shacks.[29]

Charlton was a rural township of 2,100 people that had been only slightly touched by the industrialization of Massachusetts. Its population was beginning what would be a half-century of very gradual decline. The inhabitants supported themselves mainly by farming and shoemaking. There was a woolen mill in the "Charlton City" village, and in the Northside Village a tannery was run by the Bacon family, with whom Warren was boarding in a house on the Worcester & Stafford turnpike. Next door to the Bacon house was the former Rider Tavern, which had closed a few years earlier when turnpike traffic relocated to the Central Turnpike a few miles to the south. The district schoolhouse was on a side road just a short walk away. As the Western railroad had bypassed Northside Village, running instead through the extreme northern tip of the township, Warren's new neighborhood had become something of a

Figure 2.1. Charlton Schoolhouse No. 2, Charlton, Mass. (built 1848), where Warren taught in the fall of 1849. Photo by author, 2019.

backwater even within Charlton. "The place is nothing at all," Warren wrote in his journal upon arrival.[30]

Warren had a few easy days of teaching at the beginning. Only twelve students showed up the first day, and fourteen the next. "I have got a pleasant arrangement of the classes and of the school generally. Being utterly unable to resist the school if I should bully over them I govern as Miss Shaw would and with the same result," Warren wrote.[31] His choice to model himself after the female teacher at Putnam School is intriguing. The decision followed logically from Mann's beliefs that women made the better teachers, and that the feminine quality of gentle influence was more effective at building children's character than rigid, male authority. School reformers such as Mann believed that violent discipline would produce anger, resentment, and obstinance, while gentler approaches would produce the self-governing qualities appropriate for a citizen of the Republic.[32] Warren's choice of teaching style also made sense personally, as it harmonized with the emotionally rich, partly feminized approach to Christian evangelism that he was developing.

The school grew to twenty-three students the next week. Warren reported happy feelings and recorded the things he did to keep up his spirits such as writing letters and taking walks. He envisioned staying until "about the first of March, and shall aim to be regular in the habits of bathing prayer and reading the Bible both morning and night, study exercise and shall try to do all that I can to improve my pupils." But he soon found that the gentle ways of Miss Shaw did not work as well in Charlton as they had at the Putnam school. On his eighteenth birthday, a dark, rainy day, "I had my fears a little excited this noon by a written communication from Marble 1st, Bacon 1st, Rowland, and Gould saying that if better order was not kept, their seats would be vacated." Warren told the boys that he would try to keep the younger children under better control, partly by "inculcating self government." He told himself that it was helpful to have the older students taking such an interest in good order, and he minimized the incident as an "adventure." Warren did not fully appreciate the trouble he had put himself into by adopting Miss Shaw's teaching practices. Women might very well be able to tame disruptive students through moral example and gentle encouragement (supplemented now and then by whipping), but their success depended as much on gender norms as on the superiority of these methods. Guiding the class as a mother trains and nurtures her children, the female teacher drew her authority from the habits of respect that children showed their mothers. As a fictional rustic observed in a story published earlier in 1849, "The boys would be ashamed to fight a woman." But Warren, of course, could not claim the gender status that made female teachers so effective. Loath to rely on patriarchal discipline and violent punishment, he left himself with no claim to authority but his shaky position as schoolmaster. Further, he was dealing with a poorer, rougher class of children than he had encountered in the exclusive Putnam School.[33]

Warren's account of his teaching experience is notable both for what it reveals about his ideas of teaching and as an early example of his developing style as a diarist. The voice that conveys the news of his life is that of an unreliable narrator who provides neither the true experience of the actor (Warren in the schoolhouse) nor the true feelings of the author (Warren writing in his journal by lamplight). Warren was beginning to explore the possibilities of the journal as a literary form like a play or a novel, in which the writer has the power to invent his characters and guide the reader's interpretation. One of his entries for Charlton was even written in the form of a play script, with numbered acts and stage directions.[34] Warren would more fully embrace the opportunity for self-invention when writing and revising later volumes.

His entries for that autumn revealed the bleak routine of his days: confrontations with insolent students, solitary walks to the depot in hope of mail, then supper and bed in a cold house where the family stayed aloof. Warren kept insisting on his contentment, even as he began to mark off the hours like a prisoner awaiting release. "When I think how like shot the hours have come down from 480 to 327," Warren wrote as Thanksgiving vacation approached, "I am happy as a clam." By mid-December the journal featured a daily countdown to the end of winter term, dropping almost to one thousand before Warren was fired. The point was for the imaginary reader to see the contrast between Warren's miserable conditions and his unavailing effort to be cheerful. Warren was giving a performance. He was the star of a melodrama in which a brave young Christian brought a kindly, moral style of teaching to the ungrateful natives of Charlton.[35]

The situation was obviously deteriorating in November and December, even as Warren continued to insist in his journal that it was going well. "The kind manner and conversation I desire to cultivate will I believe prove a strong addition to the more specific means of government," he reassured himself. He began to hope that some of the more troublesome older students would drop out or that his strategy of "discipline and winning hearts" would tame them. One of the boys disrupted the school by bringing a cowbell, and another bluntly told Warren he was incapable of teaching algebra. Warren's diary discusses his interactions only with the schoolboys, though New England district schools educated girls too. This is not because of any greater affection for the boys, but simply because they were the ones who caused trouble. (Schoolgirls were not perfect students either, wrote a female schoolteacher at the time, but they were more eager to win the teacher's approval, and misbehaved mainly by lying about having completed their work.) Frustrated with the disorder in Warren's school, the district committee provided Warren with written advice and a promise to support him in his efforts at discipline, even if Warren felt compelled to expel disruptive students. "I found however that for the alleged reason that I am not strict enough in preserving stillness in school and gave too much recess, but very likely because a 'Fatherly' government is not yet appreciated here and because I am—too religious—that the district decided at a school meeting held last Monday night, not to board me round but to hire my board and thus get rid of me sooner." Though he spoke in masculine terms of being "fatherly," Warren was deliberately rejecting the traditional model of the authoritarian father in favor of the emerging middle-class ideal of gentler, Christian parenting. He was aware that this style was less familiar to the farm families of Charlton than to the educated, affluent classes of the Boston area, yet he was unwilling to adapt; he regarded his new neighbors with a disdain that they undoubtedly detected.[36]

Feeling unappreciated, Warren was in a foul mood when the school committee belatedly conducted his certification exam. He "sat bolt upright full of scorn" during the "farce of an examination," giving curt answers to men he considered unqualified to judge him. "Mr. Lamb looks just like a hog, bristly hair, small dull eyes, enormously fat cheeks and monstrous body, coarse as dirt," he wrote of one of his examiners. The committee gave their certification but signaled their disapproval by forcing Warren to pay $2.25 a week to board at another house. They remained concerned about his poor classroom discipline. "On all hands I am driven to flogging," Warren wrote on December 6, choosing a term more often applied to the brutal beatings inflicted by slavedrivers and the British Navy. Though even Horace Mann held that corporal punishment was sometimes necessary, Warren was determined to run his classroom by love. He told his students in a choking voice that instead of being whipped they should learn to govern themselves. He repeated pleas for order had little effect. Students continued whispering, stamping their feet, and cracking nuts.[37] Finally, on Christmas Eve, the school committee met with Warren again and asked him to leave. School was held the next morning as usual, as most rural New Englanders paid little attention to Christmas. Warren gave brief farewell remarks, telling students that they would miss his kindness as soon as they were beaten by a cruel schoolmaster. Warren tried to comfort himself by recording the faint validation of his masculinity by the school committee: "I was assured of the respect and affection of the school and district for me, as a man." It was obvious, though, that his first attempt at teaching had been a humiliating failure. "Thus ended the Charlton episode, a time of forlorn lack of mutual adaptation between myself and my position and surroundings," Warren summarized it years later. He returned to the Putnam school for the next few months.[38]

## Too Much Familiarity

Warren had failed both to keep control of the class and to exert a moral influence on individuals. He had hoped at least to gain the affection of the younger ones. His journal records almost no individual interactions with students other than failed attempts at discipline; one notable exception occurred when Warren was out for a walk and "my feelings were exceedingly cheered for the evening by having Southwick II run after me from the depot so as to chat along." He would prove more successful in cultivating personal relationships with students in his early years at RPI.[39]

Warren's journals for his first years in Troy (1850–53) are missing, and no letters survive from this period. He briefly sketched out the experience in his later autobiographical article and in retrospective passages in later journals. His first impression of the city was not positive. Troy in 1850 was booming as a riverport at the eastern end of the Erie Canal. Its population of nearly 29,000 made it the twenty-fifth largest American city, ranked just below Chicago. Trojans pointed with pride to their bustling commerce and industry. Barges docked in the canal's West Troy terminus, filled with grain and other products of upstate New York and the Great Lakes states. From there, Troy merchants towed the barges down the Hudson River to New York City or stored their contents in "compact blocks of lofty ware-houses" that stretched for a mile and half along Troy's waterfront. Iron mills, cotton mills, woolen mills, and flour mills had sprung up in the riverfront wards. Edward A. H. Allen, upon moving to the city three years before Edward Warren, thought it "a beautiful city" with tree-lined streets, nestled in a picturesque countryside with tall hills and deep gorges that invited botanizing. Allen noted, though, that Troy lacked an adequate park and that it was a "hot dusty city" kept tolerable in the summer only by constant sprinkling of its unpaved streets. Warren recalled it much more harshly at the time of his 1850 arrival. "Almost the entire social elevation was that of moneyed 'old families,' while for the population generally, the streets were the sewers, and pigs the scavengers. In summer, screaming charcoal men, and bell ringing milkmen, who never left their carts, vied with the birds in making sleeping impossible after 4 A.M. In spring the unpaved clay streets were a level sea of watery mud from curb to curb, and school-houses were the meanest buildings to be found."[40]

Troy had two nationally prominent educational institutions. Emma Willard's Troy Female Seminary, on Second Street between Congress and Ferry, had since 1821 provided instruction both for the girls of prominent local families and for boarding students from distant cities and states. Willard became famous as a leader in women's education and as the author of textbooks; many of her graduates went on to become teachers at schools, academies, and women's colleges throughout the United States. The Rensselaer Polytechnic Institute was then located a short walk to the northeast of the Female Seminary, occupying two brick buildings at the corner of Sixth and State streets where the river valley ended and a steep slope began to rise eastward. Opened in 1825, the Rensselaer School had from the beginning encouraged active student involvement in experimentation, deemphasizing lecturing. Students went on field trips to study machinery at local factories, and botany and geology in the countryside. The renamed Rensselaer Institute expanded to offer courses in civil engineering in the 1830s. Beginning in 1849 and continuing for about five years, it undertook a major reorganization that included a more rigorous curriculum in imitation of European scientific and technical schools, the addition of "Polytechnic" to its name, and the enlargement of the student body to 123 by 1856. The civil engineering course took three years to complete in the 1850s; expanding requirements meant that by the 1860s, most students took four years to graduate. Engineering instruction in the United States before the rise of RPI had taken place mainly at military academies, most notably West Point. The military precedent was briefly reflected during RPI's transition by the adoption of student uniforms; in 1851 and for a few years thereafter, RPI students wore dark green suits with bronze buttons, black stripes on the pants, and matching caps.[41]

Entering near the beginning of RPI's transition, Warren was able to count his Putnam schooling as a partial fulfillment of college credit, and to complete his studies in a little more than a year. He received a degree in Civil Engineering upon graduating from RPI in August 1851, at the age of nineteen. He tried applying for jobs as an engineering assistant, but concluded that he was naturally better suited to teaching. "I was better pleased with an invitation to remain as assistant at Troy, than I should have been to have begun an engineer's roving life," he recalled. He was hired in November 1851 as a "repeater," akin to a graduate teaching assistant, who supervised and evaluated sections of students as they gave extemporaneous presentations in response to questions. He continued on until 1853 as an "Instructor in Descriptive Geometry and Drawing," until the ongoing expansion of RPI created a position for him as professor in that field, retitled in 1854 as Professor of Graphics. He had gone from high school student to college professor in less than four years.[42]

Warren's sudden rise into the faculty put him in the awkward position of supervising young men who had recently been his peers. The initial period of his teaching career, he wrote, was "one of great annoyances incident to the transition, which must be gradual, from a student and an equal to that of an office." He was keenly aware of his inexperience, "being a teacher by nature and by a small amount of practice, yet being very diffident and anxious as one must be who has a place yet to create." In discussing the problems of transition, Warren mentioned two students in particular, each just two years younger than he: Charles Osborne of Illinois, who went on to a career as a lawyer, and John Bagley, his dear friend from the Putnam school. John entered RPI in the fall of 1850 but did not graduate until 1853. Warren and John had a falling out at some point during these years. Warren's earlier hope of bringing about John's religious reformation proved unavailing. Commenting in 1856 on John's initial expressions of faith, Warren exclaimed, "How terribly Bagley's after life proves the insufficiency of these spasmodic exercises." John Bagley nonetheless went on to a respectable career as an engineer in New York City.[43]

Warren struggled to assert his authority over his students while simultaneously befriending them. This would have been difficult for any instructor; college students had historically cultivated a reserved independence from the faculty, often with an adversarial tone. Warren's temper and sensitivity to slights made it harder for him. When students were falling behind in one of his drawing courses in February 1854, he scheduled special sessions to help anyone who needed it; two of the students attended only to be disruptive, so Warren gave up in frustration and left the room. He was dismayed that a student friend of his, "F", had developed a friendship with the disruptive boys. When "F" came to his boardinghouse room for a social visit that same afternoon, Warren noticed that he seemed to be adopting the other boys' coarse, wicked ways, including taking an interest in an upcoming dog race—the type of disreputable amusement popular among amoral "sporting men" and "jolly fellows" whose style of rough masculinity contrasted sharply with the evangelical manliness Warren valued. "That call, instead of doing anything to restore our old friendship will probably be the point from which I can view him only as a common acquaintance," Warren wrote. Reflecting in 1855 on the disrespect shown by some students, Warren acknowledged that it was partly his own fault. "My natural disposition has been to err on the side of allowing both myself and others . . . too much familiarity or even in some cases rudness [sic] of intercourse rather than to allow myself to conduct, so as to lead others to think that I was vain—proud or cold hearted." He was infuriated that a student had been so presumptuous as to make a dirty joke in his presence. Warren resolved to "compel the treatment I deserve," yet reflected that in practicing Christian love he must also share the suffering "of Him who though Divine was mocked and buffeted."[44]

The annoyances eased as his remaining peers graduated and as Warren grew into his role as professor. "This was the period in which I learned my rights, acquired confidence, and asserted my position," he recalled at the beginning of 1857. Unfortunately, he became overconfident and relaxed his "self vigilance." He struggled to strike the perfect balance of kindness and authority, tending in moments of irritation to make sarcastic comments about students' weaknesses and misbehavior. In January 1856, Warren had just recently berated himself in the pages of his journal for his failure to maintain proper order, when he was startled to learn that the director of the Institute, Prof. Benjamin Franklin Greene, was planning "to speak of improper familiarities of intercourse between students and their instructors!" The news led Warren to write another long journal entry noting that both the professor and the students were to blame if mutual friendliness deteriorated into disrespect. He later chastised himself for his weakness "in appearing to depend for happiness on the company of genial and good students."[45]

One of his good and genial students in the mid-1850s was George Hunt. In 1856, Hunt was studying in Warren's class in the "training school," RPI's preparatory program for incoming students needing to correct deficiencies in their earlier education. Warren took a liking to him because of his comments in class, and grew more interested when his parents and family moved to California. "I shall only define my position as his brother at present," Warren told his journal, "So as during the rest of the term to test his desert of confidence, as well as to build up by uninterrupted and spontaness[sic], yet entirely natural and unof-

Figure 2.2. Warren as an RPI faculty member, ca. 1869 or 1870, AC 18, Institute Archives and Special Collections, Rensselaer Polytechnic Institute, Troy, New York.

ficious kindness a foundation for my speaking to him bye and bye, my thoughts of advice—of the extent of religion—and of the means of perfecting character." Evidently, Hunt passed the test, but the course of the friendship is difficult to trace because this is the place in the journal where Warren made his most drastic changes, removing six sheets of paper (twelve pages). The second of the two missing sections, at least, contained a discussion of two students, one unidentified and the other evidently Hunt. The first page after the gap continues discussing one of the two, as follows: "[U]pon him shall tend to the fulfillment of my high hopes; for his good and for the continuance of this friendship for many years after his course as a student has closed." Warren went on to explain his larger intentions, "starting with the fixed fact that I am so connected with a hundred young men, as to make it easy and natural to influence them." He wished to mix his teaching with

> indirect work upon their hearts, a discreet and charitable mixture of the intercourse of a social nature at all times when I casually meet one or more students, and for my special work on hearts, the watching over the interests of the two who been [sic] with me; to satisfy my future self that this is not an outbreak of the constitutional excess of the emotional over the rational, in case the question should arise "why take these only," I say—Providence has placed them in my pathway, one has lost his mother, the other's parents are far away, and both have generous hearts, susceptible consiences [sic]—willingness to be benefitted, and this is enough.⁴⁶

As long as he could control his bent toward excessive emotion, he believed, he could use friendship with students to serve the Lord.

A later entry describes a social call by Hunt at Warren's boarding house. The two went out for a long walk during which they chatted about vacations and politics, and Warren offered advice on Hunt's program of study. Warren also gave some advice on morality, telling his friend to always keep in mind the wishes of his absent mother. Hunt promised to consider Warren's urging to become a Christian, and agreed to see him again. "He is full of life, being cheered by unexpected success in his examinations, and I doubt not he is my virtuous and noble friend for many a year," wrote Warren. "I look upon his fine abilities joined to his virtue, the whole anchored to that loved mother, when taken in connection with his age as affording a ground of confidence, and love unclouded by axiety [sic], firmer than that I have discovered in others whom I have loved as well, but have been deceived." Warren may well have been referring in the last comment to the disappointing John Bagley, and possibly even to Dicky. Hunt also proved disappointing. He called at Warren's boarding house later for private tutoring, but the friendship did not endure. Warren looked back fondly in 1858 on his pleasure with Hunt and his unrealized hopes. "Many such passages never had their proposed fulfillment, and it is well, for all <u>such</u> premeditated doings are [unnatural?]." He left it unclear whether that fulfillment would be religious conversion or personal intimacy, or both.⁴⁷

Warren kept trying to socialize with his students. Disliking the cold authority that other faculty assumed toward their classes, he wished to demonstrate "a free expression of sympathy with the students as far as circumstances make it rational." One entry describes an afternoon in the fall of 1856 when he attended a cricket game with a group of pupils and then invited several to accompany him to "to go to any place of interest about Troy." The students evidently declined. When one of them, Lewis F. Rice, later acted disrespectfully in class, Warren lashed back, forcing him to make a public apology. Warren then scolded the class, blaming students for professors' habit of distant reserve. "When they were complained of for austerity of manner or lack of sympathy with the students, it did not proceed necessarily from lack of good will but from having their attempts to associate with the students as freely and socially as obvious considerations of propriety would admit, met by responses of this kind." Warren believed friendship could develop even out of an asymmetrical power relationship, but students did not seem as comfortable with the prospect. Rice later tried to conciliate Warren by inviting him to give a speech to the class near the close of the 1857 spring term; Warren seized the occasion to make new social overtures, prefacing his speech by alluding to his solitude in "my little room which several of you have seen, and which I wish each of you who has not seen it, might see before the first of May." Comfortable in his dominant roles as teacher, mentor, and evangelist, Warren would not recognize any tension between intimacy and power. Instead, he blamed age. By early 1858, Warren reached a sober acceptance of a "too decided difference of age and sphere of voluntary mental action from the students to make any healthy natural acting as one of them possible, although the peculiar affection and relationship of benevolent manhood for genial youth may be all retained." He was twenty-six years old.[48]

Warren now recognized that he and his students stood on opposite sides of a generational divide, yet he was loath to change his behavior. He remained a demanding instructor who was willing to fail the majority of a class if necessary, but willing to give generous praise if it was merited. He kept trying to befriend students. The diary of Arthur Bower, an RPI student in the late 1860s, describes Prof. Warren's friendliness. Meeting the professor on the street shortly after coming to Troy in 1867, Bower was surprised to have him offer personal assistance in finding a better boarding house. When Bower began a drawing class with Warren, the professor saved him money by providing triangles and a ruler. Meeting Warren at the reading room later that fall, they went out together "to a sale of Chinese trinkets." Arthur Bower generally kept his distance from Warren over the next two years, but on the evening after an 1869 fieldtrip, "I went and called on Prof. Warren at his down town room to see some machine drawings. This is the first time I have ever called on him, although he gives an invitation every time."⁴⁹

Warren outlined his mature teaching philosophy in two publications in the late 1860s: a short booklet and a series of articles. These revealed the persisting influence of his years at the Putnam Free School, which he believed had provided him with the equivalent of "an English collegiate course." In his *Notes on Polytechnic or Scientific Schools in the United States* (1866), Warren argued that America's engineers and scientists needed more than a narrow technical education; they, like the most esteemed doctors, lawyers, and ministers, should first receive a broad collegiate education that would give "to the awakened, eager and active mind, facilities for gaining a comprehensive view, as from a hill top of the whole field of knowledge." Collegiate education properly aimed at "the discipline of the mental faculties, as working forces." A classical liberal arts education was just one way of training the undergraduate mind, Warren asserted in a nine-part essay in the *Journal of the Franklin Institute* in 1868 and 1869. The same benefits traditionally produced by study of the humanities could be achieved by comprehensive study of mathematics and the physical sciences. A polytechnic university that inculcated general culture and habits of careful thought could prove at least as well suited for the modern, Christian civilization of the United States as a classical, liberal arts school—which remained "brooded over . . . by a crew of disreputable divinities." Once broadened and inspired, students would be ready for the professional training that would qualify them for careers. As the goal of collegiate education in both its polytechnic and humanistic forms was "to generously develop the man," Warren argued that "the *whole being* and not merely the *technical knowledge* of the teacher should be favorably brought to bear upon the *entire* life of the student." The personal influence of instructors would assist students in strengthening their will, sharpening their moral sense, and taming their ardent emotions. Universities where faculty treated students with personal kindness would not need extensive disciplinary codes, Warren wrote in *Notes on Polytechnic or Scientific Schools*, but would be more like the Putnam school, where "all the relations of teachers and pupils were those of a polite company, bound together . . . by unwritten laws of social decorum and kindness."⁵⁰ This philosophy seemed to justify or even demand Warren's personal engagement with students.

Despite all his efforts, Edward Warren remained unpopular with students, partly because of his long-windedness, his prim moral lectures, and his demanding assignments. His classroom conflict with Rice in 1856 was set off by his recommendation of a crushing study schedule. Warren spared students the boredom of hearing him read from his extensive lecture notes, yet his extemporaneous speech was so verbose and rambling that many listeners found him hard to understand. Warren assigned his own textbooks, which were so despised that students in 1865 ended the spring term with a drunken, midnight ceremony to bury his *General Problems from the Orthographic Projections of Descriptive Geometry*, which they declared would burn in hell. Student newspapers mocked him. *The Surveyor* in February 1866 ran a scathing review of "Windy's Book," Warren's *Notes on Polytechnic and Scientific Schools*, referring to him as "a little spindle legged Professor." A few pages later, the students inserted a fictitious notice from Warren that poked fun at his obvious inexperience with women. "By chance, when my washing was returned last week, a lady's *chemise* accompanied it," wrote the bogus "S. E. W.," after a pretentious preamble. "The article is one of [the] finest I ever saw—that is, it is the only one I ever saw."⁵¹ After he announced his departure for the Massachusetts Institute of Technology in 1872, the *Transit* satirized his ponderous manner of speech:

> Professor Warren having found his newly established course of ninety-nine lectures on "The Moral and Intellectual Aspects of Tobacco Chewing," unappreciated by the students of Troy, has decided, after innumerable counter-revolutions of the subject in the depths of his inner-consciousness, to project himself into the bosom—rough on the bosom!—of the University of the North, at the Hub of the Universe, Boston, Mass.

The satire continued for another 103-word sentence, before concluding: "Hooray! Amen."⁵²

Though his students do not seem to have regarded him as "a born teacher," Warren's claim still makes sense as an expression of how central teaching was to his life. Warren's most important interactions with other people were didactic. Nowhere in his extensive diaries does he describe a close connection with a boy or man of his own age. The friendships he cultivated, the romances he desired, the efforts at saving souls—almost all of these were with younger people whom he could instruct affectionately. (The exception, his triangle with Whipple and Augusta, carried more complicated dynamics.) There is no surviving proof of romance between Edward Warren and any of his students, but in the case of George Hunt, at least, he obviously desired such intimacy while simultaneously fearing "an outbreak of the constitutional excess of the emotional over the rational."

"Man is primarily a union of matter and mind, of body and spirit, and *such* a union that the highest earthly well being of each is involved in that of the other," Warren wrote in the *Journal of the Franklin Institute*. It was standard rhetoric at the time to speak of a holistic approach to teaching, of ensuring the balanced development of the student's intellectual, moral, and physical powers. Midcentury educational reformers promoted physical education in ways ranging from recess games for young children to gymnasia for college students. At the Putnam school, Warren and his friends had created a gymnasium for their fellow students. Warren himself was never an athlete, and regretted "being deficient in knowledge of all the manly [accomplishments]," but he strove to stay in adequate physical condition and admired athleticism so much that he listed "higher gymnastics" among the fine arts. In keeping with his ideal of evangelical masculinity, Warren hoped that an occupied mind, a strong moral sense, and a healthy body would keep the student on the straight and narrow path to becoming "a whole man."[53]

Warren shared the Unitarian belief in a commonality between education and religion. "I believe it is the highest object of revealed religion to lead us," he wrote, "with the Church as our Training School, Scripture for our Text Book, Nature for our Illustrations, the Ministry for our Tutors, and God in all his Threefold character and action upon us, as the . . . Chief Teacher."[54] A teacher wishing to encourage a child's development must throw his whole being into his work, not withdraw into cold professionalism, Warren believed. So too should an evangelical Christian fully engage with the individual he wished to convert, bringing to bear all the intellectual rigor and emotional earnestness he could muster. Matters of the spirit demanded even greater personal investment than teaching. The emotional intensity of evangelism—espousing the word of Christ in order to spread the faith—could prove overwhelming, imperiling the soul of the evangelist and forcing him to confront the treacherous connections between the spirit and the body.

## 3

# Evangelism

> For the flesh lusteth against the Spirit, and the Spirit against the flesh: and these are contrary the one to the other: so that ye cannot do the things that ye would.
>
> —Galatians 5:17

Edward Warren knew the truth about himself long before he dared to share it with his parents. By the winter of 1853–54, the twenty-two-year-old Warren could keep up the pretense no longer. He was, he told his outraged father, attracted to the Episcopal Church.

Warren had experimented with different faiths since his Newburyport years. He attended services at Baptist, Unitarian, Universalist, and Episcopal churches, but remained committed for years to the orthodox Congregationalism in which he was raised. In Troy, which lacked a Congregational church, he joined the next best thing: the Presbyterians, another Calvinist sect. Yet he came to prefer the calm outlook, ritualism, and sensuous liturgy of the Episcopal Church. The senses, he believed, were "avenues to the soul." Though Episcopal worship is not known for emotional fervor, Warren found it answered his spiritual needs. Attending that church also offered him the chance to deepen his connection with his young friend, Willie Gilbert.

Throughout his spiritual journey Warren found in his faith both personal guidance and a sense of social responsibility. His personal religion provided him with a code for the conduct of life, encouraging his cultivation of kindly sentiments and his adherence to a rule-bound moralism. It also mandated that he serve as an evangelist—that is to say, that he espouse the Gospel and convert other individuals to the Christian life. Both aspects of his religious experience demanded attention to his emotional state, as he could evangelize effectively only if he served as a model of Christian love. Even before leaving Congregationalism, Warren avoided the frightening allusions to damnation that pervaded orthodox sermons, preferring the promise of harmony with God. His method of evangelism, encouraged by published advice from clergymen, involved intense engagement with friends, pleading with them as an expression of his concern for their eternal well-being. Plunging into the effort of conversion, Warren again found his personal needs entangled with duty to others. His love for potential converts exceeded Christian *agape* and extended into emotional and physical *eros*. As Warren's father probed him about his apostasy from Calvinism, one question reached deepest: Who, or what, had most influenced his choice of a new church? The answer would reveal the kind of a person Warren had become.

## Quite at Home in the Congregational Church

Warren grew up hearing the echoes of Puritanism in the Rev. Lyman Gilbert's Congregational church in West Newton, known as Second Church. Gilbert forcefully expounded Calvinist doctrine there from 1828 until his dismissal in 1856. Gilbert assured his congregation at the dedication of a new meeting house in 1848 that new ideas would not be heard there. "You are not to look for a change in Christianity. . . . It will never prevail over the earth except by retaining its inflexible character." Warren's father, a deacon, listened closely as Gilbert preached each Sunday, drawing on his own deep knowledge of theology to detect any weaknesses in the pastor's argument.[1]

Yet even Gilbert's orthodoxy was a diminished version of the Puritan faith. "You know that the sinner must be converted or perish," he declared in 1847, urging his flock to vigorous evangelism. "Will we leave them to perish, rather than offer the effectual fervent prayer of the righteous man, which could and would avail to secure their conversion to Christ?"[2] Gilbert was edging into dangerous territory. Anyone who had learned the Westminster Confession—an expression of Calvinist orthodoxy still accepted by many Congregationalists and Presbyterians at the time—knew that only the grace of God produced conversion. No prayers could save the soul predestined to hell. At best, prayers and sermons would simply play the part that God had always known they would: preparing one of the elect to receive the wholly undeserved grace of God, which the convert would be powerless to resist if it ever came.[3]

Congregationalists were struggling among themselves to develop methods of evangelism that would neither dwell on the discouraging news of predestination nor fall into the heresy of Arminianism, as they pejoratively called the belief that humans had the power to choose whether to accept God's grace.[4] They had a difficult message to sell. As Calvinists, they insisted that anyone—perhaps even an infant—could be damned for sin she or he had virtually no hope of avoiding. This vision of divine omnipotence jarred with American beliefs in individual freedom, and with republican expectations that power be exerted in reasonable ways. Such a harsh God seemed hard to love. The Unitarian leader William E. Channing observed in 1820 that "[w]ere a human parent to form himself on the universal Father, as described by Calvinism, that is, were he to bring his children into life totally depraved, and then to pursue them with endless punishment, we should charge him with a cruelty not surpassed in the annals of the world."[5]

New England Unitarians began to emerge in the late eighteenth century as a liberal element within Congregationalism. Facing opposition, they sharpened and expanded their critique of Calvinism until they fully repudiated predestination, original sin, and the divinity of Christ. A good Unitarian strove to develop a balanced character in which desires and affections were controlled by the conscience. By 1833, Unitarians had helped force the disestablishment of the Congregational church in Massachusetts and had taken over nearly one hundred churches, mostly near Boston. Though Unitarianism failed to become the new orthodoxy, its challenge to Calvinism contributed to the modification and ultimate abandonment of orthodox doctrines by most mainstream American Protestants over the nineteenth century.[6]

Whether Congregational, Presbyterian, Baptist, or Methodist, most Protestant churches in the antebellum era expected that people would begin a regenerate Christian life with a conversion experience. Conversion, explained the Presbyterian Rev. Thomas Skinner and the Congregational Rev. Edward Beecher in a guide to evangelism first published in 1832, "is preceded by conviction of sin, and . . . a determination ever after to renounce it in all its forms, to fix the affection supremely on God, and to live in entire obedience to his will. It implies also a sincere affectionate reliance on the atonement of Christ as the only and sufficient ground of pardon." A conversion experience during a revival could involve self-abasement in public with lamentations about one's worthlessness in the unregenerate state.[7]

Many affluent Americans and aspiring members of the middle class found unrestrained public emotionality to be distasteful. The emerging middle-class culture of the antebellum Northeast placed high value on privacy. This was the era when private family life became celebrated as essential to respectability, and when etiquette manuals advised rigid self-control in public spaces.[8] Unitarianism appealed to affluent New Englanders for its emphasis on self-culture and its avoidance of the "coarse passions" of revival sermons. Believing that humans were born without sin, Unitarians saw no need for a rebirth and hence felt little compulsion to interfere in the private lives of others by urging repentance. Affluent people throughout Northeast were drawn to Episcopalianism for similar reasons. Putting greater emphasis on infant baptism than on adult conversion, Episcopal clergy in the Northeast tended to avoid evangelism. Congregationalists complained that affluent Congregationalists joined the Episcopal Church despite the vast doctrinal differences because the church appealed to their desire for social exclusiveness, because it tolerated dancing and the theater, and because it made no awkward demands about spreading the faith. The Episcopal Church made rapid inroads among the antebellum American elite. Bolstered also by immigration from England, the Church grew from fewer than 31,000 congregants in 1832 to nearly 140,000 in 1859.[9]

Attending Phillips Academy, starting in 1846, ensured that the teenage Edward Warren would continue to worship in Congregational meetings during his first months away from home. He brushed up on his knowledge of the Westminster catechism with the help of a divinity student from the conservative Andover Theological Seminary. Warren was swept up in the enthusiastic religiosity of many of his Phillips classmates during a revival in Andover that winter. He attended prayer meetings with classmates in their rooms and in the rooms of divinity students. He and his friend Philip Blake extended their devotion into efforts at moral reform, as they tried to stop classmates from smoking tobacco and drinking coffee. Coffee was only a minor vice in itself, but like tobacco and alcohol it was considered to have potentially demoralizing effects by stimulating boys to masturbation. Warren and Blake told one devout boy that they would no longer pray with him in his room if he kept drinking coffee, but they failed to secure the lasting reform of another friend who went back to smoking.[10]

Newburyport, where he moved in 1848, offered Warren the freedom to try out other Protestant sects. The Putnam School was nonsectarian, and Warren boarded for two years with the family of a Baptist clergyman, the Rev. Nicholas Medbery, whom he later described as "very kind." He occasionally attended Medbery's Second Baptist (Green Street) Church, and also ventured into Unitarian services at Thomas Wentworth Higginson's First Religious Society, but neither appealed to him. Warren watched with distaste as Medbery baptized converts by immersing them in the dirty water by the wharves. At the Unitarian church, a Higginson sermon on morality struck him as one that "might easily have been composed by a moral pagan and it had no more of the Gospel of Christ in it."[11] Warren attended a combined Universalist and Unitarian church on the first Sunday of his 1849 teaching stint in Charlton, politely accompanying the owner of the house in which he boarded. Universalists, a sect that flourished among New Englanders of modest status, rejected the idea of a limited elect; they believed everyone could eventually be welcomed into heaven. Warren walked out disgusted: "such bare-faced contradictions of scripture I cannot endure."[12]

Warren preferred the more familiar services of Presbyterians and orthodox Congregationalists. New Englanders at this time still worshipped in both the morning and the afternoon, with a break when people went home for a midday meal. Warren usually visited two churches in Newburyport each Sunday, often the First Presbyterian Church and one of the three orthodox Congregational meetinghouses in the city. Starting in June 1848, he came to prefer a fourth Congregational church a short distance outside the city limits, in the Belleville section of Newbury.[13] He admired the sermons and was pleased with the Bible class, which included his older friends Francis Whipple and John Blunt. Warren began the second volume of his journal on April 11, 1849, with an entry proclaiming his decision to join the church, a momentous step that required him to give an account of his spiritual regeneration. "I have resolved to boldly perform my duty and so has Mr. Blunt we were both examined this afternoon at Mr. Fiske's church meeting and shall join his church," he wrote. The ceremony in front of the congregation took place later that month. Warren was "just 17 ½," he recorded. "I tried to realize what I was doing and I hope I shall be better in the future. I have felt very happy all day." He also joined the choir, where he felt himself "quite at home."[14]

Warren regularly summarized the Rev. Daniel T. Fiske's sermons at Belleville, favorably describing arguments that conformed to Congregational orthodoxy. Preaching on the 139th Psalm, which describes God's constant scrutiny of each soul, Fiske impressed Warren with "the retributive power of the memory and conscience, and the consequences of not regulating the passions."[15] And so, when Warren walked out of the scripturally false Universalist meeting on his first Sunday in Charlton, he sought the truth in the nearest Congregational church, whose members called themselves the First Calvinistic Congregational Society of Charlton. There he heard a sermon than reminded him of his duty "to bring those about us to Jesus. I am sure that I sincerely wish to do all I can for those here by example and prayer, but I scarcely see how I can speak with those who are so much older than myself."[16]

## Overflowing with Holy Affections

To attempt to bring someone to Jesus carried implications of power and superiority: it suggested that the evangelist had God on his side and that the potential convert did not. Such implications had been more readily accepted in the hierarchical society of colonial New England, when esteemed pastors thundered warnings of damnation from the pulpit. The relatively egalitarian, fluid society of mid-nineteenth-century New England was uncomfortable with such overt exertions of religious power, and was developing new approaches to evangelism. Antebellum Americans valued gentle forms of influence, yielding a greater cultural role to the emotions and to those who were thought to deploy them most effectively—women. Guided by their nurturing instinct, women were said to exert a soft moral influence on those they loved. As described in magazines, advice books, and theological works, the practice of evangelism in the public space of the male-dominated church or revival meeting was now potently supplemented by private appeals from friends and family. These appeals drew strength from affectionate bonds between the evangelist and the convert, and were based on impulses of the heart more than the logic of the mind.[17]

Antebellum Protestant religious experience gradually shifted toward what writers at the time called "heart religion" and what the historian

Richard Rabinowitz has labeled "devotionalism" and "sentimentalism." Religious experience after 1840, Rabinowitz writes, became intensely focused on an individual's emotional connection with God, rather than on doctrine or morality. "Love was an ever more important aim and standard of religious life" for mid-nineteenth-century devotionalists, he writes. "And the love they spoke of so frequently was increasingly identical in all its manifestations—in the love between spouses, between parent and child, between friends, and between Christ and Christian. In each case, the dominant aesthetic, the main concern, of the devotionalist was establishing a one-to-one relationship." Other scholars have stressed the gender implications of heart religion: devotionalists promoted an "androgynous model of piety" by urging male as well as female Christians to adopt the emotional qualities associated with feminine moral influence.[18]

Congregationalists emphasized the power of emotions to reinforce analytical persuasion. The Rev. Horace Bushnell, in particular, took this approach in sermons and publications in the 1840s and 1850s. Faith, Bushnell told his Hartford flock, required trusting the teachings of the heart. Emotional influences were so potent that they could turn a child into a Christian long before any conversion experience, he argued in his 1847 book *Views of Christian Nurture*. When children were too young to follow reasoned arguments, parents should "rather seek to teach a feeling than a doctrine, to bathe the child in their own feeling of love to God." Influence in this form also worked outside the lines of parental authority, Bushnell believed. Every individual exerted an "unconscious influence" each time she or he came in contact with another person, whose sympathetic powers were "tinder to those sparks of emotion revealed by looks, tones, manners, and general conduct." The loving and worshipful feelings that radiated from the true Christian had lasting power because of their source in God.[19]

Bushnell freely acknowledged that similar ideas of Christian love had been expressed by many of his theological predecessors. The Unitarian William E. Channing argued that each person carried a divinely implanted principle of love, and that as he felt its power he would grow in likeness to God. "He more than believes, he feels the Divine presence; and gradually rises to an intercourse with his Maker, to which it is not irreverent to apply the name of friendship and intimacy," Channing declared in 1828.[20] Unitarians and Congregationalists disagreed about whether intimacy with God was easier or more difficult to achieve if one thought of Christ as part of a divine Trinity. Channing asserted that understanding Jesus as

God turned him into such a distant figure that "we cannot feel a sense of brotherhood and friendship with him." Bushnell argued that such an understanding helped people "believe in the particular and personal love, in which he reigns from eternity." Either way, the key point was Christ's role as an intimate friend for the believing Christian.[21]

New England clergy before 1830 had paid limited attention to dyadic friendships, despite the flourishing of Christian fellowship within their congregations. Some pastors even scorned individual intimacy as a distraction from commitment to the church as a whole. By the 1840s and 1850s, evidently encouraged by changing views of emotionality in the broader culture, clergy used friendship as a central metaphor for religious experience. Articles and books examined Biblical representations of friendship. One popular example was David and Jonathan, whose love for each other was described in 2 Samuel as "passing the love of women." Some writers tried to read meaning into a few brief allusions to the intimacy between Jesus and his disciple John, the longest of which mentions that "there was leaning on Jesus's bosom one of his disciples, whom Jesus loved."[22] Unlike worldly friendship, the love guided by religious feelings was said to overcome misunderstandings, self-interest, and outside pressures. A Christian would use his affective links with a sinner to bring about his conversion; making God the center of their relationship, the two friends would continue to offer correction whenever one risked falling back into sin. Christian friendship would persist even when the whims of fortune lifted one friend to a higher rank or plunged him into poverty. This uplifting harmony of souls could continue past death into Heaven. Another crucial distinction between worldly and Christian friendship is that the latter showed a gentle, steady affection unmarred by emotional excess.[23]

A few weeks before starting his teaching job in Charlton in the autumn of 1849, Edward Warren read "the good little book, *Hints to Aid Christians in Converting Men*." This was the popular guide to evangelism by Thomas Skinner and Edward Beecher. The two clergymen argued that, as the millennium was drawing near, each Christian should strive to hasten its coming by laboring for the salvation of whomever they could most directly influence. Skinner and Beecher urged the Christian to converse "personally and privately" with friends and family members. The Christian should begin with friendly inquiries into his target's knowledge of religion and his relations with God. Discussions of doctrine were less effective than praying together or making heartfelt appeals to eschew sin and repent. Skinner and Beecher warned that affection between the Christian and the prospective convert posed dangers as well as opportunities. The evangelist's "expression of parental, filial, or other natural affection" must remain subordinate to the love of God; it must not interfere with the effort at conversion, however uncomfortable that effort might prove. The Christian should remain most deeply identified with Christ, feeling his sufferings and imitating his example of righteousness, in order to provide a model for the prospective convert. Further, the Christian should remain in full control of his emotions, never showing frustration or imperiousness. "The moment you permit your passions to be excited, you are stripped of all your power."[24]

Skinner and Beecher observed that many Christians worried about alienating friends by discussing religion, but they reassured readers that sinners secretly wished Christians would try to rescue them. At this time, Protestant friends could be presumed to have some vestigial sense of religious duty. Friendships in antebellum America often involved discussing feelings, and—as feelings had not yet become so exclusively the province of romance and psychotherapy—this discussion could be framed by faith. A mild inquiry into the state of one's soul was likely to be received as a well-meaning expression of concern, or could be deflected gracefully rather than taken as a judgment. Though Warren had yet to succeed in bringing anyone to Jesus, he had found that Skinner and Beecher were correct about the receptivity of friends to religious discussion. In June 1849, in the midst of his flirtation with Augusta Wood, Warren went on a picnic excursion with her, John Bagley, and John's girlfriend Jenny Andrews. The long walk home was potentially awkward, given John's and Jenny's preoccupation with each other and Warren's tension with Augusta over her relationship with Francis Whipple. Warren and Augusta walked hand in hand for a while, then arm in arm, and Warren brought up the subject of a religious tract that Whipple had given him, Philip Doddridge's *The Rise and Progress of Religion in the Soul* (1745). "In the most natural manner possible I turned off onto religious subjects and talked kindly about them all the way home. I shall try hard to benefit her now I have begun." It is possible that Augusta considered this monologue a crashing bore, bearable only as a way to fill the time, and yet the friendship continued. Warren continued going on walks with her that summer, and found her "happy . . . [and] very sociable."[25]

Talk about faith had provided much of the conversational content in Warren's romantic friendships with Dicky Derby, John Bagley, and Cajah Lunt, and succeeded in building emotional affinity. Warren was not fully conscious of a distinction between his personal and his evangelical goals. "Since meeting I have been looking at Dickey's miniature and thinking over what I intend to say to him, about his greatest interests when he visits me," Warren mused on Valentine's Day 1847, as he thought about Dicky's upcoming overnight visit to Andover. "For how can I better prove my love to my best Friend [Jesus] than by trying to feed his lambs for him and where is there a more tender lamb than my brother [Dicky]." The reference here is to a passage in the Gospel of John (21:15), in which the resurrected Christ directs Simon Peter to devote himself to the work of Christian pastorhood. Warren later exclaimed, during a moment of optimism in 1848 about Dicky's increasing faith, "Oh how tender will our next meeting be now that I regard him more as a present from our common Father." In the early weeks of Warren's intimacy with John in 1849, the two boys discussed John's doubts about his faith. "I hope that he may at once be a Christian if not I hope to be guided in the best way to lead him to have a stronger faith. How many happy hours we may thus spend to-gether," Warren wrote. For him to convert a friend would be a glorious triumph, bringing him and the friend together in blissful consummation of spiritual unity and personal affection. The ecstatic tone in which Warren tells of kissing an increasingly religious friend cannot simply be deprecated as boastful conquest or teenage horniness—no more than any young lovers' first blush of pleasure can be defined so narrowly. Warren's joy embraced the spiritual, the acquisitive, the emotional, and the physical, in ways that neither he nor we can easily untangle.[26]

The emotional influence described by Bushnell, Skinner, and Beecher was said to work even on people of superior status, such as older friends, older relatives, parents, or husbands. But Warren chose to direct his influence toward younger people. "I have older friends to imitate and younger ones to imitate me let me be careful then what I imitate and what example I set before all," he wrote in the summer of 1847. This focus can be partly explained by Warren's pattern of romantic friendships only with younger males, and the circumstances of his later career teaching children, teenagers, and young men. Further, as he wrote in Charlton in 1849, he doubted his ability to "speak with those who are so much older than myself" on religious matters.

By focusing on the young, Warren was drawing on one of the strongest remaining forms of hierarchy in the antebellum Northeast. Hereditary distinctions of social rank had long since been undermined by the cultural changes of the American Revolution; chattel slavery had been discredited and then banned in the Northern states; political rights had expanded to a wider range of white men in the Jacksonian era; habits of deference to wealth were fading amid the social division of industrial cities; and even women's subordination to men was questioned by some radicals in the late 1840s. The "passion for equality," as the historian Nathan Hatch calls it, undermined older patterns of clerical authority, and encouraged a sense that religion and theology were matters of individual judgment. Old-fashioned authoritarian styles of parenting were frowned upon. Yet the belief in hierarchy persisted where children were involved. The distinction between maturity and immaturity—however vague—remained an unquestioned dividing line between those who could assert power and those who could not. While emotional influence might work on anyone, it could be deployed without hesitation on those whose youth put them in an inferior position. The youngest child could and should be molded by his parents, wrote Bushnell. "Whatever their requirement may be, he can as little withstand it, as the violet can cool the scorching sun, or the tattered leaf can tame the hurricane. . . . In all this, they infringe upon no right of the child, they only fulfill an office which belongs to them."[27] Older children and youths remained malleable to the influence of teachers and employers.

## Sweet Willie

In the early 1850s, while Warren was just beginning his career as a professor at RPI, he launched a new effort to befriend and convert younger boys—not those on the cusp of manhood whom he taught every day, but boys in their early to mid-teenage years, like Dicky, John, and Cajah had been when he fell in love with them. He created an informal social club with a group of young friends he came to call the "Dry River Brotherhood." Though the journals from these years are missing, Warren mentioned later that "the happy circumstance that led to the formation of our present friendship" occurred on April 29, 1851, a day worthy of annual commemoration thereafter. Warren erased from his journals the names of the boys involved in this small group, but he let slip in 1854 and 1855 that among its members were "Clem," "Rousseau," and "Willie." Of these only William Eaton Gilbert can be identified with certainty. Warren considered the membership to be open and tried to recruit additional boys. The group met weekly, apparently on Friday evenings in Warren's room in his boarding house.[28]

The group took its name from the "Dry River," a winding gorge on the other side of the Hudson from Troy where Warren and the boys went on several excursions. It was a beautiful place. An RPI student, Edward A. H. Allen, described the Dry River in summer as a "very romantic spot, being a circuitous fissure in the shale rock for several miles. A little rivulet runs through it, but it seems to have once been the bed of a mighty river. The banks are in many places 60 or 70 ft. high." Hemlocks clung to crevices in the cliffs, shading the cascades and pools below. Warren and the boys enjoyed excursions on which they played in the water and sketched the scenery.[29]

Most of the Dry River Brotherhood's meetings focused on reading and religious discussion, with some attention to current issues such as slavery. Warren encouraged the boys to adopt healthy habits of early rising and to keep precise records of the times at which they went to bed and got up, in keeping with a practice that he followed meticulously but discontinuously. He read to the boys from novels and inspirational tracts, and they read together from scripture. Warren also exhorted the boys to greater religious devotion; his journal includes a draft of a long and pompous speech he considered giving on the subject of friendship. In it, he urged the boys toward a loving style of evangelical masculinity in place of the "mistaken view of manliness" that demanded suppression of the emotions. "It is manly to restrain our feelings within proper bounds, and not to let ardent affection for one or a few friends, lead us into habits of partiality or neglect of our duties to all with whom we are concerned," Warren acknowledged, "but it is a sad mistake to suppose that we become more manly by trying to crush our warm feelings and act coldly to our best friends. The very beginning of the precept 'Love not in word only,' implies that love thus shown is true love if backed up by 'deed and truth.' 'Love one another with a pure heart fervently' implies a warmth of heart as a quality of perfect character." Warren was pleased by the effect the club had on his young friends; in the missing Volume Six of his journal, he recorded the boys' expressions of faith on occasions when "they so fully unveiled their spirits to me."[30]

Warren attempted to build a stronger individual relationship with Clem, to whom he gave a gilt-decorated copy of Henry Ward Beecher's *Seven Lectures to Young Men* as a Christmas present in 1854. Clem accompanied him on a vacation visit to Warren's family in West Newton in the summer of 1855. Warren spent days showing him the sights of Boston, and spent an evening with him in the company of Dicky Derby. Clem proved a disappointment. "He has real innocence and a good deal of intelligence, but is faulty and undisciplined in two ways. He is deficient in observation as indicated by forgetfulness of localities and inattention to my explanations. And in manners, he shows too much the influence of his daily business."[31]

William Gilbert was by far his favorite. "Sweet Willie," as Warren called him in poorly erased passages of the journal, was the son of the wealthy industrialist Uri Gilbert, whose Eaton, Gilbert & Co. produced railroad cars, streetcars, and coaches from a factory on Green Island. Uri Gilbert was also president of the Troy Savings Company, a trustee of RPI, had served as an alderman in the 1840s, and would go on to serve two terms as mayor of Troy after the Civil War. He was described after his death in 1888 as "one of Troy's most prominent, loved, and respected citizens." In the mid 1850s, Willie lived with his parents, his four siblings, his grandmother, and four servants in a house on Fifth Street (now called Fifth Avenue) a block from the railroad station and about five blocks from RPI.[32]

"W___ has yet to disappoint me in responding with a full heart to all my efforts to do him good," Warren wrote on Sunday, April 9, 1854, in a journal entry pocked with short erasures. The fifteen-year-old boy had come by invitation to Warren's boardinghouse room that evening, and after some friendly conversation Warren turned the talk to religion. "With satisfaction to myself I tried in my kindest manner to enkindle his interest in the subjects of confirmation, representing the church as the safe fold of Christ." He urged Willie to form a Bible study class with several other boys. Willie and Warren went for walks together on Wednesday and Thursday of that week; later Thursday evening, Warren led some of his fellow members of his Presbyterian choir to Willie's house and serenaded him. Warren at this time was attending both the First Presbyterian Church and St. Paul's Episcopal Church, where Willie worshipped with his family.[33]

The deepening friendship reached a climax on Sunday evening, April 16, 1854. Warren and Willie separately attended what Warren felt was an inspiring sermon at St. Paul's on the text of II Corinthians 3:18, which describes becoming more Christlike by contemplating Christ as if in a mirror. The beginning of what happened next is recorded in the diary despite some erasures: "The singing was sweet, the moon shone brightly and. . . . W___ was there and met me at the door," Warren wrote. From the church door at State and Church Street, Warren began walking Willie toward the Gilbert home on Fifth Street, less than three blocks away. They struck up an engrossing conversation, starting with the beauty of the sermon. As they walked, they remained fully in the public eye. Months later, Warren would favorably contrast urban living with life in a village where nosy neighbors scrutinized all their neighbors' faults—but Troy was just a modest-sized city, a far cry from the anonymous environments of New York or Philadelphia. Warren and Willie, their faces lit by the gibbous moon and Troy's new gas lamps, would have been easily recognized by neighbors, townspeople, and fellow parishioners on their own routes home from St. Paul's. Regardless, the two did not stop at Willie's house but continued north to Grand Division Street (now Grand Street). Here the story stops abruptly, as the next sheet of paper has been removed from the diary with short snips of a scissors. Perhaps they turned east, up the hill toward the more secluded Eighth Street, which would become Warren's favorite walk, "always suggesting the most cheerful thoughts of Willie." We can never know. Yet Warren apparently could not bear to destroy all record of this evening. From an incompetently erased notation in the journal's index, it is evident that the two eventually looped back southwest toward Warren's boarding house near the Hudson riverfront, where "Willie spent the night with me." Willie was fifteen years old at the time; Warren was twenty-two.[34]

Nothing in the journal explains how Willie could have stayed out without alarming his parents, or how he might have reentered in the morning without being noticed. In this upstate city in early spring, the windows of the Gilbert home would have been closed for the night and the doors locked. It is doubtful that Willie's parents would have given him a key to enter the house before the family awoke; "night latches" at the time were symbols of disreputable freedom from familial supervision. He would have had to somehow push open a window, or enlist the collusion of a servant, or pretend upon entering the house in the morning that he had just stepped out for an early stroll.[35]

In any case, the sleepover at Warren's does not seem to have been repeated, even though Warren soon moved into a new room on Ferry

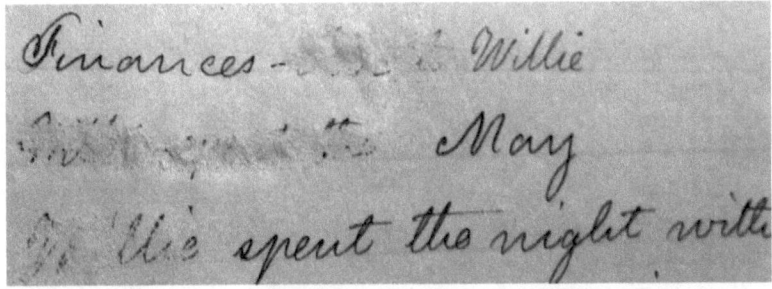

Figure 3.1 Crude erasures in Warren's Journal, volume 7, 1994–6, Samuel Edward Warren papers, Institute Archives and Special Collections, Rensselaer Polytechnic Institute, Troy, New York.

Street and decorated it to be more inviting and uplifting. "I hope I shall be better and especially fight against wandering imaginations, uncharitableness and idleness. I have taken much pleasure in thinking of it as a place where my little friends can always find a welcome, and be made both happier and better," he wrote. Willie remained friendly through the spring and summer of 1854. He began to share Warren's interest in singing, and the friends continued to enjoy walks together, one of which Warren described as "most affectionate and profitable." Warren exclaimed in a moment of optimism, "how quickly an answering chord in W___'s heart responds to any remark of mine on a delicate point of friendship." They talked about religion and made vague plans for a walking excursion to Lake George, a good fifty miles north. But Willie proved neither as friendly nor as devout as Warren had hoped. Warren worked in August on a multipart letter to Willie discussing Acts 17, in which Paul confronts Greek idolatry. Clearly, there was another topic, but Warren later erased and scribbled out several lines. He warned himself to keep his mind busy on useful things, as "thinking may be a source of evil." The corresponding entry in the index reads "Sensuousness." As autumn approached, Willie raised the idea of attending boarding school in Lansingburgh, just north of Troy but beyond convenient walking distance for Warren. Frustrated, Warren wrote him an unpleasant letter in September that utterly failed to persuade Willie to take courses instead in RPI's preparatory program. Willie responded with a note informing Warren that he had moved to Lansingburgh.[36]

The friendship revived a bit in November, as Warren and Willie spent Sunday evenings together reading Bunyan, but there was no revival of the old intimacy.[37] Warren tried to make sense of what had happened, as he so often did, by meditating on scripture. On December 22, 1854, he wrote a ten-page rumination that drifted from a religious lecture he had heard, to physical and spiritual appetites, to the trustworthiness of intuition, and to his experience of friendship, before winding up back at religion and the fall of Adam:

> By the yeilding [*sic*] of the soul to temptations proceeding from the appetites of the body the flesh obtained mastery and man fell from his high destiny. Christ is called the second Adam because as in Adam the race lives bodily so in Christ the whole race was quickened and new created and should inherit his spiritual life and realize again the supremacy of spirit over body . . . if we yeild [*sic*] to the temptation to sin against our own souls by rejecting him our souls return to utter bondage to sin.[38]

Though Warren had not given up on the possibilities of harmony between body and soul, he was worried about the flesh prevailing over the spirit.

Three days later, on Christmas, Willie surprised Warren by appearing at his door to invite him to dinner and a ride. "Why do I ever doubt his kindness?" Warren asked himself. "Laying aside all passionate kindness of blind impulse on the one hand, and all jealousy on the other . . . I will try to be ever with an even and rational kindness his sincere, and faithful and constant friend." Willie continued to visit but without as much warmth or commitment as Warren wanted. In May 1855, Warren sent another critical letter, whose intemperate preachiness he regretted the next day. "There may be <u>real selfishness</u> lurking under apparently fervent love," he admitted to himself. Continuing to agonize over his harsh words, Warren wrote that "I regard nothing with such a chill of horror, as seeing him nearly a Christian and then led away." He wished that his life could give steady testimony to his love of religion and his desire to share it with a friend.[39]

Warren had done what Beecher and Skinner had warned him not to do. He had let personal affections and strong emotions interfere with bringing his friend to God. Worse, he admitted to his journal that summer, his "manner of showing love" to Willie had been physically inappropriate as well. "When my love was more impulsive but less true than now I carressed [*sic*] him more than was seemly, and gave him a distaste for the whole thing," he confessed. "Now, it is but just and generous too, that I should wait patiently till an improved inward character and outward action on my part should acheive [*sic*] that double triumph of both removing the effect of my former errors, and then winning an intercourse that should be the happy mean between the extreme of abuse and the extreme of neglect."[40]

This is a peculiar passage that demands close reading. First, what did Warren mean by writing that he caressed Willie "more than was seemly"? Though the larger entry in the diary discusses Christian love and character, this wording implies an atypical concern with keeping up appearances. Warren was usually more concerned with righteousness than propriety. For example, an entry on his New Year's Day social calls reveals that he rejected offers of drinks with a judgmental rigidity that risked offending his hosts.[41] It is unlikely that he believed Willie's discomfort reflected a concern with public appearance. As Warren would have limited his most intimate touches to the privacy of his bedroom, Willie's distaste must have had more to do with the nature of the caresses than with how they seemed to others. So the word *seemly* is incongruous in this context—yet it may have been deliberate. Given Warren's constant reading of the Bible, it makes sense to interpret the passage as a scriptural reference. The odd wording echoes one of the few New Testament verses that condemn same-sex intercourse: Romans 1:27, in which Paul warns of the wrath of God against men who "leaving the natural use of the woman, burned in their lust one toward another; men with men working that which is *unseemly*." The caresses that Warren considered "more than . . . seemly" were probably of the sort that Paul deplored.[42]

Another peculiar aspect of this passage is Warren's hope of rebuilding his friendship with Willie in "the happy mean between the extreme of abuse and the extreme of neglect." Abuse and neglect are mismatched endpoints for a spectrum of social engagement. The opposite of abuse would be better expressed as kindness, caring, or cherishing, while the opposite of neglect would be smothering attention. Warren appears to suggest that his affection toward Willie had grown so intense that it was experienced as overbearing. Quite possibly, Warren chose the word *abuse* as a euphemism for the type of caressing that led to orgasm. The terms *abuse* and *self-abuse* were commonly used at this time as variants for "the solitary vice," which was said to have damaging effects on physical, moral, and psychological well-being.[43] Warren may have been expressing the hope that he could learn to express affection toward Willie in a way that avoided the genital play his friend disliked.

The historian Bruce Dorsey observes that the study of sexuality confronts great difficulties in meeting the strict standards of historical practice "requiring definitive empirical evidence of sexual acts." (If sexual acts were as rare as explicit documentary evidence suggests, the human species would certainly have gone extinct.) But, Dorsey continues, scholars are not so much interested in the mechanical details of long-past sex acts as in the broader erotic relationships of participants and the context in which this eroticism developed. Close examination of individual experiences allows us "to investigate the combined physical, spiritual, and sexual dimensions of men's desire for, and relationships with, other men." Warren's story, too, offers a glimpse into such erotic connections and contexts, regardless of his method of caressing Willie and regardless of how much farther the two of them went. After his encounters with Willie, Warren would change his ideas both about religion and eroticism, as he turned toward what he consider a sobered, mature manhood.

### The Use of the Senses in Religion

Warren's friendship with Willie left him with an awareness of potentially positive connections between faith and the body, a belief that rested uneasily with Christian theology but that seemed to him to be harmonious with Episcopal worship. Warren continued his slow drift into Episcopalianism, finally renouncing his Presbyterian ties and being confirmed into the Episcopal Church in 1856.

Warren criticized Calvinism and the dictatorial "Puritanism" of New England, but his doctrinal objections were not his main reason for switching churches. The Presbyterian pastor whose church he attended in Troy, the Rev. Nathan S. S. Beman, had long since embraced views that seemed provocatively Arminian. Beman had stirred controversy among Presbyterians in 1825 by publishing the argument that Jesus's sacrifice opened the gates of heaven to any sincere believer. Beman supported the divisive "new measures" of the evangelist Charles G. Finney, joined Finney in revivals in Troy and in Williamstown, Massachusetts, and supported him at an 1827 confrontation with Lyman Beecher and other leading Congregationalists. Warren was unenthusiastic about revivals but did not raise objections to Beman's views on the subject, nor did he seem repelled by what many Troy residents considered Beman's domineering manner. Beman was outspoken on social issues of interest to Warren, strongly supporting temperance and opposing slavery. Another obvious incentive for Warren to stay in the First Presbyterian Church was the fact that Beman served as president of RPI.[44]

Warren's change of religious affiliation was less a matter of fleeing Calvinism than of embracing Episcopalianism. He began to consider the Episcopal Church's attractions in the summer of 1852, and slowly drifted into the church in 1853, at the age of twenty-two. Warren's previous impressions of Episcopalianism had not been favorable. The gulf between Congregational and Episcopal doctrine was wider than that between the Congregationalists and most Protestant sects. The High Church faction, in particular, was vehemently anti-Calvinist. There was a minority evangelical faction which like some of its counterparts in the Congregational and Presbyterian churches believed that "the liveliest emotions of admiration, wonder, love and gratitude" could be conduits for the Holy Spirit. Yet evangelical Episcopalianism was weaker in the Northeast than in the Midwest and the Washington, D.C., area. The trend in New York State, particularly, was toward the High Church persuasion that had been gaining strength since the beginning of the century and had been reinforced by the influence of England's Tractarian movement in the 1830s. Welcomed in New York State by Bishop Benjamin T. Onderdonk, Tractarianism encouraged a return to older ritual that struck critics as suspiciously Roman Catholic. Indeed, some of the Anglican Tractarians eventually converted to Catholicism, as did seventeen American Episcopalian clergy between 1850 and 1853 alone. Encouraged by Tractarianism, the High Church sought in its own way to appeal to individual affections. Echoing the trend within Anglo-American Protestantism, the Episcopal Church in America placed new emphasis on the individual's devotional experience and on a sense of intimacy with Christ, displayed in each service by the splendor and mystery of the Eucharist. Churches began to take a greater interest in the effects of beautiful architecture and church music.[45]

Warren admired the look and feel of Episcopal worship. Attending St. Paul's frequently in 1854 and 1855, he decided that "so long as man inhabits a mortal body, whose senses are avenues to the soul, all these senses should be appealed to." The Episcopal Church "educates the sentiment of <u>Reverence</u> and Provides for the love of <u>appropriateness</u> and <u>beauty</u> without tending to superstition," he wrote in 1855. In a long rumination titled "The Use of the Senses in Religion," he argued that

God intended mankind to use its senses, especially sight and hearing, as an aid to faith. Episcopalianism was the happy medium between the excesses of Catholicism and the austerity of Puritanism.[46]

For Warren, the beauty of the church was more than just smells, bells, and stained glass. "The Church's theory is that the noblest work and highest duty of man is to build up and restore to its ideal beauty and strength his own character," he wrote in 1856, in a time of doubt about his ability to influence others through direct appeals. In contrast to the spasmodic passions of evangelical revival meetings, High Church Episcopal worship worked a steady improvement on the individual soul. He wrote admiringly of a sermon by St. Paul's new pastor, Thomas W. Coit, that echoed Horace Bushnell in urging parents to "educate the <u>hearts</u> of their children." The patient cultivation of a beautiful soul through Episcopal devotion would exert a subtle influence on other people in one's life. "Created as we are our fullest affections can only be given to <u>embodied</u> excellence, we love Christianity better as embodied in a living, sympathizing person," Warren wrote in a draft of an 1858 letter to his cousin, Henry Freeman Allen, on the occasion of Henry's adult baptism as an Episcopalian.[47]

Warren's enthusiasm about beauty and sentiments was harmonious with the culture of antebellum Romanticism, but it took him farther from Protestant doctrine, and even Christianity broadly, than many contemporaries were willing to go. In one ill-considered effusion, he toyed with the idea that "the spontaneous life of free impulse is the only fascinating life and is the highest idea of the true life, as distinguished from a laborious life of painstaking principles." Warren meant that the impulses of a properly cultivated soul would be good ones, but his words would have made theologians uneasy. Christian thinkers ever since Paul have distrusted sensuality, emotional impulses, and the body as potential enemies to the spirit and to revealed religion. Body and soul are distinguished but problematically linked in most varieties of Christian theology through the figure of Christ: God made flesh. Christians understand themselves to be corporeal forms combining body and soul, and they understand some spiritual relations in corporeal terms as well. The central sacrament of Christian liturgy is the Eucharist, in which believers celebrate their unity through the physical act of consuming Christ's symbolic (or transubstantiated) body and blood. The Christian church itself is considered the body of Christ. Early Christians struggled over the extent to which their individual bodies had to be disciplined for the good of the church and for the good of their individual souls. The letters of Paul—whom Warren admired—suggested that the physical body was a source of dangerous temptations. Paul warned in his first letter to the Corinthians against indulging in the fornication endemic in that promiscuous Greek city. "Know ye not that your body is the temple of the Holy Ghost which is in you?" he asked. Being part of the body of Christ, Christians should not bring their own bodies into lustful congress with prostitutes. Here and in his letter to the Romans, Paul specifically condemned sex between men, yet he did so in the context of condemning all forms of sexuality that distanced a Christian from God, and, more broadly, all forms of sin. Paul urged that sexuality be tamed through marriage between men and women, "for it is better to marry than to burn." An 1854 exegesis on Romans, by the Unitarian theologian Abiel Abbot Livermore, interpreted the passage on sex between men as forbidding not just "unnatural" sex (evidently sodomy) but licentiousness in general. "The whole aim and spirit of the Gospels is to purify the bodies as well as the souls of men, to carry the beauty of holiness into all the relations of the sexes, and to throw the check of self-denial over all the animal instincts," Livermore added.[48]

Puritan clergy had frequently discussed the Christian's love of God in erotic terms, at times using explicitly sexual metaphors. Yet they and their Congregational descendants were ambivalent about the intense emotions of Christian zeal, especially when roused in revivals. Expressions of fellowship might readily slip into fleshly indulgence and sin. "Certainly the mutual embraces and kisses of persons of different sexes under the notion of Christian love and holy kisses, are utterly to be disallowed and abominated, as having the most direct tendency quickly to turn Christian love into unclean and brutish lust," wrote the theologian Jonathan Edwards.[49] In the early nineteenth century, the Boston Unitarian Joseph Buckminster argued that affectionate sentiments between people were worthless or harmful if they did not center on God. "The love of sensual gratification is yet more degrading. All the passions of those who cherish it seem to be converted into appetites; all their affections into lusts. . . . No, christians, the love of pleasure and the love of God are irreconcilable." Horace Bushnell declared in 1848 that "It is the very life of the soul to feel, desire, love, to stretch itself out in holy yearnings after all good." But he warned that one must be careful the desires were truly for God, writing in 1853 that "allowing any lust to have its freedom, any passion to go unbridled, this lust, this passion will even take possession of your head" and lead one to justify wicked habits.[50]

The dangers of conflating love with lust were amply illustrated by stories of lustful clergy in the newspapers and literature of mid-nineteenth-century America. News reports were published in both the sensational penny press and in religious journals, while fictional tales appeared in George Lippard's *Quaker City* (1845) and Nathaniel Hawthorne's *The Scarlet Letter* (1850). Observers from more restrained churches, such as the orthodox Congregationalists and High Church Episcopalians, had for decades looked askance at the tendencies of unbridled evangelicals. The emotional style of worship and conversion erupting in revivals and camp meetings struck such observers as dangerous. One early scandal involving evangelical clergy was the 1833 Rhode Island murder trial of the Methodist Rev. Ephraim K. Avery, resulting from the death of a pregnant millgirl named Sarah Maria Cornell. Bruce Dorsey has meticulously analyzed the scandal in the 1830s surrounding the behavior of revivalist preacher Eleazar Sherman. The forty-year-old Sherman was subjected to a church trial in Providence in 1835 by other ministers in the Christian Connection; he was accused of kissing and fondling his evangelical male bedmates and of attempting sodomy, and was found "guilty of gross immoral conduct." Sherman's actions, though bolder than some of his contemporaries felt comfortable with, were extensions of what Dorsey calls the "close, intimate, and loving relationships" common among itinerant preachers, whose physical and spiritual affections often blurred.[51]

Clergy and laity found that the sentimental style of Protestant devotion encouraged private discussion of feelings, a situation in which piety could easily lead to intimacy and in which rogue pastors could abuse their privileges. New York Episcopal Bishop Benjamin T. Onderdonk was accused in 1844 of habitually groping women, and was suspended from his clerical duties after a church trial. Cynics scoffed that his behavior was nothing out of the ordinary given the "caressing character of the intercourse between the clergy and the women in their parishes." The popular Baptist preacher Isaac Kalloch was tried in a criminal court in 1857 for alleged adultery with a female parishioner. The Unitarian pastor Horatio Alger Jr. was dismissed from his Cape Cod church in 1866 for the "abominable and revolting crime of unnatural familiarity with *boys*." He later went on to success as an author of children's literature. The most spectacular scandal involved revelations in 1872 of Henry Ward Beecher's affair with a parishioner, and the subsequent slander and adultery trials. Sexual misconduct by clergy was publicly portrayed as the result of an unusually close relationship between American pastors and their female churchgoers, but the historian Karin E. Gedge has suggested that the reality was much more complicated. Although pastoral counseling could drift into emotional and sexual intimacy, it was more common for a pastor's relationship with his female flock to be awkward, even tense. Differences in the communication styles of men and women, combined with female resentment of male clerical authority and the troubling specter of sexuality, created a sense of distance. Interactions with men were not so fraught.[52]

The Onderdonk scandal was fresh in public memory in New York State in the 1850s, as Onderdonk retained the title of Bishop until his death in 1861. Onderdonk's sympathizers believed he was targeted not so much for his behavior as for his embrace of Tractarianism, which had divided the church in New York until the two factions reached an uneasy compromise in 1853. Warren indicated that the Onderdonk controversy did not deter him from joining the Episcopal Church; in a separate passage, he expressed a general outlook that would have allowed him to overlook the problem: "I am disposed literally to 'Judge no man,'" he wrote, quoting a passage in the Gospel of John where the Pharisees bring to Christ a woman caught in adultery. Warren acknowledged that the timing of his move to Episcopalianism in 1856 might seem odd, given the recent blistering exchange of articles on doctrinal issues between his former Presbyterian pastor Nathan Beman and his new Episcopal minister Thomas Coit. He insisted in a meeting with a skeptical Beman, though, that his decision was unaffected by their conflict.[53]

Warren was troubled by the Episcopal Church's avoidance of what he considered the major issue of the day: abolition. Though the marginalized evangelical Episcopalians sympathized with antislavery, the church hierarchy sought to avoid an issue that might cause a regional schism. Yet Warren could take comfort from the abolitionism of his friends at St. Paul's, the Gilbert family. Uri Gilbert was both an active member of the church and an adherent to antislavery politics in the Whig party and then the Republicans. He later hired as his coachman a fugitive slave from Virginia, Charles Nalle, whose 1860 rescue from slavecatchers in Troy received extensive coverage in local newspapers and in the abolitionist *Liberator*. Though the Episcopal Church as a whole did not share Gilbert's views, Warren comforted himself with scraps of evidence that the church did good work among Southern blacks.[54]

Warren told Willie Gilbert that his preference for Episcopalianism over Presbyterianism resulted from his "investigation of the merits of the different systems." But privately he confessed that he had been drawn to the Episcopal Church by Willie himself. Willie's example left him receptive to the Church's appeal, which he found "answered to the cravings of my own soul." In a journal entry interrupted by a short erasure, Warren hoped that he himself could develop such an admirable character that he might "excite in my parents the same inquiry that W___ . . . did in me, and I pray God that it may lead to the same results in their case that it has in mine." Warren hoped in 1855 that he and Willie could receive the rite of confirmation into the Episcopal Church together—implicitly solemnizing their friendship before God. As it turned out, when Warren was confirmed the next year, Willie did not join him.[55]

## Beyond My Control

Dr. Samuel Warren was angered and perplexed to learn of his son Edward's interest in the Episcopal Church. He hoped this was a problem he could handle, given the theological knowledge he had amassed in the spare hours of a life spent dabbling in farming and avoiding the practice of medicine. When Edward Warren broached the subject during his winter vacation in 1853–54, Dr. Warren attacked Episcopalianism at what he considered one of its weak points: the claims about apostolic succession made by New York bishop John Henry Hobart and given new prominence in the 1830s by English theologian John Henry Newman's *Tracts of the Times*. The Episcopal view of apostolic succession was that the Anglican and Episcopal clergy drew their legitimacy from a direct succession of bishops extending all the way back to Christ. By focusing on this point, Dr. Warren called attention to the Episcopal Church's descent from Catholicism, which he considered a grave flaw. Edward knew little about the subject; on his return to Troy he borrowed a book on the subject from his Presbyterian pastor, Rev. Beman. The topic failed to interest him, and he was distressed that his father was so hostile to his faith.[56]

The sparring over apostolic succession set the tone for the arguments between Warren and his father over the next year and a half. Dr. Warren referred to the Episcopal Church insultingly as "the erring sister of Rome" while Edward privately called his father's harsh argumentation "a direct legacy of Puritanism." By June 1854, Edward Warren was counseling himself to stay calm and not continue their correspondence on theological questions. Dr. Warren would not drop the matter, and Edward struggled to hold his ground in a manner representing the calm and loving spirit of the Episcopal Church. In a partially effaced journal entry, Edward contrasted his relationship with father, who had failed to serve as a loving role model in religious matters, to his friendship with Willie.[57]

The conflict reached a flashpoint while Edward Warren was on vacation in West Newton in August 1855. He and his parents had repeated discussions of church matters. Edward joined his parents at their church one Sunday and heard "a most intolerable sermon of hell and despair." His mother devoted that afternoon to reading and discussing with Edward a recent sermon by Congregational theologian Mark Hopkins that attacked the Episcopal High Church's quasi-Catholicism. The following Saturday, Dr. Warren summoned his son into his study for an inquisition. Dr. Warren had prepared a list of written questions and remarks, which Edward considered "worthy of preservation as fruits of the whining formalism of New England religion." Among other issues, Dr. Warren warned Edward that his apostasy might create a permanent breach from his parents—"a sentiment every way worthy of Puritanism," Edward fumed later. "I do not envy the heart that could conceive it, and yet more write it, and read it off, to the face of a dutiful and affectionate son." Ten years later, Edward Warren added a note to indicate that he and his father were reconciled, yet he chose not to efface his expression of resentment; it still lurked on the page, ready to ambush his grieving parents if they should read the diary after his death.[58]

Dr. Warren interpreted his son's change of church as a challenge to paternal authority, and he wondered about the motivations. He asked Edward whether the influence for his decision was internal or external; who or what was luring him away from the religion of his family? This question cut to the heart of the matter, and Edward responded honestly, though stiffly. "An outward circumstance arrested my attention, in the course of Providence, and led me to make an investigation," he admitted, according to his journal. "Viz., the spontaneous and beautiful expressions of religion from the lips of W___ & others in contrast to the coldness of friends in the Presbyterian body, and to respond to it in the way I did, and with the results that have followed, is from within, is constitutional and beyond my control."[59]

Edward Warren was not approaching religion as his father did—as a matter of learned reasoning on theological questions. Fully committed to a religion of the heart, he had followed his heart in loving Willie Gilbert and the church to which he belonged. Warren would stay true to the Episcopal Church for the remaining half-century of his life. But even as he stood his ground that summer day in his father's study, Warren knew that his passionate nature was a mixed blessing. He knew that his friendship with Willie had failed like all the earlier friendships that had been animated by both yearning and faith. Warren felt he had become a person he could not fully respect, an immature man at the mercy of emotions that at times exceeded even his love of God. His challenge as he moved farther into adulthood was to become a man who could feel deeply without losing control, a man possessing the steady love he wished he could find in his own father.

# 4

# Fatherhood

> For all that is in the world, the lust of the flesh, and the lust of the eyes, and the pride of life, is not of the Father, but is of the world.
>
> —1 John 2:16

Warren's friendships kept ending in disappointment. His hopes would rise with the first feelings of fellowship and he would press on for more, engaging his new friend with sympathetic questions about his inner life and his relation with God. If a sense of intimacy developed, he would try to carry it farther into physical affection, only to see the friendship dissipate into awkwardness or estrangement.

Warren reconsidered his efforts at intimacy after the failure of his friendship with Willie in 1855. He despaired of a friendship that might marry romantic feeling with religious devotion, an ideal by which he had sought to justify eroticism in terms acceptable to nineteenth-century Protestant culture. Having attained a mature age, Warren decided, he was permanently exiled from the garden of youthful love and would have to settle for other ways to enjoy the company of younger men and boys. Warren now tried to understand his adult role as that of a loving father rather than as a romantic friend. He hoped to express his affection in a more restrained, less sensual way that would be less likely to damage a relationship. Imagining himself as a "universal father" would also help preserve his dignity and bolster a sense of mature manhood that was otherwise elusive for a young bachelor.

## A Single Life without Hope of Leaving a Name

The religious tension between Edward Warren and his father began to ease after their showdown in Dr. Warren's study. Edward told his journal shortly afterward that he felt no bitterness toward his parents, and that the conflict reflected merely the influence of bad theology on good Christians. His parents might be taking his resistance personally, but Edward hoped in time "to prove that I may love <u>them</u> and hate <u>it</u>," meaning Calvinism. Looking back on the dispute in the fall of 1865, Edward Warren wrote, "how blessedly now 10 yrs. after are we knit together."[1]

His father redirected his annoyance toward Edward's failure to marry and have children. Dr. Warren in late 1855 counselled his twenty-four-year-old son to find a "mate"—advice that Edward had no intention of following. "Almost the only thought of marriage which I have had for a long, long time, has been an occasional starting as it were, from a reverie, to find that I neither knew one who is to be thought of in that connection—see any immediate prospect of knowing any one—or what is of more importance feel at all uneasy at this state of things," Edward Warren wrote. Pondering his father's letter, he concluded that he would continue to devote himself to his work, "not turning to the right or left, and shall expect that whatever little 'Wild-Flower' arrests me by the wayside will be found in my path by as little forethought or contrivance of mine, as any other event in my life."[2]

Warren's journal entries to that point had contained very little about women. In Newburyport, he had shown far more desire for his male friends than for his closest female friend, Augusta; even his mild interest in her seemed guided to some extent by his wish to interact with her beau, Francis Whipple. But in June 1855, when his friendship with Willie had cooled and the religious dispute with his parents had grown heated, Warren reported an interruption "in my daily routine so unusual, and so amazing in its total overthrow of my aforementioned declarations of a cast iron insensibility to all sentimental influences, that I must record it." Warren, along with other Rensselaer faculty members, was attending the public examinations at the Troy Female Seminary when he was charmed by one of the graduating students. His eye was drawn to her "modest beauty and natural grace" as she sang a duet. "A faultless figure dressed in perfect taste the natural ringlets, the expression of earnest soul, the subdued yet cheerful face, and the fair bosom adorned by the holy symbol of the cross, all formed a beautiful picture. She sang sweetly and with feeling." He murmured to a man sitting next to him, "she is an angel," and returned the next day to admire her performance in a philosophy examination.[3]

The odd thing about this incident is not that Warren felt attracted to a woman for the first recorded time since his friendship with Augusta. His reaction to this young woman was in some ways in character; the juxtaposition of physical beauty and piety that drew him to her had previously sparked his interest in several boys. The odd thing, rather, is that Warren made a public display of his interest without making any effort to meet the woman, Katharine W. Kirby of Cromwell, Connecticut. "Possessed with infatuation I went to the Depot this morning thinking to get a last look at her," Warren wrote the day after her graduation. He saw her talking with three RPI students he knew but did not approach the group. She boarded the train for her journey back to Connecticut while he stayed on the platform. At that point, Warren met another RPI instructor, William Tweeddale, and a friend from church, George Loveland, and told them of the situation. Tweeddale tried to engineer a last-minute introduction by urging Warren to board the train with Kirby as far as Albany. He suggested that Warren enter her train car from one end while Loveland, who was acquainted with her, would enter from the other; they would meet in the middle beside her seat as if by accident, and she and Warren could be introduced. Warren refused. He and Kirby were still strangers as the train carried her away from Troy for the last time. In the days that followed, Warren continued asking his acquaintances about her. On a walk with Loveland that Sunday after services at St. Paul's, he learned that she had been in the St. John's Church choir. "So she is an Episcopalian!" he exclaimed. Despite his claim to have been smitten by her beauty, Warren had never gotten close enough to see her face clearly; he learned from Loveland that she was afflicted with acne, but that "we never think of her face she is so good." Warren made no effort to get her address from the seminary so that he could write her a letter. He recorded the experience in his journal, "vowing if Providence should place her in my way to make her acquaintance"—but Providence evidently never did.[4]

It is possible that Warren was so shy around young women that he could not bear to approach Katharine Kirby, although his shyness was not enough to stop him from making social calls in Troy like everyone else. Another possibility is that he intended merely to put on a public performance of an attraction to women, in an unusual situation where he would never actually have to be introduced. Warren's inquiries ensured that people in both his church and work communities learned of his interest, possibly allaying any suspicions that might have developed. The incident also provided material for three pages of journal entries, perhaps written with his parents in mind as readers. He wrote a sentimental poem concluding, "Oh that 't 'were true/ You were the bud and I the dew," and later added a pious wish "to make myself worthy of anyone so good."[5]

Ten years later, Warren had still not found himself a suitable bride. His bachelorhood had become "a period of forlorn extent. . . . But there are glimmerings in the <u>eastern</u> and southern sky." Warren's father made no secret of his impatience. In 1867, he published a theological article in which his son undoubtedly saw a personal attack. Dr. Warren's article in *Bibliotheca Sacra* was an exegesis on an obscure Old Testament story from Judges. The story goes that Jephthah, leading the Israelites in battle, foolishly vowed to make a burnt sacrifice of whatever creature he met first upon returning to his home after victory. Unfortunately, the first creature he saw was his only child, his daughter. She asked for a reprieve of two months to go into the mountains to bewail her virginity, after which "she returned unto her father, who did with her according to his vow." Warren's father argued that Jephthah did not actually kill his daughter, but rather committed her to a life of service of God as a temple virgin. Father and daughter wept, Dr. Warren insisted, not because she was to die, but because "she submitted to live a single life without hope of leaving a name behind in the earth. This no good person desires to do." Dr. Warren's only child—also unmarried and unlikely to leave offspring—must have noticed the subtext of disapproval toward his own life choices, even if his father did not explicitly point it out. In his father's eyes, Warren's failure to marry made him "no good person."[6]

Failure to marry had consequences for a nineteenth-century man that went beyond the lack of a life companion, regular sex partner, and bearer of children. In an era when maturity was defined by one's social context rather than simply by age, a young bachelor's claim to full manhood was still somewhat tenuous. Until he took a wife and became the head of a household, unsympathetic observers saw him as lingering in the irresponsible state of youth. Some men internalized this view. One of Warren's near contemporaries, a Michigan store clerk named Henry Parker Smith, wrote on the eve of his 1854 marriage that he was experiencing his "last boyish day"—at the age of twenty-eight. The historian Stephen Frank has found that diarists and advice writers alike believed marriage and children gave a man a new patriarchal authority, helped him develop the character traits of patience and self-restraint, and strengthened his morality. Only then did the youth become a real man. Dr. Warren, in his letter urging Edward Warren to find a mate, recommended that his son build a house big enough to include both parents as boarders. He was offering, in effect, to retire as patriarch if Edward would assume that position.[7]

The opportunity to head the family was more appealing than the prospect of marriage, and Edward Warren began calculating how to achieve it. As he wrote his textbooks, he figured they would make him wealthy enough to become a homeowner. He estimated his anticipated twelve-volume series would sell at an annual rate of six thousand books, which with royalties of twenty-five cents per book would bring him $1,500 a year. By then, he expected, his RPI salary would have reached $1,000 a year. If he inherited his father's estate, he would receive another $700 from interest and dividends. Adding in his own future return from investments, he hoped for a very comfortable yearly income of $3,340. Even as little as $1,100 a year would allow him to get married, he wrote, though it would be best to complete all his books first. "I may then feel free to follow my inclinations from this time, without misgivings or forebodings in regard to any one who may seem a desirable partner for me." Reassuring himself that he need not feel unworthy to marry, Warren began fantasizing . . . about his dream house. It would be an Italianate villa complete with a three-story tower, a library with a stained glass bay window, enough space for his parents to take meals by themselves—and even a "housewife." He did not mention space for children. For Warren, it seems, the financial ability to provide for a household was a more important marker of manly achievement than marriage itself. Warren put all these plans on hold in 1858 when he realized that he had overestimated his book income. "This marriage question is all summed up thus. I am not indifferent to it. I am not opposed to it, but I have objects to accomplish which interest me greatly, and I can not in such wise court marriage as to slight those objects." he wrote. He resolved to devote himself to his career instead of marriage.[8]

The unexpected death of Dr. Warren in the autumn of 1867 changed Edward Warren's plans again. Dr. Warren was returning from his woodlot in Waltham, riding on the front of a wagon loaded with the winter's firewood, when the wagon hit a big bump. Thrown to the ground, he felt a wheel roll over his head. He lingered in his brother's house in Waltham for more than a week, in and out of consciousness, allowing his son to return from Troy to see him before he died. Edward's mother began her widowhood in their home in West Newton. She shared summer vacation cottages with Edward in rural New England, then moved to Troy in 1871 to live with her son. Edward Warren arranged for them to rent a cottage on the hill above Troy. He described it in a letter to his cousin Henry Freeman Allen as "15 minutes walk from the Institute, and with Horse Cars going by the door. I shall get a good housekeeper and make Mother a pretty little house for the rest of her days, which with the rare beauty of the situation, in sight of hills and groves and pond; and my book-children; and solid enjoyment of the Institute, is enough, perhaps, for one man, in this world of hopelessly unattainable ideals." In a reversal of his childhood experience, Warren found himself caring for his mother. He had become master of a household without having to marry a woman and beget children.[9]

## The Things Which Remain

Long ago, at boarding school in Andover, Warren had imagined a future home for himself, his parents, and Dicky Derby. By 1871, only he and his mother survived, though Dicky lived on as a fond memory. We need to look back at the last years of this defining friendship in order to see how Warren sought a new fatherly engagement with younger males.

Warren and Dicky had drifted apart in the 1850s, keeping in touch only occasionally by mail. Warren reported exchanging a series of letters with him in 1855 that emphasized religious subjects. Dicky showed signs of growing piety at that time. "He has for sometime attended frequently the Episcopal service at [Newton] Corner," Warren wrote. "How joyful a sight to see him voluntarily walking off three miles alone, with his Bible under his arm." The two old friends had an affectionate discussion of faith one September day in Newton, beginning by considering a verse from Revelation: "[S]trengthen the things which remain, that are ready to die" They ended up sharing a bed that night. Warren's emotions on this occasion can only be imagined, as he did not explicitly describe them. A week or so later, when Warren went to give Dicky a present of gold studs for his twenty-first birthday, Dicky invited him upstairs to talk about the Episcopal Church and to read the Bible together. "Behold how marvelous are the guidings of Providence," Warren exulted later that autumn. "Just as I had learned the powerlessness, and more the mischeif [sic] of intense emotion appearing in my attempts to influence others, through my mortifying experience in the case of [Willie] last Summer, and just as I had begun to act steadily on the principle that deliberate and studied personal religious advice should not be given till asked for . . . Dickey begins to excite my interest." Warren continued to reach out to his friend, although with diminishing success. In an 1857 letter he expressed hopes that Dicky would feel in his soul the Divine presence that reassures believers "that our relations to the vast two fold universe of matter and of soul, and to the world's Creator, are correct and healthful." Some conflict between Warren and Dicky's mother put a chill on the relationship in 1857 and 1858; Dicky's mother had treated Warren with what he considered an intolerable rudeness that was "damaging to my proper social progress and reputation." As Dicky seemed to sympathize with his mother, Warren felt the situation was hopeless. He feared he was losing his friend forever.[10]

Dicky had his own difficulties in achieving mature manhood. He had attended the Lawrence Academy boarding school in Groton for three and a half years as a teenager, with the intention of preparing for college, but he was forced to withdraw when his health failed again. He studied privately in Northborough with the Unitarian pastor Joseph Allen, the uncle of West Newton Model School principal Nathaniel T. Allen. Eventually giving up his goal of a university education, Dicky studied bookkeeping at a commercial college and took a position in a wholesale store in Boston selling millinery and silk goods. It was neither the most prestigious nor the most traditionally masculine of employments. The term "man-milliner" had been used to signify effeminacy for more than a century before the New York politician Roscoe Conkling famously hurled it as an insult against reformers in 1877. As the historian Brian Luskey has shown, clerks who sold women's clothing and accessories were ridiculed in mid-century America for their supposedly emasculating work. Mocked as a "third sex," they were even suspected of secretly playing a feminine role in their sexual lives as "molly coddles."[11]

Dicky worked in the women's hat business nearly four years before deciding to try his luck in the West. He took a job as a sales clerk in Beloit, Wisconsin, and later in Minneapolis. Troubled again by poor health, he moved to remote Meeker County, Minnesota, where he devoted his days to hunting, fishing, and nature study, and built a log cabin by the shore of what he named "Lake Manuela" in honor of one of his nieces.

He reportedly befriended local Indians and the children of poor settlers in the area. After a visit home in 1858, he surprised Warren by dropping in on him in Troy one June morning. "We had a beautiful time," Warren recorded. They visited a mill and strolled through the Albany cemetery before Dicky boarded the train late that afternoon. Dicky returned to his cabin in Minnesota, this time sharing it with two other young men from New England. He came back East for good in 1859 and took a job in Boston with another wholesale millinery dealer.[12]

The Civil War erupted when Dicky Derby was twenty-six years old and Edward Warren was twenty-nine. Warren managed to avoid military service. His name does not appear in the draft registration records for Troy or Newton; perhaps he told officials in each place that he was registered in the other. Dicky, however, volunteered as soon as the war began in April 1861. He was eventually commissioned as a lieutenant in the 15th Massachusetts Regiment. A photograph shows him as a slender, light-haired young man in uniform, posed stiffly at the base of staircase, a somber expression on his clean-shaven face. Dicky narrowly survived the Union disaster at Ball's Bluff by swimming across the Potomac, and saw action also at Malvern Hill. Warren feared the worst was coming; he composed "an epitaph; which may I never live to see," during the Peninsula Campaign in April 1862. "Here sleepeth . . . under the wing of Christ's Angel of Death; and in Christian Hope of a Blessed Resurrection. A dear lad, Fair Earnest and true and loved of many Hearts. His spirit; early ripe; early gathered by Angel Reapers to the Father of Spirits." From reports after his death, Lt. Derby was popular and well respected in the army. His friend Walter Gale from Newton was at his side on the morning of Sept. 17, 1862, when Derby was shot through the temple at the beginning of the battle of Antietam. "I had found him such a genial companion, with so much love and respect, that I could not quite reconcile myself to the thought that we were parted for this life," Gale wrote to Dicky's mother. Similar letters flooded into Newton over the next few weeks; writers praised both his manly heroism and his gentle personality. "From his childhood up to the hour of his death, I loved your Richard as if one of my own family," wrote the Rev. Arthur B. Fuller, an army chaplain and the brother of the author Margaret Fuller. "He was a noble, pure, and saintly young man, and his death was as heroic and honorable as his whole life had been worthy." Richard Derby willed his Minnesota land, his sporting equipment, and his art supplies to his nephew, and his books and pictures to his nieces. His journals and sketches, which he had sealed upon leaving for war, were all burned at his request. Dicky's remains were eventually brought home and buried next to those of his father in Medfield.[13]

It is possible to read the insistence on Dicky's manliness as a strategy to deflect any possible stigma associated with personality traits that might signal gender nonconformity. But, as noted in the introduction, there was no single standard of masculinity at this time. Even among mercantile clerks, themselves a distinct subculture focused on accumulating capital and achieving economic independence, there were different styles of striving to be a "self-made man." Some devoted their free time to the coarse pleasures of macho urban "sporting" life in theaters, saloons, and brothels. Others labored to build character through church attendance, introspection, prayer, and devotional reading—techniques of moral self-discipline that struck skeptics as effeminate but that signaled Christian manliness to Protestant evangelicals.[14]

Dicky's Christian manliness was the central theme in a memorial biography published in 1865 by a friend of Arthur Fuller, Phebe Hanaford. This 226-page hagiographic text revealed both the high esteem in which Dicky was held by his many friends, and how marginalized Warren had become in Dicky's social network. Short on material, Hanaford padded her early chapters with contextual information about the towns in which Dicky lived, the history of Lawrence Academy, and the beauties of the western prairies. She does not seem to have gathered any information from Warren, even though she acknowledged him as Dicky's "earliest friend; they were like David and Jonathan." Hanaford did reproduce the condolence letter that Warren had sent to Dicky's mother, Mary Ann Allen Derby. "For seventeen long years I knew and loved him," Warren wrote. He recalled Dicky as bedfellow, table-companion, and cherished playmate, emphasizing the age difference between them. "How his little self, in old times, fancied my strength to be great! while I felt as a sort of champion for him. He once threw his arms around my neck . . . and told me I seemed to him more like a father than a brother." No previous declaration of a fatherly relationship with Dicky can be found in Warren's writings; this was something new. Warren acknowledged "bungling" his effort to save Dicky's soul, but hoped that it still had a good influence.[15]

## Reveries of a Pelted Turtle

Warren had ended the final surviving volume of his daily journal in the summer of 1858, and thereafter recorded his impressions in more abstract terms in the pages of two diaries of thoughts, titled "Thoughts, Taken on the Wing" and "Thought Sketches." His habits of writing had already evolved toward abstraction in the scant pages of the preceding years. Much of his free time was now filled with reveries and philosophical reflections rather than personal interactions. Warren by his own admission was withdrawing from human society into the solitary haven of his mind. He appears to have grown reluctant to communicate about his life even in private writing. After Dicky died in 1862, there are no surviving journals, diaries, account books, or commonplace books by any name.

Warren had written in the summer of 1854 that he was making a "fixed practice of not seeking acquaintances, but allowing myself to be sought out," which apparently did not happen very often. By 1858, he observed that "I have felt for the last six months a rapidly growing independence of society as a source of happiness." Reflecting in 1865 on earlier expressions of what he called his "exclusiveness," Warren wrote that this habit was "emphatically so with me now. My Dept., my study, my home, being mostly my world, though I love people."[16]

Warren claimed to draw pleasure increasingly from his own thoughts and daydreams. There is at least a hint of self-pity in his description of this lonely habit. Warren wrote of one June evening in 1856, when "I sat alone upon the hill, from half past eight till nearly ten, engaged in reveries," after saying a final farewell to a departing friend. He wrote in 1858 of his "power to create pretty thoughts such as now make my solitary life independent of outward excitements for happiness." Later that year, Warren described his retreat from a cold world where mean-spirited people "proceed to pelt and vilify their more fortunate neighbors while these retire to the fireside of their own interior natures, and there find every satisfying resource and are safe as is the pelted turtle when withdrawn into his shell to escape the pebbles cast by the infantile school-boy, and feel no loss except that of the pleasures of loving and being loved by all."[17] This is another of those passages, like the ones in which he expressed false cheer about teaching in Charlton, where Warren evidently expected his readers to see through his words to the troubled soul beneath.

Daydreaming—the free play of the imagination—was ambivalently regarded in antebellum America, linked as it was both to idleness in a world of industriousness and to the creative insight valued in Romantic culture. Henry David Thoreau told of days at Walden when he "sat in my sunny doorway from sunrise till noon, rapt in a revery" and reaped richer rewards than if he had wasted the morning on productive labor.

William Ellery Channing described reveries as the exercise of human faculties not fully employed in mundane tasks; freed to wander, the mind might "mingle the greatest of all thoughts, that of God, with household drudgery." Warren had read praises of the imaginative powers in Emerson, and was aware that "the disciples of Kant" believed intuitions could discern truths that were invisible in the dim light of empirical understanding. Warren had been impressed with the exposition of similar ideas by the clergyman and itinerant lecturer Edwin H. Chapin, who defended the power of the imagination to call forth the individual's highest virtues and noblest deeds.[18] On the other hand, Christian advice literature for young men warned that idle thoughts might drift into sinful fantasies and thence into sinful action. Some warnings against undisciplined daydreams emphasized that they were the route by which young men strayed into self-pollution or the brothel, while others implied that the greatest harm came from the thoughts themselves. "When once you have the beautiful chambers of the imagination stained and soiled and polluted, there is no recovery," wrote the Congregational clergyman John Todd.[19]

Those who feared the imagination and those who praised it agreed that flights of fancy often began with sensory stimulation, especially visual perceptions that evoked powerful emotions. Clergymen such as John Todd, Daniel C. Eddy, and Henry Ward Beecher warned that sensory pleasure would lead to sensual indulgence at the expense of spirituality. Youths would surrender their moral sense when "dazzled and blinded" by urban nightlife. On the other hand, Romantic writers, artists, and lecturers argued that the sight of beautiful art or dramatic landscapes could invigorate the moral feelings. One whom Warren had heard, the Rev. E. L. Magoon of New York, wrote that "[i]n viewing magnificent scenes, the soul, expanded and sublimed, is imbued with a spirit of divinity, and appears, as it were, associated with the Deity himself." Magoon asserted that one could not help but feel the sublimity of mountain scenery and raging ocean waves. Sensitive souls like Warren or Thoreau could be moved as well by the beauty of suburban Brookline or the sounds of the Concord woods.[20]

Warren knew from reading and experience that imagination could be dangerous if not guided by the will. He had concluded from the Willie debacle that "thinking may be a source of evil," and that it was safest to keep the mind busy on pure and useful matters. "In reviewing many past reveries, and in comparing them to the impulse which is constitutional, to communicate them to some one else," he was glad that he had shown the self-restraint to hold most of them inside. Yet on the whole Warren regarded his reveries—whether rapturous or brooding—as welcome signs of his capacity for strong feeling. "It is at most the joy and the misery of a man to be possessed of feelings at once deep and mercurial in their sensibility," he wrote. The heart of a sensitive man might shrink inward during adversity like a frostbitten bud, until "in prosperous times the heart opens wide and inhales the sunny atmosphere of joy."[21] A rich interior experience—nurtured by scriptural knowledge, appropriate reading, and fond memories—could sustain the spirit through bleak hours.

After his missteps with Willie, Warren lost confidence in the power of the will over the passions. He worried about the treachery of the body and noted its role in the fall of Adam—the original sin, answered only by Christ's resurrection in a triumph of the spirit over the flesh. Warren's defense in 1855 of the uses of the senses in religion included a note of caution about which senses were most appropriate: sight and hearing, because they "minister directly and largely to the enjoyment of the mind and only indirectly to bodily pleasure."[22]

Less than three months later, on Dec. 31, 1855, Warren made an index of his long-completed Volume One and discovered "in a greater or lesser state of development all or very nearly all of my present virtues and faults." He then attempted a searching self-examination. His journal entry for New Year's Day 1856 enumerates three principal failings that he believed his early journals had revealed. The first was his vain desire for prominence. The third was overanxiety about things beyond his control, and his futile urge to control them anyway. The second fault was so troubling that Warren could describe it only in vague, contorted phrases, and he eventually found even these cryptic words too disturbing. Warren scribbled over the first five lines, which can now be uncovered only through painstaking scrutiny of magnified images. The effaced lines indicate that the second fault was "that which, by some of the mysterious connections between flaw—the sense of touch—and . . . some emotions, has been fostered by great yet innocent familiarity of intercourse with a warm hearted friend." Warren could not bear to name the fault directly, only to trace its origins in friendship, and in the combination of touch and emotion. (The word *intercourse* at the time simply meant interaction.) Warren went to say that this fault had "grown so as to have expressed"—and here the concealing scribbles ended—"itself in the now concealed passages of my last two journals, showing the sad fact that the traces of evil upon the mind may deepen even after its outward fruits have been rejected. An iron heel must be set on the neck of this fault and innocent and untiring industry must come to its rescue."²³ The cryptic language and the efforts at erasure in this passage make it impossible to know exactly what transgressions stemmed from the confluence of touch and feeling, but a notation immediately following the passage makes it clear who he had in mind: "D.R.B. $ G-W.E." The initials "D.R.B." refer to the "Dry River Brotherhood," the group of boys in Troy that Warren had befriended; "G-W.E." is William E. Gilbert—Warren's favorite member of the group. The dollar sign remains mysterious; possibly it was intended as an ampersand.²⁴

Warren was in anguish over a list of sins that included poor classroom management and "every season of intercourse with friends in which I have given any one an excuse for acting ever afterwards differently from what my position begs of me to be worthy to receive." Without clearly indicating the cause of his remorse, he vowed later in January 1856, that

> [t]he means of this moral warfare need to be increased and strengthened as the power of sin increases, for [erasure] sin which is at first purely outward + at most but a rare visitor to the thoughts may after his power to act has been stopped may worm and burn and fight his way into the heart and challenge dislodgment with a power that shall almost dishearten the forces of good. Ah, but die in the contest rather than yield!²⁵

Troubled by the dangers of sensuality in 1858, Warren suggested a radically curtailed role for the body in religion. In the final entry of the final volume of his journal before he switched to the "thoughts" diaries, Warren observed that the Albany sculptor Erastus Dow Palmer

> makes his angels as busts enveloped in clouds; and is it not true that the human body seems to have a boundary at the diaphragm so that if pared off at the lower rib it would be a beautiful object, with brain the seat of <u>Reason</u>, the Lungs feeding on the pure and beautiful air, and whose breathings are the emblem of our souls' aspirations, the heart the seat of life, energy, vitality, the emblem of the solemn sacredness of life and of the other hearts beatings of affection. So that to cultivate health and beauty in this nobler bodily region may very likely secure perfection in the freight train of animal life below.²⁶

Figure 4.1. Erastus Dow Palmer, "Morning Star," (c. 1851–1855), marble, 20 in. diameter. Minneapolis Institute of Art, anonymous gift in memory of Mr. and Mrs. Palmer Jaffray, accession number 89.124.2. Photo: Minneapolis Museum of Art.

A body sliced off at the lower rib, of course, would leave the Christian with the higher senses intact and receptive to inspiration, while sparing him the worst distractions of fleshly desires. It would be easier to be an angel that way. This disturbing image of bodily amputation echoes passages in the Gospels of Matthew and Mark where Christ urges drastic action to avoid sin: "[I]f thy hand or thy foot offend thee, cut them off, and cast them from thee: it is better for thee to enter into life halt or maimed, rather than having two hands or two feet to be cast into everlasting fire." Warren also discerned valuable wisdom in the Apostle Paul's emphasis on the conflict between the body and the spirit. Erring men in need of help, Warren wrote, should turn to the passage in Romans that begins with the injunction, "Let not sin therefore reign in your mortal body, that ye should obey it in the lusts thereof." Warren concluded his first "thoughts" diary with a prayer that "our immortal spirits may reign supreme over our mortal bodies," and his second with a meditation on the need for unmarried men to remain "sacredly pure" and think pure thoughts.[27]

Warren had reached a deeply sad place in his life's journey, choosing to leave behind the sensual love that had once given him joy. He now linked sensuality to sin, and sin to a form of slavery. Literally, in tirades against American chattel slavery, and implicitly, in ruminations on sin, Warren identified enslavement as the destruction of masculine identity. "What must be the character of a system which, inch by inch and hour by hour, eats out my manhood?" he wrote in 1860, imagining himself in the position of a Southern slave.[28] He resolved to put away childish things and adopt the manly self-discipline of celibacy. Warren's acceptance of defeat reminds us that, while the emotional culture of the antebellum Northeast did validate love between young men, it still imposed limits. Warren's possibilities for intimate relationships shrank once he aged out of youth culture. Perhaps he might have found satisfying companionship among other evangelical men if he had been less shy or if he had lived in a larger city, but opportunities were scarce for a socially awkward man in a town the size of Troy. Mature manhood for Warren meant feeling abandoned, lonely, and ashamed.

The scholar Heather Love observes that early scholarship on homosexuality downplayed the negative feelings of shame experienced by lesbians and gay men. With eyes fixed on a brighter future, scholars preferred more affirming narratives of queer experience. Writing about gay-themed literature since the late nineteenth century, Love insists on the value of looking backward at the psychic injuries that queer people have endured, and at the persisting negative feelings of loss and regret manifested in their writings.[29] Though Warren's experience predates modern homosexuality, his too is a story of looking backward in sorrow on broken intimacies.

## A Universal Father

Warren still believed that feelings, affections, and impulses were essentially good if a man had the ability to guide them judiciously. It was true that misguided love could lead a man to heedless indulgence and great distress, he wrote in 1862, at the age of thirty. Nonetheless, it would be a foolish overreaction if the man were to "blame his love rather than its ignorantly or carelessly misguided exercise, and thence to cultivate sternness on principle." In the late 1850s and early 1860s, Warren reconsidered how best to experience and express kind feelings. "Our affections which we send forth to different persons seem to be differently flavored from the different parts of our nature," he observed in 1860. "Towards some our affections are peculiarly reverential, towards others peculiarly limpid sweet and spiritual giving a foretaste of the mutual love of fellow angels, to others our affections are more sensuous and so of less permanence and value." Warren tried during these years to turn away from the troubling sensuality of romantic friendship toward the safer framework of paternal love.[30]

In his interactions with children, Warren enjoyed thinking about what he had lost in attaining adulthood: days of play instead of work, freedom instead of responsibility, and innocence instead of knowledge. He continued to hope that his influence would lead boys to deeper spirituality. Warren regularly taught Sunday school classes in Troy from the 1850s at least into the late 1860s. He still felt twinges of nostalgia toward his lost intimacy with Dicky, writing in a partially effaced passage that one of the boys at the First Presbyterian Church "reminds me so much of . . . that I want very much to . . . him."[31] Yet he tried now to use the knowledge of his past as an aid to empathy with the young. Thinking in 1859 of a struggling Sunday school student, he wrote:

> How the embarrassed look and involuntary silence of injured boyhood, pleads eloquently for kind charity for poor human nature in its tender and sympathy craving age. Save me it says from the iron rule of cold reason which tolerates not one repetition of fault, but pray remember I am but a young boy struggling through the mists of my own imperfection to the healthful sunshine of human gentleness and sympathy and charity.[32]

Warren's reading sometimes set him off on reveries about playing with young children. Recalling an anecdote he had seen in a magazine article, he recorded in 1859 "the lesson of wisdom . . . of associating freely and as a brother with the young. Socrates after discoursing gravely on the deep truths of philosophy refreshed himself by playing leap frog with some boys . . ." Warren went on to tell of a similarly wise Boston merchant who enjoyed treating street urchins to sleigh rides, welcoming so many that the sleigh was packed with "intertwined and clasping and laughing little rosy cheeked curly heads, himself the merriest of the whole half fairy crew." From these examples, Warren concluded that "one need not fear to find his hearts delight in making young eyes sparkle and young hearts beat with joy." Mid-nineteenth-century fathers, and writers of advice literature such as Horace Bushnell, considered it a worthy part of modern fatherhood to romp and play with their children, especially with the boys. Indeed, Warren and Bushnell believed that the bonds of affection developed through play would help the man lead the boy to Christ. "The cords of human sympathy which age throws around the heart of childhood, are like the ropes which bind the canal boat to the tow boat," Warren wrote, in one of his characteristically florid metaphors. "Wherever it goes they go. So love me well and love me long, then where I go you can go by staying close to me in heart. Then as you grow older learn of Him who helps me to lead you truly as much as the Pilot guides the steamer which leads the boats."[33]

Declaring his wish to escape enslavement by sin, Warren found "mingled grace and sweetness" in playing with "those dear little one's [sic] whose hearts know all our hearts, though their heads never dream of the thoughts that fill our heads in our own peculiar hours of study." He particularly enjoyed giving gifts and doing other kind deeds for children. A child who felt neglected by his parents and ignored for want of gifts, he wrote, would grow up gloomy and hateful; cheering his heart with a gift would be an important step toward making him a sympathetic and confident man. Children should not grow up too fast, he wrote. Those who "mistake the green for the ripe fruit" will fail to achieve their potential, while those who are nurtured wisely in all their purity will be "both beautiful to look upon and laden with fair fruit of abundant good works."[34]

Encounters with youth and innocence evoked strong sentiments in Warren. In his Sunday school class at St. Paul's Episcopal Church, he wrote in 1858 that "little Walter Thomson is my pet and honorary member."[35] Warren also indicated affection for little girls, whose immaturity he similarly exaggerated. After an awkward social call to the Gilbert family on New Years' Day 1856, he wondered about his behavior toward Willie's four-year-old sister: "[W]as it in good taste to seize little Josie and shower a score of kisses on her for no apparent special cause?—It caused a look of embarrassed wonder in Addie's sprightly face." (Addie was Willie's fourteen-year-old sister). Moving on to the Adancourt family that day, he was disappointed that little Julia was growing out of her adorable baby talk. These references to girls are unusual; Warren rarely mentioned them. Even his feelings and reactions to young boys are difficult to follow with any certainty, given the extensive editing of the journals. If there was any sexual element to his thought and behavior toward prepubescent children in his adult years, it is not clearly shown by the surviving words of the journal.[36]

Warren also admired older youths who retained the childlike qualities of play, freedom, and innocence. On an 1858 expedition up the Dry River, he wrote, "It was a blessed sight to see those youths . . . so perfectly absorbed as children, in building the dam, while Mr. Wylie made whistles, and I a rude water wheel, to which Mr. Williams added a trip hammer." Warren hoped to recover some of what he considered his own lost innocence. Describing a new daily regimen of rising early and taking a sponge bath, Warren hoped that this bodily discipline was purifying his spirit as well: "I . . . sometimes feel as if something of the pure innocence of Dickie's life were becoming natural to me, so that there is not so much left in me to be overcome only by hard fighting."[37]

It is doubtful that any of the teenagers Warren knew were as innocent or childlike as he liked to imagine. Student newspapers at the Rensselaer Polytechnic Institute reveal a rowdy undergraduate culture of drinking, smoking, flirting with the Female Seminary students, and seeking sexual encounters—though rarely with success. The diary of Arthur Bower describes an elaborate practical joke in which students tricked a friend into believing that an illegitimate baby had been left at his door.[38] Regardless of the reality, Warren liked the appearance of innocence in both children and youths, and used the word frequently in expressing praise.

Fatherhood was a reassuring way for Warren to rethink his affection for both children and young men. It allowed him to cultivate affectionate bonds in a relationship that preserved the dignity of his social position and that precluded sensual engagement. It also reaffirmed a masculine identity that may have felt weakened by his lingering condition of being unmarried and childless. Looking back years later, Warren reassured himself that his journals provided "agreeable evidence that my interest in Juveniles did not prevent doing much manly work, but was a beautiful diversion, far better indeed than many which might be engaged in."[39] Here, he seemed to insist that playing with boys did not diminish his adult status; instead, he had matched the ideal of evangelical masculinity by performing as a paternal role model and making brave efforts to spread the faith. In an undated and partially legible scrap of paper tucked into the eighth volume of his journal, Warren reflected on his relationship with Willie and wondered if "an affection essentially paternal in . . . its character and manifestation [is] . . . to take the place of the reality for me?"[40]

Another chance for surrogate parenthood came when his younger cousin Henry Freeman Allen got married. Warren had been close to Henry through childhood, and was pleased when Henry joined the Episcopal Church in 1858. After graduating from Harvard in 1860, Henry for some reason chose to study for the ministry at the Andover Theological Seminary, which espoused Calvinism. While there, it seems, Henry met the family of one of the Andover professors, Calvin Stowe, and courted the professor's daughter, Georgiana. Warren appears to have discussed the courtship with Henry at this time. After a visit to Henry's family home in the summer of 1861, Warren mulled over the sacredness of marriage and the heightened consciousness of divinity that he believed would come with raising children. Several other diary entries that summer and fall considered the implications of marriage between people of different faiths. These entries presumably referred to the religious difference between Henry and Georgiana, who was the daughter and niece of Congregationalist ministers and theologians, and the granddaughter of the eminent Lyman Beecher. Warren may also have been thinking ahead to prospective wives for himself. He wrote that the spouse whose religious affiliation was merely inherited from parents should defer to the one who had come to his faith through careful deliberation.[41] Fortunately, Georgiana's mother, the author Harriet Beecher Stowe, was sympathetic to her daughter's turn to the Episcopal Church, into which Georgiana was confirmed along with two sisters and an aunt in April 1862. Henry and Georgiana married in 1865.[42]

Warren paid visits to the new couple on his way back and forth from Troy to Boston, expressing envy of their comfortable home life in Stockbridge, Massachusetts, where Henry was rector of St. Paul's Church. In an October 1870 letter congratulating them on the birth of their son Freeman, Warren digressed into telling about his new home in Troy before saying that he accepted his own childlessness "with contentment, willing to be 'the superfluous man' who gives perhaps a sort of unique flavor to society, and is of some use as a universal father to even up the deficiencies of many other fatherhoods." He assured Henry that he was prepared to come to Stockbridge for a weekend to attend the baptism ceremony and serve as little Freeman's godfather. But Edward Warren never took that small step toward universal fatherhood. He was unable to attend the ceremony after all, and so Calvin Stowe took his place.[43]

## The Father and the Son

Warren envisioned becoming a father figure much like the Christian friend he had tried to be, just more reserved and in firmer control of himself. In his "thoughts" diaries and in notations to older journal entries, he resolved that his mature reason would prevail over his emotional nature. He would not let himself get annoyed at the errors of a child or a youth, knowing that the young were just learning their way in life. Warren was determined to guide gently, and mostly through example. If his advice on religious matters was rejected, he hoped to have the maturity to "look on in unruffled spirit," secure in his faith and in his knowledge that other people were free to make their own mistakes. He would avoid the "inordinate sentimentalism" that had afflicted him with Willie, yet would remain sympathetic to the tender feelings of others. He would be a kindly father to whoever needed one, not a stern and punitive patriarch like Dr. Warren. It went without saying that he believed sensuality had no place in any father-son relationship.[44]

Warren's kindly model of parenthood reflected the prevailing advice of his era. Commentators since the 1830s had complained that American fathers were retreating from the business of child rearing and leaving it in the hands of mothers. These warnings were exaggerated, as historians such as Shawn Johansen have cautioned; real fathers retained an important role in child rearing. Nonetheless, the complaints contained an element of truth. Part of this shift reflected the fact that men in an industrializing and urbanizing America were more likely than women to work outside the home; part of it reflected a growing belief that in parenting, as in teaching, women could be more effective because of their supposed gentleness and sensitivity. As children were now considered to be essentially good and malleable, instead of innately depraved, a gentle approach was deemed best for shaping them. Some commentators worried that Americans had gone too far in placing mothers in charge. Fearing that family discipline would deteriorate without a strong paternal presence and that the American social order and system of government would crumble, antebellum New England writers including author and educator Theodore Dwight Jr. and Amherst College president Heman Humphrey urged fathers to get more involved with raising their children. They did not advocate a return to Puritan patriarchy or to discredited practices of breaking the will of the sinful child. They urged fathers to become more kindly and caring toward their children, so that they could effectively supplement the mothers' work. The father would remain the supreme authority, a more reserved, less emotive presence. "The father may instruct, but the mother instils; the father may command our reason, but the mother compels our instinct. . . . The empire of the father is over the head, of the mother, over the heart," wrote the Unitarian pastor Artemas Bowers Muzzey in his 1854 *Fireside Book*. "The head of a pious and well-ordered family affords a beautiful counterpart of the God of all families; he is in the likeness of our Divine Guardian, the object of an affection which is chastened by a becoming reverence." The Congregationalist Horace Bushnell argued that as God himself took a fatherly pleasure in children's play, the Christian parent should show his own pleasure by playing with the child; this would not undermine his authority but strengthen it by bringing the child closer to him.[45]

Warren noted that differing conceptions of God reflected Americans' evolving ideas about fatherhood. He observed approvingly that Unitarianism "recognizes God as the Universal Father, where High Calvinism sees only the stern Judge." In place of an irritable Jehovah who went around smiting and chastening, Unitarians celebrated a genial deity who was all about love. "We believe that God is infinitely good, kind, benevolent," declared William E. Channing in his celebrated 1819 expression of the Unitarian creed. "To give our views of God in one word, we believe in his Parental character. We ascribe to him, not only the name, but the dispositions and principles of a father. We believe that he has a father's concern for his creatures, a father's desire for their improvement, a father's equity in proportioning his commands to their powers, a father's joy in their progress, a father's readiness to receive the penitent, and a father's justice for the incorrigible." The love between parent and child was the purest expression of human affection, and the model that would lead the child to religious devotion, wrote the Rev. Joseph Tuckerman in 1838. Tuckerman used a phrase that Warren would later apply to himself: "God is the universal Father. Every human being is a child of God. This, I repeat, is a great central doctrine and light of Christianity."[46]

Mid-nineteenth-century Protestants who believed in the Trinity tended to ascribe a more distant demeanor to God the Father, and they thought of Jesus when imagining personal intimacy with the divine. God might love his children and wish them well, but it was Jesus who offered warm sympathy as a friend or brother.[47] As in early colonial days, when Puritan clergy wrote in sensual terms of becoming as a wife to Christ (figured in the Gospels as a bridegroom), the Christ-centered devotionalism of the nineteenth century could take on erotic overtones. Examining Victorian-era Anglicanism, Frederick S. Roden has detected "a queer relationship to the Divine" in the writings of John Henry Newman and other High Church Anglicans, Anglo-Catholics, and converts to Roman Catholicism. Newman praised male celibacy as a preparation for entering into a metaphorical marriage with Christ. Newman and likeminded Anglicans and Catholics experienced the sacrament of communion as a quasi-sexual reception of God's body into their own, Roden asserts.[48]

Such a relationship with Jesus was certainly too much for Edward Warren once he had undertaken his mature effort to stifle sensual imagination. Warren did seek a personal relationship with Christ, but he imagined Christ offering paternal protection for his soul, much as "the strong arm of a loving father in a dark forest keeps harm from his little son," he wrote in 1859. A fatherly Christ—more loving than either God the Father or Dr. Warren the father—would provide the model for the chaste affection he would like to show his younger friends. Warren would follow Christ's lead, and his friends would follow his until they came to love Christ themselves. "Love Him and catch the echo of his words, 'that where I am ye may be also.'"[49]

## Thoroughly Revised

It is difficult to track Warren's emotional life through the 1860s. He left hardly any introspective writing after he stopped making entries in the second "thoughts" diary in the summer of 1862, at the age of thirty. He appears to have stopped keeping any sort of journal; at least, no journal can be found. Nonetheless, some signs of his matured thinking can be seen in his revision and rethinking of earlier journals. The notes inscribed in the margins, the blacking out of certain passages, the erasure of others, the new words written in the gaps, the removal of whole sheets of paper—all these reveal an effort to make the record of life better match his new self-image and the new image he wished to present to others.

Warren decided in 1865 that a lot of incautious entries needed to be altered or removed before anyone saw the journal. By then he had already done quite a lot of editing. On January 1, 1856, when beginning Volume Eight, he alluded to personal faults that had appeared in the "now concealed passages" in the preceding two volumes. The concealed passages of Volume Seven are numerous and in some cases extensive, appearing on least sixty of the journal's 159 numbered pages. In several dozen instances, the ink has been scraped away to reduce names to initials, though the erasures are inconsistent enough to divulge some identities; most of these erasures reduced the name of "Willie" to the initial "W." Adjectives have been removed before the name of Willie Gilbert in at least eleven places. On at least twenty other pages, passages ranging in length from a few words to eleven lines have been scribbled out, or erased, or both. The great majority of these alterations concern interactions with boys, particularly Willie; some concern conflicts with his father. The most drastic alterations of the journal are the removal of the top of one leaf (probably with entries on both sides), and the removal of four entire leaves (eight pages). Warren's index for the journal hints only vaguely at the contents of three of these missing leaves, but the contents of the other missing leaf are clearly summarized in the April 16, 1854, notation that "Willie spent the night with me."[50]

Warren's alterations to Volume Seven suggest that he had come to reevaluate both his behavior and the journal's purpose. "There are two theories of a journal," he explained near the end of Volume Eight. "1st That it should be a complete record of both the good and the bad in life, in which case it should evidently be destroyed, or else expurgated. 2nd, That it should only record the good acts—including self discipline in reference to errors—i.e. such parts as might usefully be left to those who wish to know the writers life . . . from pure affection, or to find limits at self improvement . . ." At the time he wrote these lines in January 1858, Warren realized that his journal more closely reflected the first theory: the tell-all. He regretted having produced such a candid document, and yet he did not want to lose what had evolved into an eight-volume account of his life for the past dozen years. Looking back on his New Year's Day inventory of faults two years previously, he resolved that his journal should be made suitable "for influencing others for good, and if a record of my life can have such an effect I ought not to destroy it. I propose therefore that all my journals be revised, so as to be willingly left in the possession of whoever of parents—wife children or confidant, shall be alive at my demise, but in no case to be kept by any except those of the direct line of my descendants so long as any such shall exist. And the last living one of all the above category of persons however far in the future he may live, shall destroy all these Journals by fire." The presumption was that relatives would be more sympathetic or reliable than strangers, a presumption that was already called into question by Warren's fraught relationship with his parents, and that would ultimately be proven false by the journals' survival to this day.[51] As Warren continued that same entry, on January 31, 1858, he offered an explanation for the absence of three leaves earlier in Volume Eight, which have been torn out close to the binding. "Experience shows that the record either of ill-advised acts or of self condemnation need not be preserved, for the annihilation of evil and the knowledge of it should be the rule. There will be enough of it present at all times. Neither are characteristic acts forgotten, by the only one concerned in knowing them."[52]

Warren completed his major editing of Volumes Two, Seven, and Eight in the fall of 1865. "Fully revised Nov. 1865," reads a notation on the opening flyleaf of Volume Seven; "Thoroughly revised" is written inside the front cover of Volume Two, just above a two-sentence overview of the journal dated Oct. 20, 1865. A slip of paper tucked inside the front cover of Volume Eight reads "Sept 65 Final thorough revision of first 13 p." Warren ended up making the fewest changes to Volume One, but an undated notation inside the front cover declares that it too had been made "ready for inspection."

Warren could remove offending passages with great skill when he was determined to do so. He was an authority on the subject of erasure, having provided detailed instructions in his 1865 textbook, *A Manual of Drafting Instruments and Operations*. Unwanted ink lines, he advised, "are removed by a sharp erasing knife, which has a short, sharp triangular blade fastened to a wooden or ivory handle." Repeated scrapes in one direction with moderate pressure could remove the thin top surface of the paper and obliterate any sign of the error. Alternatively, a compound of vulcanized rubber and ground glass could be used to gently rub away the marks. Once the scraped page was smoothed with the handle of the knife, the clean paper could be written over again.[53] So meticulous are some of the erasures in Warren's journal that no complete words can be recovered from the lower layer of the palimpsest even using digitally enhanced photographic techniques; minute traces can be found of swirling indentations on the paper, probably from the knife handle used to burnish the erased surface, but only microscopic ink flecks remain of the original letters.[54]

Figure 4.2. Digitally enhanced image of an erasure from Warren's Journal, Volume 2. Courtesy, Archives and Special Collections, Thomas Dodd Research Center, University of Connecticut, Storrs, Conn. Digital enhancement by Mark R. Smith of Macroscopic Solutions, LLC.

Given that Warren could make words vanish when he wanted to, it is notable that his alterations were not always thorough. Sometimes he erased passages only partially or scribbled over them, leaving visible ghosts of the elided words. In editing an 1854 entry in November 1865, for instance, he removed two or three words from the following passage: "a very . . . gentlemanly boy whom I have noticed lately politely handed me a book." The end of the erasure is fairly thorough, but the first missing word can still be read as "pretty." Elsewhere in the journals, selective erasures left surprising passages intact. It is notable, for instance, that Warren erased part of the passage about his delightful night with John Bagley in June 1849, but not the suggestive statement that they had "frolicked" in bed. Perhaps the erasures removed some embarrassing words while preserving sufficient reminders to spark pleasant reveries.[55]

Warren was reluctant to remove pages from the journals, excising only four leaves from Volume Seven and six from Volume Eight. The most effective editing technique would have been to rewrite the journals into new blank books, but Warren chose not to do that. He made it obvious to readers that they were looking at an altered document. Warren may have wanted it that way; he may have wanted readers to know of his repentance without knowing of the sin. At other points in the journals, he cross-hatched so thinly over phrases that he practically invited his readers to discern the original words and to learn that the hero of the story had risen above some minor transgression. Thus, the completed document bore graphic testimony that the journals served—in the words with which Warren began Volume Eight—as "records of my mental and moral and social progress." His example of self-improvement might even be the means of "influencing others for good." The trick was to disguise his strongest temptations and divert attention to something less serious.[56]

Other efforts at diversion can be seen in Volume Two, the volume that covers his romances with John Bagley and Micajah Lunt Jr. in Newburyport. On the back of the opening flyleaf, Warren wrote in pencil that "[a]ll my journals to be read by no one but my parents in the case of my death as a single man or widower. Others may see the index only, and may have such portions read to them as are not marked Private. Or else my relict or heirs, only shall use them as above directed." This directive is undated; the wording proves merely that it was written before the death of Warren's father in 1867.[57] The selection of the "private" passages is quite peculiar; all three involve comparatively tame interactions with Warren's friend Augusta Wood. The first of these mentions an evening social gathering when Warren "had a fine time especially when I waited on Miss Wood home." In the second, Augusta and her friend Jenny laughed at a ridiculous white neckerchief that he wore. The third, the only one that is even mildly erotic, is where Warren reports having "a splendid cozy time with Augusta."[58] The most charitable explanation for Warren's special treatment of these passages would be that he thought any hint of a romantic connection with a female carried more powerful sexual overtones than similar intimacy with a male; a reference to a "cozy time" might be damaging to the lady's reputation. But there is another possible explanation. The "private" marks were ostensibly to prevent his parents from reading the entries aloud to another interested person, yet perhaps the true purpose of the marks was to call attention to just those passages. Warren might have imagined this as an effective device to persuade his father of his interest in girls.

Warren added two inscriptions in October 1865 that emphasize the ordinariness and innocence of the events described in Volume Two. Inside the front cover of the volume, he summarized his account of early months in Newburyport as "variously 'rich' in youthful freshness ardor, tirelessness and happy unconcern." Here, and in a footnote to a passage on holding hands with Augusta, Warren adopted the same tone of bittersweet nostalgia that his contemporary writers often used when remembering their youth: " 'Sweet sensibility. Oh! Lah!' Yet how pure and sweet was this rosy young life." Evidently, even after his adult decision to retreat from sensuality, he still saw his young romances with multiple boys as unproblematic.[59]

As a result of all this editing—particularly the deletions—the journals became less reliable as records of Warren's original experience, feelings, and ideas. The removal of pages discussing his relationships with Willie in 1854 and two RPI students in 1856; his concealment of passages dealing with his sins and with the Dry River Brotherhood; and his possible destruction of whole volumes—these tactics succeeded in their apparent purpose of concealing details of interpersonal relationships. Among other questions, we simply cannot know whether there was a sexual aspect to his adult friendships with boys younger than Willie, or whether Warren practiced sodomy. The altered journals are now complicated documents with multiple layers of meaning. They reflect the actual events, Warren's first judgment about which events should be recorded, his thoughts when he wrote the original entry, his later reconsideration of the events, his reassessment of his original entry, his revised judgment of what his readers should know, and his strategy of interpreting the material to help readers improve their own character. The revised journals have two authors: the younger and the older Warren, the second of whom consciously adapted the story for public consumption.[60]

It is impossible to know whether Warren proved successful in adopting a paternal relationship with younger males, and whether such a relationship brought him a sense of satisfaction and peace. As the journals end in 1862, the dated alterations end in 1865, and only a handful of his letters survive, there is a scarcity of evidence revealing his later experience and thinking. And so a historian cannot go much farther with the story of Warren's struggle to control what he called his various "native peculiarities."[61] Yet there are tantalizing hints that Warren's life took surprising new turns in the 1870s and 1880s. The epilogue that follows will trace what can be known of events that must ultimately remain mysterious.

# Epilogue

## *The Cross, the Grave, the Skies*

> And the dead were judged out of those things which were written in the books, according to their works.
>
> —Revelation 20:12

Warren's professional stature rose in the 1860s as he turned his attention to publishing. Converting his lecture notes into manuscripts, he produced a series of textbooks with the New York firm of John Wiley & Sons, starting with *General Problems from the Orthographic Projections of Descriptive Geometry* in 1860.[1] These works brought him to the attention of rival engineering schools, which began to take interest in recruiting him just as he grew frustrated at the Rensselaer Polytechnic Institute.

After its ambitious expansion in the 1850s, RPI suffered hard times in the 1860s and 1870s. The institute's buildings near the railroad station burned down during Troy's great fire of May 10, 1862. The institute operated out of temporary quarters until private donations and state aid allowed it to rebuild at a new hillside location on Eighth Street overlooking the city. The new facilities that opened in 1864 and 1866 seemed to augur an expansive future for RPI, and Warren outlined a vision for expanding the curriculum to match. The recommendations that he published in his *Notes on Polytechnic or Scientific Schools in the United States* (1866) and his 1868 and 1869 articles in the *Journal of the Franklin Institute* were for a comprehensive scientific school with an expansive general education and intellectual rigor to equal that provided by liberal arts colleges. But that would have taken money that RPI did not have. Facing financial difficulties in the 1860s, the institute raised tuition sharply while allowing faculty salaries to lag behind those of comparable schools. Trustees and faculty discussed plans in 1870 to expand the scope of the curriculum, but decided instead on retrenchment: starting in 1871, RPI became narrowly focused on civil engineering.[2]

Warren did not oppose the retrenchment but he made no secret of his displeasure with RPI. He shared the widespread dislike of RPI director Charles Drowne, who was said to be tyrannical to his subordinates but "ready to lick the boots of a trustee." Warren complained privately in 1865 of "a total absence of all efficient leadership around which the faculty can rally in resisting the wicked invasion of their rights by the trustees." He griped publicly, in letters to the trustees, about the lack of proper equipment, his heavy workload, and his low salary—a problem that had bothered him for years. In early 1871, at the age of thirty-nine, he considered the offer of a job at the newly founded Stevens Institute of Technology, in Hoboken, New Jersey, which was trying to recruit distinguished faculty from other engineering schools. Warren tried to use the job offer to improve his situation at RPI, telling the trustees that Stevens was offering him better facilities, better equipment, and a 50 percent raise over his current $2,400 salary. He said that he felt a sense of loyalty to RPI and would prefer to stay there if he were offered sufficient inducements. It is unclear whether the trustees gave him any of what he wanted, but in any case Warren decided not to move to Hoboken. He explained later that "but for long habit in living close to my work, and a dreary March day to visit the place, both which made me forget the possibility of living in pleasant country a few miles out, I might have accepted the call."[3]

Warren had already begun to inquire into the possibility of a job at the Massachusetts Institute of Technology, located at this time in Boston. MIT president John D. Runkle was building up the new institution by luring faculty away from competing programs; he was interested in recruiting Warren, who was by far the leading American expert in his narrow field. Warren wrote to Runkle after rejecting the Stevens offer to remind him of his availability. At Runkle's request, MIT created a position for Warren as professor of descriptive geometry, stereotomy, and drawing, and offered him $2,500 a year, a nominal raise over what he received at RPI. Warren submitted his resignation to RPI in the spring of 1872, telling the trustees that he had hoped to spend the rest of his career in Troy but had lost hope that RPI would ever have the resources it needed for adequate improvements. He would leave there "only wishing, in vain, that Troy and the Institute . . . had been such that no human agency could have detached me from them." Warren added that personal considerations also entered into his decision: "My Mother's life, which is everything to me, seemed to depend on a return to her native air, and life long associations."[4]

Warren and his mother moved to a house on the border of Newton and Brighton from which Warren could commute to work. The Massachusetts Institute of Technology, colloquially known as Boston Tech, was a much newer school than RPI but had quickly surpassed it in size and wealth. At the time Warren began his new job in the 1872–73 academic year, MIT was rapidly expanding its student body and had recruited an energetic, distinguished group of young professors. It boasted twenty full-time faculty members and 375 students, slightly more than double the numbers at RPI. The professors were supplemented by another fifteen instructors, unlike at RPI. MIT was already outgrowing its new building on Boylston Street near Copley Square in the Back Bay neighborhood.[5]

Warren almost immediately encountered trouble at MIT, as students complained that his courses were too difficult and colleagues were annoyed by the uproar in his poorly supervised drawing rooms during lunch hour. Warren had assistants but apparently they were unable to provide adequate supervision. The faculty voted to drop MIT's requirement for machine drawing and urged Warren to make his "Shades and Shadows" course easier. Classroom discipline remained a problem as it had at RPI. A short publication by the Class of 1874 described Warren flying into a rage in the classroom on Nov. 27, 1872, in response to some student misbehavior that Warren later called a "disorderly manifestation." The commotion drew President Runkle, who spoke with the students, obtained their written apology, and asked Warren to forgive the disruption. The mercurial professor eventually calmed down, according to the article, in a reference that played on Warren's initials: "[A] S.E. Wind seldom blows long; and this one . . . was reduced to a gentle zephyr." An article in the student newspaper, the *Spectrum*, blamed Warren for student misbehavior in the drawing rooms while avoiding mention of his name: "It remains almost entirely with a teacher whether a class is well behaved. If he is gentlemanly, respectful, and firm himself, he will always inspire respect: if weak, inefficient, and vacillating, contempt and disrespect are his sure rewards." Warren's colleagues continued to complain of his inability to keep down the noise in his drawing rooms. The faculty began to wonder whether mechanical drawing was really that important, and in early 1874 decided to further reduce the requirements. Warren found himself "embarrassed . . . by great contrast between the new and former conditions under which his duties were performed."[6]

So Warren was in a vulnerable position as MIT struggled through a financial crisis caused by the nationwide economic depression of 1873. Enrollment shrank by sixty-five students at the beginning of the 1873–74 academic year, then by another twenty-two students the following year. President Runkle put the blame mainly on the depression but also noted that students were dropping out before graduation because of the difficulty of the curriculum. Warren was asked to resign his position at the end of the 1874–75 academic year. He later explained that he was merely one of several instructors affected by a "policy of retrenchment," but this explanation is less than candid. Warren knew very well that other considerations were involved. It was no coincidence that Warren was the only one of MIT's twenty professors to be laid off that year. Runkle wrote privately in January 1875, when he was considering laying off Warren and another professor, that the economic crisis was a good excuse for doing what he would have liked to do anyway: "[I]f Hunt & Warren were our most valuable men, we should undoubtedly look for some other solution—But it is a little singular that all the circumstances conspire to point out this solution—Now we can simply rest the case on the question of the economy sought, & the ease with which the work can be satisfactorily done by distribution; or we may bring in the question of cause in addition." T. Sterry Hunt was ultimately allowed to remain as a geology professor, but Warren's position was eliminated. "Warren will understand, whether it is expressed or not, that he has failed to give reasonable satisfaction, & that the occasion is used to get rid of him," Runkle wrote. "If the occasion did not exist, I should feel it my duty to tell him that his resignation would be accepted at the end of the present year; which I rather think he expects."[7]

Runkle did not say what "cause" would justify the dismissal of a full professor who had been recruited just three years before; dismissal would seem a rather extreme response to concerns about classroom disorder, so there is reason to believe there were deeper issues at stake. Warren not only left MIT, he abandoned the teaching profession altogether. He would appear to have had abundant opportunities for new positions with the rapid expansion of engineering programs in late-nineteenth-century America. Thanks in part to federal assistance provided by the Morrill Act of 1862, the number of engineering schools and university engineering departments rose from seventeen to eighty-five during the 1870s alone. In addition, Warren's skills could have helped him find work in art schools. Indeed, at the time he was fired from MIT he also held a temporary position as a lecturer at the Boston Normal Art School, where he been assisting since 1873 in training the instructors for this new school. But Warren left the Normal Art School in 1875 after losing his position at MIT. He tried to obtain work by printing a flyer offering his services as a lecturer for preparatory scientific schools, colleges, and professional scientific schools, yet never secured another steady job. Could he have committed such a grievous offense that he found himself no longer employable as an educator? Could he have faltered in his determination to find intimacy only as a father figure, and confronted the harsh difficulty of returning to the world of youthful love? There is no way of knowing, as MIT officials preferred to keep their firings quiet. In an earlier case when the institute was considering the dismissal of an allegedly incompetent professor, they offered that "no permanent record of this request need be made" if the professor resigned without a fuss. In Warren's case, there is no surviving explanation in the MIT records. S. Edward Warren, who had believed himself to be a born teacher, ended his prestigious career without recording any protest.[8]

## A Teacher without Students

Though the reason for Warren's firing remains mysterious, it was clearly a traumatic event that scarred his life. Warren later wrote that he "withdrew from active life in 1875, and . . . devoted his life to the preparation of textbooks on technical subjects." Actually, ten of his twelve textbooks were written before he was fired, though he did continue to make modifications to several of them for later editions. In some editions published after his dismissal, Warren concealed his former connection with MIT, saying instead that he was "formerly Professor at the Rensselaer Polytechnic Institute, etc." His 1875 book on *Stereotomy: Problems in Stone Cutting*, came out after he was fired; Warren described himself as a professor at the Massachusetts Normal Art School and formerly RPI, and he dedicated the book to his former RPI students.[9]

Losing his job was obviously a financial blow, but Warren and his mother were not entirely dependent on his salary. Warren's father in

1867 had left the lifetime use of his estate to his wife Ann Catherine Warren, after whose death the property would pass to Edward Warren. This estate in 1867 included the house in Newton, worth about $5,000, and corporate stocks and other assets worth nearly another $8,000, totaling an amount that roughly corresponds to the purchasing power of $228,000 in 2018 dollars. The family investments performed well over the next two decades. By the time of Catherine Warren's death in 1889, she owned no real estate but the total value of her property had grown to $28,830—roughly corresponding to the 2018 purchasing power of $812,000. Edward Warren had his own investments and royalties in addition to the family wealth that he inherited. It is unclear whether he had to dip into the principal to cover his expenses, but he died in 1909 with an estate that had grown only modestly to $34,901, corresponding to the 2018 purchasing power of $994,000. Warren, like his father, could live without the income from a full-time job.[10]

Warren continued to identify himself as a "teacher" or a "professor" for the rest of his life, but he does not appear to have done much productive labor after his premature retirement at the age of forty-four, other than completing and revising his textbook series. He did some private tutoring and wrote a few articles on educational topics that he published or presented in the late 1870s. Thereafter, his interests turned more to religion; he published a deeply conservative essay in 1890 about the sanctity of the Sabbath, and an 1895 plea for "Moral Instruction in the Schools" that ignored the growing religious diversity produced by mass immigration. He wrote a book of advice to the young, titled "Training for Success," and attempted unsuccessfully in 1900 to have it published. A reader for the press dismissed it as "well-meant but entirely commonplace." Warren remained an Episcopalian. He had joined the Grace Episcopal Church on his return to the Newton area in 1872, and in 1874 had helped recruit the new rector, George W. Shinn, having met Shinn in his previous position as rector of St. Paul's Church in Troy. Warren remained a church member after that but was never particularly active in church affairs. He also joined the Newton Natural History Society and the New England Historic-Genealogical Society.[11]

The most extraordinary event in Warren's seemingly humdrum existence was his marriage to his housekeeper, Margaret Miller. Warren barely mentions her in his surviving writings except to say that she was originally from Paisley, Scotland. Public records show her to have been nineteen years younger than Warren and to have immigrated in 1872, the same year Warren and his mother returned to Newton. She is listed in the 1880 U.S. Census as living as a servant in the Washington Street home of Warren, his mother, and his aunt. Their marriage on November 18, 1884, was the first for both of them. Though she was still of childbearing age at the time, their union proved childless. He referred to her in his 1904 will, somewhat formulaically, as "my faithful and dearly beloved wife Margaret, whom God in his goodness has given me."[12]

What could a man in his fifties want from a woman in her early thirties? Asking the question that way seems to unfairly suggest an answer about sex, but let's not be so hasty. Warren's previous apathy about women should make us hesitate to jump to such a conclusion Another possible explanation is that getting married added to Warren's respectability as the head of a family, a consideration that may have been especially weighty if there was a cloud of suspicion hanging over him since his firing. Marriage would also strengthen his claim to masculine authority. It would yield what Robert Connell calls the "patriarchal dividend" of power over a woman, it would resolve the questionable masculinity associated with bachelorhood, and it would heighten Warren's manly status in comparison with other males. Warren's mother might have been relieved to see her son finally reach that milestone of maturity. Margaret might have welcomed a marriage of convenience if it raised her status from an immigrant servant to the wife of an affluent man, with a servant of her own; the marriage also allowed her to bring her two nieces to live with them as part of their family.[13]

Yet it is not that hard to believe that Edward and Margaret might have genuinely loved each other for their personal qualities, despite their differences in age, status, and life experience. During her years as his housekeeper he may have come to think of her as a family member, then gradually grew to admire her. The fact that she was so much younger and comparatively uneducated may have made her seem less intimidating to him, and may have evoked the same sort of affections that were stirred by his earlier friendships with younger males. Perhaps he found in her the companion that had been missing from his lonely life. Perhaps one day he looked up from his reading as she entered his study and was suddenly reminded so much of Dicky that he wanted to kiss her. Perhaps he reached out fearfully, hoping for love in return . . . and was joyfully accepted. Perhaps as the years passed the couple became a familiar sight in the neighborhood, taking their daily walk together as Warren spoke earnestly to his wife about matters of faith. Perhaps.

## I Have Made My Bed in the Darkness

More than a century later, Edward and Margaret lie together beneath lichen-splotched slabs of stone on a knoll in Newton Cemetery, next to his parents Samuel and Catherine. The mumble of traffic can be heard from surrounding streets. Newton is now a dense inner suburb of Boston. There is a distant hum—possibly from off to the north where a river of cars and trucks flows along the Massachusetts Turnpike, over land where half of West Newton village once stood. The graveyard itself in early winter is tranquil and pretty, as it was designed to be back in the 1850s. Clumps of gravestones stand amid the snow along gently curving lanes. One can easily imagine why nineteenth-century visitors found the cemetery a soothing place to meander and reflect.[14]

As part of the larger "rural cemetery" movement of the mid-nineteenth century, Newton Cemetery originated from the same culture of sentiment that put its mark on other aspects of Edward Warren's life: the growing emphasis on emotional intimacy in friendship, teaching, faith, and parenthood. Starting with the creation in 1831 of Mount Auburn Cemetery on the outskirts of Cambridge, the designers of rural cemeteries worked to create a space totally different from the crowded urban graveyards where each new burial risked disturbing old bones. The old graveyard, though usually adjacent to a church, was a gloomy, functional space for disposing of the dead. The stones, for those who could afford them, bore grim reminders of mortality in the form of verse and decorative death's heads. The new cemetery was what one scholar calls "a landscape of hope," where the bodies of family members were buried together amid peaceful greenery, under stones carved with weeping willows. Reflecting the increasing optimism about the prospects for entering heaven, these new "cemeteries" got their name from the Greek word for "sleeping chambers." Each family member would slumber alongside his loved ones in the earth until awakened to meet God on Judgment Day.[15]

Though their identity is recorded on the stones, the dead lose their individuality in nineteenth-century cemeteries. Formally dressed in earth and granite, surrounded by the symbolic language of botany, they join an ensemble that murmurs counsel to a living audience: acceptance of the past, peace in the present, hope for eternity. Here a concluded life can be contemplated calmly, without the friction that marks the daily experience of living individuals. The machine-carved messages on the stones are almost interchangeable. Even if we can trust that a certain man or woman put some thought into choosing a particular message, how much feeling should we read into such formulaic expressions? We know that a man and woman were married on such a date, and died on such and such dates, but we can't know how they felt about the experience. Had they taken comfort from each other's company and pleasure from their bodies, or had their days been filled with bickering and petty resentments? We'll never know. These stones are memorials for forgetting, their public words helping to cloak the private space below. Almost none of the forgotten souls in Newton Cemetery matched Edward Warren's achievement in leaving behind rich diaries that might have helped us see dimly into their lives, now that their tongues have ceased and their knowledge has vanished away. But each of them was an individual who felt disappointments, loneliness, sorrows, comforts, joys—perhaps love—for one precious moment on earth, and who like each of us faced an ending in death, nothingness, and eternity.

†

This has been a story told by a historian, using uncertain scraps of evidence left behind in the course of a nineteenth-century life. Like almost all such stories, it has relied upon the evidence of whatever written texts have survived to this day. Warren helped me to tell this story by leaving a text he created himself for the purpose of making sense of his life, though of course he did not expect that it would be used in the ways I have used it here. Rich though his journals are, their usefulness is limited by his own difficulty in understanding his life, his inconsistency in recording his experience, and his vacillating attempts to alter the record for other eyes. There is an awkward misfit between Warren's day-by-day recording of events in the journal, and the goal of both of us to discern the longer pattern of his character and his mind. Moreover, he and I see time differently. There is a deep incompatibility between the limited understanding I seek—examining part of one man's life with the tools of inductive reasoning and with questions of interest to people in my own era—and the Judgment that most concerned Warren. The journals are not the text that Warren most valued as the key to exploring his heart. His preferred text was the one he scrutinized throughout his life to contemplate a story of eternity instead of days, and to prepare for that eternity with fear of justice and hope of mercy.

And so, in a spirit of humility, I would like to end my tale of Warren by stepping out of the role of historian. There is a gulf between the knowledge my craft can bring and the knowledge that ultimately mattered to my subject. This is Edward Warren's story, and I would like to end it in a way that he would have found meaningful, envisioning what he might have anticipated as the future dawning of the last day.

Imagine that we are back amid the snowy knolls of Newton Cemetery, waiting. It is utterly silent now. Night fades to dawn, black stones fade to gray, and rosy sunlight pours across the lawns and through the trees. The trumpet sounds. Amid a multitude of long-forgotten others, Edward Warren rises from the grave. His soul, as he and his fellow Episcopalians had expected, had been waiting in joyful hope for this consummation, when it would be reunited with his body, now renewed and incorruptible. He feels a new peace between spirit and flesh as he ascends to his judgment before God—and to his final reunion with warm-hearted friends.[16]

# Abbreviations in Notes

Note: In notes for journal entries, the number immediately following the abbreviation indicates the page number given in the journal. For instance, "SEW I: 14" would indicate page 14 in Warren's "Journal Vol. I. S. E. W."

**HBSC**  Harriet Beecher Stowe Center Library, Hartford, Conn.

**MIT**  Institute Archives and Special Collections, Massachusetts Institute of Technology, Cambridge, Mass.

**RPI**  Institute Archives and Special Collections, Rensselaer Polytechnic Institute, Troy, N.Y.

**SEW**  Samuel Edward Warren.

**SEW I**  Samuel Edward Warren, "Journal Vol. I. S. E. W.," Sept. 1846 to March 1849, *MS 97*, Item 079, Special Collections, University of Delaware Library, Newark, Del.

**SEW II**  [S. Edward Warren], "Journal Vol. II. S. E. W.," April 1849 to Jan. 1850. Archives and Special Collections, University of Connecticut Library, Storrs, Conn.

**SEW VII**  [S. Edward Warren], "S. Edw. Warren Journal. Vol. VII," Feb. 1854 to Dec. 1855, Institute Archives and Special Collections, Rensselaer Polytechnic Institute, Troy, N.Y.

**SEW VIII**  [S. Edward Warren], "Journal Vol. VIII," Jan. 1856 to July 1858, Doc. 1305, Winterthur Library, Winterthur, Del.

**Thoughts I**  S. Edward Warren, "Thoughts Taken on the Wing," Aug. 1858 to Oct. 1859, Vol. I. Diaries Collection Box I, Archives and Special Collections, University of Connecticut Library, Storrs, Conn.

**Thoughts II**  S. Edward Warren, "Thought Sketches," Mar. 1860 to July 1862, Vol. II. Diaries Collection Box I, Archives and Special Collections, University of Connecticut Library, Storrs, Conn.

# Notes

## Introduction

*All Biblical quotations will be from the King James Version, as this was the version in common use among American Protestants in the nineteenth century.*

1. SEW, Thoughts II: 5–6 (22 April 1860). All citations of Warren's journals will be given in similarly abbreviated form. See Abbreviations.
2. On male romantic friendships, E. Anthony Rotundo, "Romantic Friendship: Male Intimacy and Middle-class Youth in the Northern United States, 1800–1900," *Journal of Social History* 23, no. 1 (Fall 1989): 1–25; quotation from E. Anthony Rotundo, *American Manhood: Transformations in Masculinity from the Revolution to the Modern Era* (New York: Basic Books, 1993), 85; John D'Emilio and Estelle B. Freedman, *Intimate Matters: A History of Sexuality in America* (New York: Harper and Row, 1988), 121–29; William Benemann, *Male-Male Intimacy in Early America: Beyond Romantic Friendships* (New York: Harrington Park Press, 2006), xv. Richard Godbeer explores romantic friendships among adult men in the early Republic: Godbeer, *The Overflowing of Friendship: Love between Men and the Creation of the American Republic* (Baltimore: Johns Hopkins University Press, 2009). Martin Dubermann finds what he considers clear evidence of adult homoeroticism in "'Writhing Bedfellows' in Antebellum South Carolina," *Journal of Homosexuality* 6, nos. 1–2 (Fall/Winter 1980–81): 85–101. Caleb Crain considers the belief that the affective bonds that characterized romantic friendship provided a model for egalitarian relations between republican citizens: Caleb Crain, *American Sympathy: Men, Friendship, and Literature in the New Nation* (New Haven: Yale University Press, 2001). Carroll Smith-Rosenberg's article is the classic exploration of women's romantic friendships, also suggesting a spectrum of intimacy: "The Female World of Love and Ritual: Relations between Women in Nineteenth-Century America," *Signs* 1, no. 1 (Autumn 1975): 1–29.
3. Rotundo, "Romantic Friendship"; Benemann, *Male-Male Intimacy*, xvi.

4. Timothy J. Gilfoyle, *City of Eros: New York City, Prostitution, and the Commercialization of Sex, 1790–1920* (New York: W. W. Norton, 1992), 99–116; Howard P. Chudacoff, *The Age of the Bachelor: Creating an American Subculture* (Princeton: Princeton University Press, 1999), 33–38.

5. Jessica Warner, "Evangelical Male Friendships in America's First Age of Reform," *Journal of Social History* (Spring 2010): 681–705; SEW VIII: 236 (18 July 1858).

6. SEW II: 25 (8 June 1849).

7. Sidonie Smith and Julia Watson, *Reading Autobiography: A Guide for Interpreting Life Narratives* (Minneapolis: University of Minnesota Press, 2001), 47.

8. The textbooks provided meticulous instruction in aspects of mechanical drawing, which Warren defined as "the geometry of drawing; or, more exactly, as the system of principles, and exact operations founded upon them, by which all regular objects . . . can be so truly represented upon flat surfaces, that, from the drawing, the original can be constructed as it exists in the mind of the designer"; *Massachusetts Institute of Technology, President's Report for the Year ending Sept. 30, 1873* (Boston: A. A. Kingman, 1873), 20. Warren also wrote *Notes on Polytechnic or Scientific Schools in the United States* (New York: John Wiley and Sons, 1866), *The Sunday Question, or, The Lord's Day* (Boston: Earle, 1890), and several pamphlets and articles on matters of pedagogy and religion.

9. Warren described his changing journal habits in SEW VIII: 128 (1 Jan. 1857). I will follow Warren's lead in calling the numbered volumes "journals" and the entire scattered collection "the journals" or collectively "the journal." When speaking of journals in general, I will use the terms *journal* and *diary* interchangeably. I will refer to the keepers of journals, including Warren, as "diarists."

10. The archivists at the University of Connecticut, the University of Delaware, Rensselaer Polytechnic Institute, and the Winterthur Library do not know the reasons for their institutions' acquisition of the journals, and do not know the journals' full provenance. Email to author from Betsy Pittman, University Archivist, Archives and Special Collections at the Thomas J. Dodd Research Center, University of Connecticut, Jan. 26, 2015. Conversation with John F. Dojka, Head of Special Collections, Folsom Library, Rensselaer Polytechnic Institute, Aug. 2012. Email to author from L. Rebecca Johnson Melvin, Head of the Manuscript and Archives Department, University of Delaware Library, Sept. 12, 2014. Records of the Winterthur Library show that the library purchased its volume on July 31, 2002, from William Reese Rare Books & Manuscripts, but do not indicate the reason for the purchase; the provenance cannot be traced any farther back (email to author from Bill Reese, William Reese Co., July 25, 2011).

11. Most of this information can be found in a brief autobiographical sketch that appeared posthumously in *New England Historical and Genealogical Register*, 1910, Vol. 64 (Boston: New England Historic Genealogical Society,

1910), lxiii–lxv. The autobiographical sketch gives a misleading explanation for the firing, which I will discuss in the Epilogue.

12. See for example Estelle B. Freedman, "'The Burning of Letters Continues': Elusive Identities and the Historical Construction of Sexuality," *Journal of Women's History* 9, no. 4 (Winter 1998): 181–200.

13. Graham Robb, *Strangers: Homosexual Love in the Nineteenth Century* (New York: W. W. Norton, 2003), 18; Craig M. Loftin, "Secrets in Boxes: The Historian as Archivist," in *Out of the Closet, Into the Archives: Researching Sexual Histories*, ed. Amy L. Stone and Jaime Cantrell (Albany: State University of New York Press, 2015), 51–52.

14. Harry G. Cocks, "Approaches to the History of Sexuality Since 1750," in *The Routledge History of Sex and the Body, 1500 to the Present*, ed. Sarah Toulahan and Kate Fisher (Abingdon, UK: Routledge, 2013): 38–54; Eve Kosofsky Sedgwick, *Between Men: English Literature and Male Homosocial Desire* (1985; New York: Columbia University Press, 2016), 23; Eve Kosofsky Sedgwick, *Epistemology of the Closet, Updated with a New Preface* (1990; Berkeley: University of California Press, 2008), 11.

15. David M. Halperin, "How to Do the History of Male Homosexuality," *GLQ: A Journal of Lesbian and Gay Studies* 6, no. 1 (2000): 87–123; 91; Sean Brady, "All about Eve? Queer Theory and History" *Journal of Contemporary History* 41, no. 1 (Jan. 2006): 185–95.

16. Heather R. White, *Reforming Sodom: Protestants and the Rise of Gay Rights* (Chapel Hill: University of North Carolina Press, 2015), 1–6, 17–18; quotation at 10.

17. Godbeer, *Overflowing of Friendship*, 3–5; quotation at 3; Moses Stuart, *A Commentary on the Epistle to the Romans* (Andover, MA: Flagg and Gould, 1832), 108; Jonathan Ned Katz, *Love Stories: Sex Between Men before Homosexuality* (Chicago: University of Chicago Press, 2001), 6–9, 27; Thomas W. Laqueur, *Solitary Sex: A Cultural History of Masturbation* (New York: Zone Books, 2003), 202–11, 224, 236–37; Anna Clark, "Twilight Moments," *Journal of the History of Sexuality* 14, nos. 1/2 (Jan.-Apr. 2005), 140.

18. William N. Eskridge Jr., *Dishonorable Passions: Sodomy Laws in America, 1861–2003* (New York: Viking, 2008), 20–22, 50; Stephen Robertson, *Crimes Against Children: Sexual Violence and Legal Culture in New York City, 1880–1960* (Chapel Hill: University of North Carolina Press, 2005), 18, 58–63. The rape law is New York statute Title 2, Article 2, Section 22; the sodomy law is Title 5, Article 3, Section 20; these appear in *The Revised Statutes of the State of New York, as Altered by Subsequent Legislation*, 5th ed., Vol. III (Albany: Banks and Brothers, 1859), 942, 970. The special abhorrence for those who habitually practiced sodomy complicates the Foucauldian characterization of the pre-homosexual period as one in which sexuality was understood as "acts" rather than orientations; see Thomas A. Foster, "Antimasonic Satire, Sodomy, and Eighteenth-Century

Masculinity in the 'Boston Evening-Post,'" *William and Mary Quarterly* 60, no. 1 (Jan. 2003): 171–84.

19. Rachel Hope Cleves, *Charity and Sylvia: A Same-Sex Marriage in Early America* (New York: Oxford University Press, 2014), 41; Peter N. Stearns, *American Cool: Constructing a Twentieth-Century Emotional Style* (New York: New York University Press, 1994), 67.

20. SEW VIII: 90 (n.d., June 1856).

21. Karen Halttunen, *Confidence Men and Painted Women: A Study of Middle-Class Culture in America, 1830–1870* (New Haven: Yale University Press, 1982), 57; Stearns, *American Cool*, 54–57, 68–69; John Corrigan, *Business of the Heart: Religion and Emotion in the Nineteenth Century* (Berkeley: University of California Press, 2002), 1–3; Daniel Walker Howe, *Making the American Self: Jonathan Edwards to Abraham Lincoln* (Cambridge: Harvard University Press, 1997), 260–61.

22. Shelby M. Balik, "'Dear Christian Friends': Charity Bryant, Sylvia Drake, and the Making of a Spiritual Network," *Journal of Social History* 50, no. 4 (2017): 632.

23. Marc Brodie and Barbara Caine, "Class, Sex, and Friendship: The Long Nineteenth Century," in *Friendship: A History*, ed. Caine (London: Equinox, 2009), 230–35.

24. Carl F. Kaestle, *Pillars of the Republic: Common Schools and American Society, 1780–1860* (New York: Hill and Wang, 1983), 63–101; Richard Rabinowitz, *The Spiritual Self in Everyday Life: The Transformation of Personal Religious Experience in Nineteenth-Century New England* (Boston: Northeastern University Press, 1989), 157; Paula S. Fass, *The End of American Childhood: A History of Parenting From Life on the Frontier to the Managed Child* (Princeton: Princeton University Press, 2016), 16–19. These matters will be explored in detail in the chapters that follow.

25. Roy Rosenzweig, *Eight Hours for What We Will: Workers and Leisure in an Industrial City, 1870–1920* (Cambridge: Cambridge University Press, 1983), 35–38; Herbert G. Gutman "Work, Culture, and Society in Industrializing America, 1815–1919," *American Historical Review* 78, no. 3 (June 1973): 531–88.

26. On Jacksonian hypermasculinity, see Michael Kimmel, *Manhood in America: A Cultural History*, 3rd ed. (New York: Oxford University Press, 2012), 25–27, 31. The sociologist Stephen Valocchi, reviewing the literature on twentieth-century homosexuality, cautions against a scholarly tendency to treat masculinity as the normative gender of gay men; this caution is worth keeping in mind also when considering same-sex desire in the period before the invention of modern homosexuality. Stephen Valocchi, "Where Did Gender Go? Same-Sex Desire and the Persistence of Gender in Gay Male Historiography," *GLQ: A Journal of Lesbian and Gay Studies* 18, no. 4 (2012): 453–79.

27. Janet Moore Lindman, "Acting the Manly Christian: White Evangelical Masculinity in Revolutionary Virginia," *William and Mary Quarterly* 57,

no. 2 (April 2000): 393–416; Bret E. Carroll, "The Religious Construction of Masculinity in Victorian America: The Male Mediumship of John Shoebridge Williams," *Religion and American Culture* 7, no. 1 (Winter 1997): 27–60.

28. Benemann, *Male-Male Intimacy in Early America*, xvi; Howard P. Chudacoff, *How Old Are You? Age Consciousness in American Culture* (Princeton: Princeton University Press, 1989), 9; Heman Humphrey, *Domestic Education* (Amherst: J. S. and C. Adams, 1840), 72.

29. My thinking here is influenced by Anna Clark, "Twilight Moments," and by Bruce Dorsey, " 'Making Men What They Should Be': Male Same-Sex Intimacy and Evangelical Religion in Early Nineteenth-Century New England," *Journal of the History of Sexuality* 24, no. 3 (Sept. 2015): 345–77. In Edward Warren's case, the fact that certain common forms of erotic play were not usually discussed openly made it easier for him and a friend to delicately test the boundaries of their mutual interest.

30. Richard Godbeer, *Sexual Revolution in Early America* (Baltimore: Johns Hopkins University Press, 2002), 52, 55, 79–80, 83–84; Dorsey, " 'Making Men What They Should Be' "; Warner, "Evangelical Male Friendships," 691; Janet Moore Lindman, " 'This Union of the Soul': Spiritual Friendship among Early American Protestants," *Journal of Social History* 50, no. 4 (Summer 2017): 680–700; Cleves, *Charity and Sylvia*.

31. SEW VIII: 3 (1 Jan. 1856).

32. SEW VIII: 205 (n.d., early 1858).

33. S. Edward Warren to Henry Freeman Allen, Oct. 1, 1870, in Henry Freeman Allen Scrapbook, HBSC.

34. One strength of such a "microhistorical" approach is that a fine-grained study of the particular can reveal nuances overlooked by broader overviews, nuances that may force us to rethink previous conclusions. A microhistorical approach may be especially effective in exploring subjective experiences that cannot be effectively surveyed in the aggregate. For discussion of the genre of microhistory, see Jill Lepore, "Historians Who Love Too Much: Reflections on Microhistory and Biography," *Journal of American History* 88, no. 1 (June 2001): 129–44; Richard D. Brown, "Microhistory and the Post-Modern Challenge," *Journal of the Early Republic* 23, no. 1 (Spring 2003): 1–20; Sigurður G. Magnússon and István Szíjártó, *What Is Microhistory? Theory and Practice* (London: Routledge, 2013).

## Chapter 1. Friendship

1. John Angell James, *The Young Man from Home* (1838; New York: American Tract Society [1845?]), v.

2. Ibid., v, vi, 10. See also Joseph S. Buckminster, "The Temptations of the Young," in *Sermons by the Late Rev. Joseph S. Buckminster* (Boston: Carter and Hendee, 1829).

3. James, *Young Man from Home*, 31–39; 31 and 37; see also Joel Hawes, *Lectures to Young Men on the Formation of Character*, 5th ed. (Hartford: Cooke, 1831), 35–37.

4. Population data is derived from Campbell Gibson, "Population of the 100 Largest Cities and Other Urban Places in the United States: 1790 To 1990," Population Division Working Paper No. 27, U.S. Bureau of the Census, June 1998; http://www.census.gov/population/www/documentation/twps0027.html. The change in living arrangements is discussed in Paul E. Johnson, *A Shopkeeper's Millennium: Society and Revivals in Rochester, New York, 1815–1837* (1978; New York: Hill and Wang, 2004), ch. 2, and Allan Stanley Horlick, *Country Boys and Merchant Princes: The Social Control of Young Men in New York* (Lewisburg, PA: Bucknell University Press; London: Associated University Presses, 1975). For an 1840s expression of concern about young men in American cities, see John Todd, *The Moral Influence, Dangers, and Duties, Connected with Great Cities* (Northampton, MA: J. H. Butler, 1841), esp. "Lecture VI."

5. Paul Boyer, *Urban Masses and Moral Order in America, 1820–1920* (Cambridge: Harvard University Press, 1978), ch. 1; David Paul Nord, "Religious Reading and Readers in Antebellum America," *Journal of the Early Republic* 15, no. 2 (Summer 1995): 241–72, quotation at 247.

6. David Magie, *The Spring-Time of Life; Or, Advice to Youth* (New York: Robert Carter and Brothers, 1853); Daniel Wise, *The Path of Life, or Sketches of the Way to Glory: A Help for Young Christians* (New York: Carlton and Porter, 1847), 162–63, 171, 174; Janet Moore Lindman, " 'This Union of the Soul': Spiritual Friendship among Early American Protestants," *Journal of Social History* 50, no. 4 (Summer 2017): 683, 684; Jacob Abbott, *The Young Christian: Or, a Familiar Illustration of the Principles of Christian Duty* (New York: American Tract Society, 1832), 31–35; Edward L. Lach Jr. "Abbott, Jacob," *American National Biography Online* (2000); http://www.anb.org/; Jay MacPherson, "Scriven, Joseph Medlicott," *Dictionary of Canadian Biography*, Vol. XI: 1881–1890; http://www.biographi.ca/en/bio.php?id_nbr=5823, accessed Dec. 20, 2014. On the location of Warren's room and its proximity to the Theological Seminary, *New England Historical and Genealogical Register*, 1910, Vol. 64 (Boston: New England Historic Genealogical Society, 1910), lxiv; F. A. Barton, "Plan of the Real Estate of Phillips Academy, Andover, Mass" (1836), available online from Norman B. Leventhal Map Center at the Boston Public Library, http://maps.bpl.org/id/18974. Abbott's first year at the seminary coincided with Warren's father's senior year at Phillips; *A Catalogue of the Trustees, Instructor and Students of Phillips Academy, Andover, August 20 . . . 1822* (Andover: Flagg and Gould, 1822), 6.

7. Dirk Baltzly and Nick Eliapolis, "The Classical Ideals of Friendship," *Friendship: A History*, ed. Barbara Caine, ch. 1 (London: Equinox, 2009); Constant J. Mews, "Cicero on Friendship," in *Friendship*, ed. Barbara Caine, ch. 2; David Garrioch, "From Christian Friendship to Secular Sentimentality: Enlightenment

Re-Evaluations," in *Friendship: A History*, ed. Caine, ch. 5, 174–75; Cicero, *De Officiis, with an English Translation by Walter Miller*, Book 3: 45 (London: William Heinemann; New York: G. P. Putnam's Sons, 1928), 313; Richard Shiel [John Banim], *Damon and Pythias, A Play, in Five Acts* (Philadelphia: Neal and McKenzie, 1829). Damon and Pythias continued to be mentioned in American writing through the mid-nineteenth century, but usually just as shorthand for a close friendship, or for loving self-sacrifice more in the spirit of Christ than of the characters in the original story. For example, see H. B., "The Power of Love," *Trumpet and Universalist Magazine*, Feb. 29, 1840; "Bigelow as a Preacher," *Ladies Repository*, Sept. 1845; "Dr. Bushnell's View of Language Considered," *New York Evangelist*, Nov. 15, 1849.

    8. Godbeer, *Overflowing of Friendship*, 10, 12; Caleb Crain, *American Sympathy: Men, Friendship, and Literature in the New Nation* (New Haven: Yale University Press, 2001).

    9. Crain, *American Sympathy*, 32.

    10. Barbara Caine, "Introduction," in *Friendship*, ed. Caine, xii–xiii; Garrioch, "From Christian Friendship to Secular Sentimentality," 182–84; Marc Brodie and Barbara Caine, "Class, Sex and Friendship: The Long Nineteenth Century," in *Friendship*, ed. Caine, ch. 7, esp. 235; "Friendship," *Boston Cultivator*, Feb. 27, 1847.

    11. M. A., "Friendship," *Lowell Offering*, July 1843; William B. Glazier, "College Friends," *The Knickerbocker*, April 1850; "Friendship," *Christian Watchman and Christian Reflector*, Dec. 7, 1848; Kate, "Youthful Friendship," *Boston Cultivator*, April 21, 1849; E., "College Friendship," *Nassau Monthly*, Nov. 1846.

    12. Kate, "Youthful Friendship"; "Friendship," *Trumpet and Universalist Magazine*, June 29, 1850; D. P., "True Friendship," *Christian Ambassador*, Jan. 6, 1855; quotations from "Real Friendship," *Boston Cultivator*, April 18, 1846.

    13. Quotation at SEW II: 10 (May 4, 1849).

    14. Warren provided some basic genealogical information about his parents, Samuel Edward Warren and Ann Catharine Reed Warren, in an 1880 autobiographical sketch for the New England Historic Genealogical Society, reprinted in *New England Historical and Genealogical Register*, 1910, Vol. 64 (Boston: New England Historic Genealogical Society, 1910), lxiii–lxv. On the siblings of the elder Samuel Edward Warren, see Mary Frances Peirce, ed., *Town of Weston. Births, Deaths, and Marriages, 1707–1850* (Boston, McIndoe Bros., 1901), 579–80; the children listed there were all born between 1788 and 1804 and all survived to adulthood, evidently having been raised with the help of their stepmother, Lucy Jones Warren. The parents of Ann Catharine Reed Warren—Joseph Reed and Elizabeth Keyes Reed (also spelled "Read")—are recorded as having baptized nine children in the First Church of Charlestown between 1801 and 1818: Elisabeth Adams, Elisabeth, Ann Catharine, Harriet Jane, Joseph Warren, Reuben, child identified elsewhere as Ellen Augusta, Elisabeth Maria, and Charlotte Louisa. The

baptismal information is reproduced in James F. Hunnewell, *A Century of Town Life: A History of Charlestown, Massachusetts, 1775–1887* (Boston: Little, Brown, 1888), 217–19, 222, 226, 228, 230, 232–33. On Ellen Augusta Reed Winslow, see "Marriages Registered in the City of Boston for 1857," in "Massachusetts, Town and Vital Records, 1620–1988," Ancestry.com; and "Commonwealth of Massachusetts, City of Boston, Return of a Death-1908," in "Massachusetts, Death Records, 1841–1915," Ancestry.com. The first two Elisabeths died in infancy before Ann was born; see records of their deaths, "Charlestown Archives Part I: 1800–1843," p. 255, in "Massachusetts, Town and Vital Records, 1620–1988," Ancestry.com. It is uncertain whether the Warren and Reed families might have included additional children who died before baptism or before maturity. Warren's status as an only child seems certain. There is no record of the birth or death of any other child of Samuel Edward Warren and Ann Catharine Reed Warren in Newton in the years before 1850; *Vital Records of Newton, Massachusetts to the Year 1850* (Boston: New-England Historic Genealogical Society, 1905), 205, 512; Manuscript volume titled "Newton Births, Marriages, Deaths, 1780–1845," in "Massachusetts, Town and Vital Records, 1620–1988," Ancestry.com.

15. Gloria L. Main, "Rocking the Cradle: Downsizing the New England Family," *Journal of Interdisciplinary History* 37, no. 1 (Summer 2006): 35–58; Elaine Tyler May, *Barren in the Promised Land: Childless Americans and the Pursuit of Happiness* (Cambridge: Harvard University Press, 1997), ch. 1; Susan E. Klepp, *Revolutionary Conceptions: Women, Fertility, and Family Limitation in America, 1760–1820* (Chapel Hill, NC, and Williamsburg, VA: University of North Carolina Press for the Omohundro Institute, 2009), 250, 258. Couples in Amherst and Hadley who married in the 1830s had an average of 4.47 live births, compared with an average of 7.72 thirty years earlier; Christopher Clark, *Social Change in America: From the Revolution Through the Civil War* (Chicago: Ivan R. Dee, 2006), 142.

16. Dr. Samuel Warren house, Newton, Massachusetts Cultural Resource Information System, MACRIS, http://mhc-macris.net/Details.aspx?MhcId=NWT.1703MhcId=NWT.1703; accessed March 15, 2015.

17. *The New England Historical and Genealogical Register*, vol. 64 (Boston: New England Historical and Genealogical Society, 1910), lxiii–lxv; "Sad Accident," *Newton Journal*, Oct. 19, 1867.

18. SEW 8: 155–56 (n.d.; April 1857); consumer price index conversion figure in http://www.measuringworth.com; accessed March 25, 2019. The younger Warren appears to have estimated his father's assets more or less correctly. At the time of his death in 1867, the elder Samuel Warren's estate was calculated to be $12,829.75, with the house and land worth $5,000, corporate stocks $6,800, and the rest in household property; Executor's Inventory dated Jan. 2, 1868, in Middlesex County probate records for Samuel Warren, no. 44010, Massachusetts State Archives, Boston.

19. *The New England Historical and Genealogical Register*, vol. 64 (Boston: New England Historical and Genealogical Society, 1910), lxiii–lxv; "Sad Accident," *Newton Journal*, Oct. 19, 1867; M. F. Sweetser, *King's Handbook of Newton* (Boston: Moses King, 1889), 30, 186; Sharlene Voogd Cochrane, "Private Lives and Public Learning: Family Academy for the New Middle Class. The West Newton English and Classical School. 1850–1910" (Boston College PhD, 1985), 34–35; Julian Hawthorne, *Nathaniel Hawthorne and His Wife: A Biography*, vol. 1 (Boston: Houghton Mifflin, 1893), 430, 431.

20. *New England Historical and Genealogical Register*, lxiv; on drawing trains, SEW I: 26 (16 Jan. 1847), SEW II: 9 (2 May 1849), SEW II: 113 (12 Jan. 1850). Mentions beauty of hometown: SEW I: 46 (17 June 1847). Analogy to Bunyan: SEW I: 54 (3 Aug. 1847). Quotations from John Bunyan, *The Pilgrim's Progress from this World to that which is to Come* (1678; New York: Grosset and Dunlap, 1910?), 25, 175.

21. *New England Historical and Genealogical Register*, lxiv.

22. Mrs. P. A. Hanaford, *The Young Captain: A Memorial of Capt. Richard C. Derby* (Boston: Degen, Estes, 1865), 17–20, 24, 27–29, 42, 195; "Return of the Births, Marriages and Deaths which have taken place in the Town of Medfield, for the Year Ending May 1, 1843," via Ancestry.com; Dane A. Morrison, "Derby, Elias Hasket," *American National Biography Online*; Nathaniel Hawthorne, *The Scarlet Letter* (New York, Dodd, Mead, 1900), 3; Mary Jane Peabody, "Autobiography," Derby-Peabody Family Papers, Box 3, folder labeled "Mary Jane (Derby) Peabody, Autobiog, Part I," Massachusetts Historical Society, Ms. N-126; SEW I: 127 (1 Jan. 1849); William S. Tilden, ed., *History of the Town of Medfield, Massachusetts, 1650–1886* (Boston: George H. Ellis, 1887), 371. I will use the spelling "Dicky" consistently except in quotations.

23. Hanaford, *The Young Captain*, 25–34, 38–44, 192; SEW I: 2 (9 Sept. 1846).

24. Rotundo, *American Manhood*, 31–55. Interest in machines, etc.: SEW I: 10 (11 Nov. 1846); SEW I: 16 (11 Nov. 1846); SEW I: 17 (14 Nov. 1846); SEW I: 21 (18 Dec. 1846). Quotation ending with "I love him": SEW I: 28 (27 Jan. 1847). Warren's fantasy about living together: SEW I: 31 (13 Feb. 1847).

25. SEW I: 15 (8 Nov. 1846); SEW I: 99 (27 Sept. 1847); quotations from *New England Historical and Genealogical Register*, lxiv.

26. SEW I: 1 (6 Sept. 1846).

27. Frederick S. Allis Jr., *Youth From Every Quarter: A Bicentennial History of Phillips Academy, Andover* (Andover: Phillips Academy, and Hanover, NH: University Press of New England, 1979), 132–33, 147.

28. Ronald J. Zboray and Mary Saracino Zboray, *Everyday Ideas: Socioliterary Experience among Antebellum New Englanders* (Knoxville: University of Tennessee Press, 2006), xvi–xxv, 5–11; David M. Henkin, *The Postal Age: The*

*Emergence of Modern Communications in Nineteenth-century America* (Chicago: University of Chicago Press, 2006), 27–30.

29. Tamara Plakins Thornton, *Handwriting in America: A Cultural History* (New Haven: Yale University Press, 1996), 43, 47, 52–53. Some nineteenth-century diarists used slates for drafting diary entries; B. R. Burg, *An American Seafarer in the Age of Sail: The Erotic Diaries of Philip C. Van Buskirk, 1851–1870* (New Haven: Yale University Press, 1994), xvi.

30. Louis P. Masur, "'Age of the First Person Singular': The Vocabulary of the Self in New England, 1780–1850," *Journal of American Studies* 25, no. 2 (Aug. 1991): 189–211; 191.

31. Jacob Abbott, *The Young Christian: Or, a Familiar Illustration of the Principles of Christian Duty* (New York: American Tract Society, 1832), 370, 385; Zboray, *Everyday Ideas*, 6, 7, 11.

32. Charles Dickens, *Oliver Twist* (1838; Philadelphia: Lea and Blanchard, 1850), mentioned in SEW VII: 64 (30 Nov. 1854). Henry Wadsworth Longfellow, *Evangeline: A Tale of Acadie* (1847: Boston: William D. Ticknor, 1848), mentioned in Thoughts I:50 (7 Jan 1859) with commentary on its moral message. Charlotte Elizabeth [Tonna], *The Siege of Derry, or, Sufferings of the Protestants: A Tale of the Revolution* (1833; New York: J. S. Taylor, 1841), plot element mentioned in SEW I: 87 (9 July 1848). Warren refers to *Atlantic Monthly* articles in SEW VIII: 197 (30 Jan. 1858) and SEW VIII: 207 (21 Feb. 1858). His use of a distinctive anecdote shows that he had read "Artists' Excursion," *Harper's Monthly*, June 1859, 11, mentioned in SEW Thoughts I:80 (22 May 1859); I am grateful to my colleague Roger Travis for identifying this source. Warren transcribes a poem from the May 1855 issue of *The Knickerbocker* in SEW VII: 104–105 (May? 1855). Warren's *Scientific American* subscription is mentioned in SEW I: 114 (8 Nov. 1848. Warren also mentions reading "Robin Hood," probably Stephen Perry [Joseph Cundall], *Robin Hood and His Merry Foresters* (Boston: Munroe and Francis, 1852), mentioned in SEW VII: 64 (30 Nov. 1854); and the works of Oliver Goldsmith, most noted for his sentimental 1766 novel, *The Vicar of Wakefield*, mentioned in SEW VII:100 (15 May 1855).

33. John Bunyan, *The Pilgrim's Progress, From this World to That Which is to Come* (1678; Hartford: S. Andrus and Son, 1844), plot elements mentioned in SEW I: 54 (3 Aug. 1847); John Bunyan, *The Holy War Made by Shaddai upon Diabolus, for the Regaining of the Metropolis of the World: or, The Losing and Taking Again of the Town of Mansoul* (1682; Philadelphia: American Sunday-School Union, 1841), mentioned in SEW I: 101 (1 Oct. 1848) and SEW VII: 64 (30 Nov. 1854); Legh Richmond, *The Young Cottager: an Authentic Narrative*, abridged (Andover: New England Tract Society, n.d.), mentioned in SEW I: 92 (20 July 1848); Frederic Adolphus Krummacher, *Parables* (Philadelphia: Hooker and Agnew, 1841) mentioned in SEW I: 129 (7 Jan 1849) and SEW VII: 133 (19 Aug. 1855). Krummacher's *Parables* is among the gifts Warren mentions

receiving, as are Thomas C. Upham, *The Life of Faith* (Boston: C. H. Peirce, 1846), mentioned in SEW I: 127 (1 Jan 1849); Lyman Matthews, *Memoir of the Life and Character of Ebenezer Porter* (Boston: Perkins and Marvin, 1837), mentioned in SEW I: 127 (1 Jan 1849); Philip Doddridge, *The Rise and Progress of Religion in the Soul* (1745; New York: American Tract Society, 1840), mentioned in SEW II: 26 (9 June 1849). He mentions giving *Dew-drops* (New York: American Tract Society, 1850), in SEW VIII: 124 (30 Oct. 1856) and Beecher, *Lectures to Young Men*, in SEW VII: 77 (3 Jan. 1855). Quotation about tracts is from SEW I: 93 (30 Aug. 1848). He mentions reading Beecher's lectures in SEW I: 90 (16 July 1848). He quotes from Emerson's "Spiritual Laws," [R. W. Emerson, *Essays: First Series* (Boston: Phillips, Sampson, 1856)] in SEW VIII: 164 (24 April 1857). The discussion of consistency, and the quote with "beauties" and "fog," appear in SEW VII: 74 (22 Dec. 1854). The consistency reference appears to be to the section of "Self Reliance" that follows the famous "hobgoblin" quote: Emerson, *Essays: First Series*, 50–52. Warren's gift of twelve tracts to a sick friend is mentioned in SEW I: 93 (30 Aug. 1848).

34. Zboray and Zboray, *Everyday Lives*, 13–15.

35. SEW I: 7 (4 Oct. 1846); SEW I: 10 (18 Oct. 1846); SEW I: 32 (14 Feb. 1847); Anne Ayer Verplanck, "Facing Philadelphia: The Social Function of Silhouettes, Miniatures, and Daguerrotypes, 1760–1860" (PhD Dissertation, College of William and Mary, 1996); SEW II: 25 (8 June 1849); SEW I: 41 (16 May 1847); SEW I: 48 (27 June 1847); SEW SEW I: 2 (11 Sept. 1846); SEW I: 88 (12 July 1848); SEW I: 6 (2 Oct. 1846).

36. SEW I: 2 (11 Sept. 1846); SEW I: 6 (2 Oct. 1846); SEW I: 41 (16 May 1847); SEW I: 48 (27 June 1847); SEW I: 88 (12 July 1848); SEW I: 117 (18 Nov. 1848); Rotundo, "Romantic Friendship": 1–25.

37. Hanaford, *The Young Captain*, 29, 189; quotation at 169.

38. Henkin, *Postal Age*, 2–3, 17–19, 22–23, 31, 94.

39. Ibid., 99–101, 110–11, 117; Karen Halttunen, *Confidence Men and Painted Women: A Study of Middle-class Culture in America, 1830–1870* (New Haven: Yale University Press, 1982), esp. ch. 4.

40. On contents of the letters, SEW I: 3 (14 Sept. 1846); SEW I: 6 (2 Oct. 1846); SEW I: 30 (9 Feb. 1847); quotation from SEW I: 17 (14 Nov. 1846). On including notes inside letters, SEW I: 7 (6 & 7 Oct. 1846); SEW I: 9 (13 Oct. 1846); SEW I: 11 (23 Oct. 1846); SEW I: 14 (31 Oct.1846); SEW I: 25 (11 Jan. 1847); SEW I: 29 (6 Feb. 1847). On mailing separate letters, SEW I: 24 (4 Jan. 1847); SEW I: 26 (16 Jan. 1847); SEW I: 62 (22 April 1849).

41. Admiring Dicky's appearance, SEW I: 42 (5/19/47); SEW I: 45 (6/13/47). Sleeping together, SEW I: 20 (12 Dec. 1846); SEW I: 34 (25 Feb. 1847); SEW I: 46 (17 June 1847); SEW I: 49 (5 July 1847); Rotundo, "Romantic Friendship," 10–12. Warren had a vacation in Newton in March 1847: "the happiest three weeks I ever spent, anywhere at any time"; SEW I: 40 (10? May

1857). Overview of fall and winter back in Newton, SEW I: 55 (June 9 1848). Quotation about kissing, SEW I: 144 (23 Feb 1849).

42. William S. Tilden, ed., *History of the Town of Medfield, Massachusetts, 1650–1886* (Boston: George H. Ellis, 1887), 214–15, 219, 227; Hanaford, *The Young Captain*, 39, 42; Francis Greenwood Peabody, *A New England Romance: The Story of Ephraim and Mary Jane Peabody (1807–1892) Told by their Sons* (Boston: Houghton Mifflin, 1920), 116; Phillips Brooks, "A Century of Church Growth in Boston," in Perry, *The History of the American Episcopal Church*, 489–91; Sharlene Voogd Cochrane, "Private Lives and Public Learning: Family Academy for the New Middle Class. The West Newton English and Classical School. 1850–1910" (Boston College PhD, 1985), 3; Sweetser, *King's Handbook of Newton*, 70; Smith, "Newton," 238; SEW II: 15 (19 May 1849).

43. Receptivity to advice: SEW I: 30 (7 Feb. 1847). Talk on religion at Andover: SEW I: 33 (24 Feb. 1847). Plans for future and interlude in Newton: SEW I: 34 (25 Feb. 1847); SEW I: 41 (17 May 1847); SEW I: 55 (9 June 1848).

44. Joshua Coffin, *A Sketch of the History of Newbury, Newburyport, and West Newbury, from 1635 to 1845* (Boston: Samuel G. Drake, 1845), vi–vii; *Address of Albert E. Pillsbury, in Celebration of the Fiftieth Anniversary of the City Charter of Newburyport, Mass.* (Newburyport: News Publishing Co., 1901), 51; John J. Currier, *History of Newburyport, Mass., 1764–1905* [vol. 1] (Newburyport, n.p.: 1906), 161, 173–77, 196; "A Brief Sketch of Newburyport," in Wooster Smith, *The Directory of Newburyport, January, 1849* (Newburyport: C. Nason, 1848), 51–53; Stephan Thernstrom, *Poverty and Progress: Social Mobility in a Nineteenth Century City* (Cambridge: Harvard University Press, 1964), 9–13.

45. George Lunt, ed., *Old New England Traits* (New York: Hurd and Houghton; Cambridge: Riverside Press, 1873), 17; Joseph H. Bragdon, "Sketch of Newburyport," in John E. Tilton, *The Newburyport Directory Containing a New Map of the Town . . . January, 1851* (Newburyport: John E. Tilton, 1850), 85–97; H. F. Walling and O. W. Gray, "City of Newburyport," in *Official Topographical Atlas of Massachusetts, from Astronomical, Trigonometrical, and Various Local Surveys* (Philadelphia: Stedman, Brown and Lyon, 1871), via David Rumsey Map Collection www.davidrumsey.com; Coffin, *Sketch of the History*, vii; Currier, *History of Newburyport*, vol. I, 372–74.

46. Thernstrom, *Poverty and Progress*, 18–26; Currier, *History of Newburyport*, vol. I, 186; Merrimac, "Correspondence of the Herald," (Newburyport) *Daily Herald*, Sept. 14, 1848; *Directory of Newburyport, January, 1849*, 54–55.

47. John J. Currier, *History of Newburyport, Mass., 1764–1909*, vol. II (Newburyport, n.p.: 1909), 385–88; Currier, *History of Newburyport*, vol. 1, 200–201, 211–12, 327; *Exercises at the Celebration of the Fiftieth Anniversary of the Putnam Free School, April 12, 1898* (Newburyport: News Publishing Co., 1899), 20–22.

48. SEW I: 78 (20 June 1848); "Deaths Registered in the Town of Newton, from May 1ˢᵗ 1848 to Jan. 1 1850," in "Massachusetts, Death Records 1841–1915," Ancestry.com; SEW I: 86 (7 July 1848); SEW I: 87 (9 July 1848); SEW I: 8 (10 July 1848); *A Catalogue of the Trustees, Instructors, and Students of the Putnam Free School, Newburyport Mass., July 1848* (Newburyport: Abel Whitton, 1848), 6; SEW I: 90 (16 July 1848); SEW I: 91 (19 July 1848).

49. SEW I: 93 (30 Aug. 1848); "Deaths Registered in the Town of Newton"; John L. Lord Diary, Newburyport Public Library, Microfilm Reel #1, vol. 4., entry for Sept. 22, 1848 (microfilm page 820); "Deaths Registered in the Town of Newburyport in the County of Essex for the Year 1848," in "Massachusetts, Death Records 1841–1915," ancestry.com; SEW I: 95–96 (8 Sept. 1848); SEW I: 96 (11 Sept. 1848); SEW I: 97 (20 Sept. 1848).

50. SEW I: 99 (24 Sept. 1848); SEW I: 101 (1 Oct. 1848); SEW I: 117 (18 Nov. 1848); SEW I: 118 (5 Dec. 1848); SEW I: 1 25–26 (30 Dec 1848).

51. On Dicky's schooling and Warren's response, SEW I: 118 (5 Dec. 1848); SEW I: 122 (17 Dec. 1848). The effect of mail on Warren's moods: SEW I: 5 (23 Sept. 1846); SEW I: 38 (13 March 1847); SEW I: 81 (26 June 1848); SEW I: 100 (28 and 29 Sept. 1848); see also Henkin, *Postal Age*, 4. The gap in correspondence in early 1849: SEW I: 127 (1 Jan. 1849); SEW I: 130 (11 Jan. 1849); SEW I: 1 33 (24 Jan. 1849); SEW I: 137 (31 Jan. and 2 Feb. 1849); SEW I: 138 (3 Feb. 1849).

52. SEW I: 140 (11 Feb. 1849); SEW I: 150 (11 March 1849); SEW II: 1(11 April 1849); SEW II: 2 (15 April 1849).

53. SEW II: 10 (6 May 1849); SEW II: 15 (19 May 1849); SEW II: 16 (21 May 1849); SEW II: 31 (16 June 1849); SEW II: 37 (23 June 1849); SEW II: 53 (29 Aug. 1849).

54. SEW II: 81 (28 Oct. 1849); SEW II: 109 (1 Jan. 1850); SEW VII: 85 (23 Feb. 1855); SEW VII: 137 (3 Oct. 1855); SEW VII: 149 (4 Nov. 1855); SEW VIII: 207 (21 Feb. 1858). "To the last": SEW II: 53 (1 Oct. 1865 addendum to the entry for 29 Aug. 1849).

55. Rotundo, "Romantic Friendship," 14–16, 19; William Benemann, *Male-Male Intimacy in Early America: Beyond Romantic Friendships* (New York: Harrington Park Press, 2006), xvi.

56. In addition to the examples discussed below, see also his response to two "pretty" boys and a Sunday school "pet" in the following entries: SEW I: 90 (16 July 1848); SEW VII: 60 (17 Sept. 1854); SEW VIII: 218 (17 April 1858). See also the heavily redacted passage on SEW VII: 96 (15 April 1855), which contains the following words: "reminds me so much of [word elided] that I want very much to [word elided] him."

57. SEW I: 16 (11 Nov. 1846); SEW I: 21 (18 Dec. 1846); SEW I: 47 (23 June 1847); SEW I: 30 (7 Feb. 1847); SEW I: 42 (19 May 1847); Card

for Samuel Locke Lamson, Phillips Academy student records; SEW I: (21, 23, and 24 July, 1847).

58. *Catalogue of the Putnam Free School* (1848), 5; *Vital Records of Newburyport, Massachusetts, to the end of the Year 1849. Volume I.—Births* (Salem, MA: Essex Institute, 1911), 25; 1850 U.S. Census schedules for Newburyport, via ancestry.com.

59. SEW I: 63 (24 April 1848); SEW I: 65 (4 May 1848); SEW I: 66 (6 May 1848); SEW I: 72 (28 May 1848); SEW I: 73 (1 June 1848); SEW I: 122 (17 Dec. 1848); SEW I: 130 (11 Jan. 1849); SEW I: 131 (14 Jan. 1849); SEW II: 30 (14 June 1849).

60. *Catalogue of the Putnam Free School* (1848), 5–6; SEW I: 135 (24 Jan 1849). Blunt's age is difficult to determine with certainty, as the evidence is given in public records is conflicting. He is said to have been twenty-five at the time of his wedding on Oct. 11, 1853, fifty-two at the time his U.S. census information was taken on June 10, 1880, and ninety-four at the time of his death on Feb. 20, 1923; "Massachusetts, Town and Vital Records, 1620–1988," ancestry.com; 1880 US Census schedules, ancestry.com; Obituary, *Chicago Tribune*, Feb. 21, 1923; "Notable Alumni—Long List—1800s," Phillips Academy, http://www.andover.edu/About/NotableAlumni/LongList/Pages/1800s.aspx; *A Catalogue of the Trustees, Instructors, and Students of Phillips Academy, Andover, Mass., August, 1847* (Andover: William H. Wardwell, 1847), 13, 18. Examples of Whipple's and Blunt's interactions with Warren: SEW I: 60 (15 April 1848), SEW I: 62 (22 April 1848), SEW I: 64 (28 April 1848), SEW I: 73 (31 May 1848), SEW I: 77 (18 June 1848), SEW II: 8 (29 April 1849).

61. Warren's unpleasant feelings toward Blunt in 1849: SEW II: 28 (13 June 1849), SEW II: 30 (14 June 1849), SEW II: 34 (20 June 1849), SEW II: 45 (10 July 1849). Correspondence with Whipple: SEW II: 19 (29 May 1849), SEW II: 74 (16 Oct. 1849).

62. Benemann, *Male-Male Intimacy in Early America*, xvii; Thomas Hughes, "The Public Schools of England. Part II," *North American Review*, July 1879, 37–42; Thomas Hughes, "The Public Schools of England," *North American Review*, April 1879, 356–57; Paul Nash, "Training an Elite: The Prefect-Fagging System in the English Public Schools," *History of Education Quarterly* 1, no. 1 (March 1961): 14–21.

63. *Exercises at the Celebration of the Fiftieth Anniversary*, 23; *New England Historical and Genealogical Register*, lxv; *Directory of Newburyport, January, 1849*, 32; Walling and Gray, "City of Newburyport." On the housing of students in Newburyport, SEW I: 75 (10 June 1848); SEW I: 79 (24 June 1848); SEW I: 85 (4 July 1848); SEW I: 96 (9 Sept. 1848); SEW II: 18 (27 May 1849); SEW II: 37 (23 June 1849); *A Catalogue of the Trustees, Instructors, and Students of the Putnam Free School, Newburyport, Mass., For the Year Ending July 14, 1849* (Newburyport: Charles Nason, 1849), 5–8, 14.

64. *Catalogue of the Putnam Free School* (1848), 8; *Vital Records of Newburyport,* 418; 1850 U.S. Census schedules for Newburyport, via ancestry.com.

65. SEW I: 127 (2 Jan. 1849); SEW II: 9 (1 May 1849); SEW II: 11 (8 May 1849); SEW II: 16 (16 May 1849); SEW II: 16 (21 May 1849); SEW II: 17 (23 May 1849); SEW II: 19 (29 May 1849); SEW II: 2 0 (1 June 1849); SEW II: 22 (3 June 1849); SEW II: 23 (5 June 1849); SEW II: 24 (7 June 1849); SEW II: 25 (8 June 1849); SEW II: 27 (11 June 1849); SEW II: 28–29 (13 June 1849); SEW II: 30 (14 June 1849); SEW II: 32 (17 June 1849); SEW II: 33–34 (19 June 1849); SEW II: 38 (23 June 1849).

66. Eve Kosofsky Sedgwick, *Between Men: English Literature and Male Homosocial Desire* (1985; New York: Columbia University Press, 2016), 21, 66; SEW II: 50 (9 July 1849); SEW II: 56 (4 Sept. 1849); SEW II: 61 (14 Sept. 1849); SEW II: 72 (13 Oct. 1849); SEW II: 74 (16 Oct. 1849); SEW II: 83 (30 Oct. 1849); SEW II: 87 (7 Nov. 1849); SEW II: 106 (19 Dec. 1849); SEW II: 110 (5 Jan. 1850); SEW II: 114 (15 Jan. 1850); "Massachusetts, Town and Vital Records, 1620–1988," ancestry.com.

67. Examples of activities with John and Micajah: SEW II: 15 (19 and 20 May 1849); SEW II: 18 (27 May 1849); SEW I: 20 (1 June 1849); SEW II: 24 (7 June 1849); SEW II: 57 (6 Sept. 1849); SEW II: 114 (15 Jan. 1850). On religion, SEW II: 10 (6 May 1849); SEW II: 44 (8 July 1849); SEW II: 81 (28 Oct. 1849).

68. SEW I: 150 (11 March 1849); SEW I: 142 (17 Feb. 1849); SEW I: 143 (19 Feb. 1849); SEW I: 144 (22 Feb. 1849); SEW I: 145 (24 Feb. 1849); SEW I: 148 (5 March 1849); SEW I: 147 (4 March 1849).

69. John A. Bagley passport application, Sept. 23, 1878, "U.S. Passport Applications, 1795–1925," ancestry.com; Martha (Bagley) Anderson and Norton Russell Bagley, "Some Descendants of Orlando Bagley of Amesbury, Massachusetts," vol. 1 (n.p.: 1973), 80, 137, typescript reproduction of original at American Antiquarian Society, Worcester, Mass., via Heritage Quest Online; SEW II: 54 (31 Aug. 1849); SEW I: 146 (27 Feb. 1849); SEW I: 145 (24 Feb. 1849); SEW I: 30 (9 Feb. 1847); SEW I: 45 (14 June 1847); SEW II: 55 (2 Sept. 1849); SEW II: 66 (30 Sept. 1849); SEW II: 79 (26 Oct. 1849); SEW II: 112 (9 Jan. 1850). On smoking, SEW II: 69 (5 Oct. 1849).

70. *Vital Records of Newburyport,* 17; SEW II: 14 (16 and 18 May 1849); SEW II: 17 (24 May 1849); SEW II: 20 (1 June 1849); SEW II: 27–30 (11–14 June 1849).

71. SEW II: 25 (9 June 1849).

72. Henry B. Nason, ed. *Biographical Record of the Officers and Graduates of the Rensselaer Polytechnic Institute, 1824–1886* (Troy, NY: William H. Young, 1887), 286; SEW II: 12 (9 and 11 May 1849); SEW II: 21 (2 June 1849); SEW II: 35 (20 June 1849); SEW II: 38–39 (24–25 June 1849); SEW II: 40 (29 June 1849); SEW II: 42 (2 July 1849). John appears to have lived with

his elderly grandparents (Abner and Sarah Bagley, who died in 1851 and 1849 respectively), and two aunts in their forties (Mary and Sarah); it is unclear which of the aunts Warren is referring to; 1850 U.S. Census Schedules for Newburyport, ancestry.com.

73. *Vital Records of Newbury, Massachusetts, to the End of the Year 1849. Volume I. Births* (Salem, MA: Essex Institute, 1911), 109, 113, 299; *Directory of Newburyport, January, 1849*, 58; U.S. Census Schedules for Newbury, Massachusetts, 1850, Ancestry.com; Currier, *History of Newburyport*, vol. II, 251–52, 509; Walling and Gray, "City of Newburyport." On rides, e.g., SEW II: 50 (18 July 1849).

74. SEW II: 12 (10 May 1849); SEW II: 14 (17 May 1849); SEW II: 15 (20 May 1849); SEW II: 20 (1 June 1849); SEW II: 28 (12 June 1849) SEW II: 36 (22 June 1849). The phrase "and came off" is peculiar, but probably just means that Warren parted from Cajah after kissing him.

75. SEW II: 109 (3 Jan. 1850); SEW II: 111 (6 Jan. 1850); SEW II: 115 (18 Jan. 1850); 1850 U.S. Census Schedules for Newburyport, ancestry.com; U.S. Passport Application of James K. Medbery, Aug. 3, 1870, Ancestry.com. The Jan. 6, 1850, walk home was carefully edited to insert "nice" in place of an erased adjective about the walk and to insert "parted" in place of an erased verb.

76. SEW II: 49 (16 July 1849, and footnote); SEW II: 52 (23 July 1849); SEW II: 111 (6 and 8 Jan. 1850); SEW II: 114 (14 Jan. 1850); SEW II: 116 (19 Jan. 1850); Garrioch, "From Christian Friendship to Secular Sentimentality," 198.

77. SEW II: 109 (1 Jan. 1850); SEW II: 113–14 (12–14 Jan. 1850); Burg, *An American Seafarer in the Age of Sail*, xi, 22–29, 48–56, 73–82, 87–93, 126–27, 140.

78. SEW II: 113–114 (12–14 Jan., 1850); entry for March 4, 1857, Newburyport Births, Marriages and Deaths, "Massachusetts, Town and Vital Records, 1620–1988," ancestry.com; 1860 U.S. Census schedules for Newburyport, ancestry.com; "Died," *Salem Register*, Jan. 26, 1865; SEW II: 10 (undated footnote). Other footnotes in the early pages of the journal date from 11 May 1856 and 1 Oct. 1865; Warren's use of the past tense suggests that the later date is more likely, after Cajah's death.

79. SEW II: 116 (19 Jan. 1850); SEW II: inside front cover (20 Oct. 1865).

## Chapter 2. Teaching

1. Quotation from *New England Historical and Genealogical Register*, 1910, Vol. 64 (Boston: New England Historic Genealogical Society, 1910), lxv.

2. Julie A. Reuben, *The Making of the Modern University: Intellectual Transformation and the Marginalization of Morality* (Chicago: University of Chicago Press, 1996), 22; Kenneth Nivison, "'But a Step from College to the Judicial

Bench': College and Curriculum in New England's 'Age of Improvement,'" *History of Education Quarterly* 50, no. 4 (Nov. 2010), 484–85; Carl F. Kaestle, *Pillars of the Republic: Common Schools and American Society, 1780–1860* (New York: Hill and Wang, 1983), 96–101. Warren explicitly stated his continued allegiance to Scottish Common Sense philosophy in an 1869 article: Warren, "On the Future Development of Scientific Education in America [part nine]," *Journal of the Franklin Institute* 58, no. 1 (July 1869): 62–63.

  3. *New England Historical and Genealogical Register*, lxiii-lxiv; quotation at lxiv; Henry B. Nason, ed., *Biographical Record of the Officers and Graduates of the Rensselaer Polytechnic Institute, 1824–86* (Troy: William H. Young, 1887), 139; Samuel F. Field, "Newton," in *History of Middlesex County, Massachusetts, Containing Carefully Prepared Histories of Every City and Town in the County, By Well-Known Writers; and A General History of the County, From the Earliest to the Present Time*, ed. Samuel Adams Drake (Boston: Estes and Lauriat, 1880), 231; "Fuller Academy in Newton," *Boston Recorder*, Aug. 29, 1834; Warren's mention of Davis appears in SEW II: 119; "Fuller Academy, for Sale," *Boston Recorder*, Feb. 18, 1842; "Prof. Beckwith's Family School," *Boston Recorder*, March 20, 1840; U.S. Census schedules for Newton, 1840, via ancestry.com; "Death of Rev. Dr. Beckwith," *Lowell Daily Citizen*, May 13, 1870; S. N. Dickinson, *Boston Almanac for the Year 1843* (Boston: Thomas Groom [1843]), 35; *Public Schools of the City of Boston, September, 1838* (Boston: J. H. Eastburn, 1838), 8–10, 15; "The School Exhibitions," *Boston Courier*, Aug. 17, 1843; *Report of the Annual Examination of the Public Schools of the City of Boston* (Boston: J. H. Eastburn, 1848), 66; "Common Council," *Boston Courier*, March 4, 1844; Arthur Wellington Brayley, *Schools and Schoolboys of Old Boston* (Boston: Louis P. Hager, 1894), 55, 429; *Remarks on the Seventh Annual Report of the Hon. Horace Mann, Secretary of the Massachusetts Board of Education* (Boston: Charles C. Little and James Brown, 1844), 4.

  4. David Hogan, "Modes of Discipline: Affective Individualism and Pedagogical Reform in New England, 1820–1850," *American Journal of Education* 99, no. 1 (Nov. 1990): 1–56; Kaestle, *Pillars of the Republic*, 63–101; Horace Mann, *Lectures on Education* (1845; Boston: Ide and Dutton, 1855), 38, 55–56, 124; *The First State Normal School in America: The Journals of Cyrus Peirce and Mary Swift* (Cambridge: Harvard University Press, 1926), 278, 281, 285; Calvin E. Stowe, *Common Schools and Teachers' Seminaries* (Boston: Marsh, Capen, Lyon, and Webb, 1839), 100; J. Blanchard, *On the Importance and Means of Cultivating the Social Affections among Pupils, by J. Blanchard, Delivered Before the American Institute of Instruction at its Annual Meeting, Boston, August 1835* (Boston: s.n., 1835).

  5. *Seventh Annual Report of the Board of Education, Together with the Seventh Annual Report of the Secretary of the Board* (Boston: Dutton and Wentworth, 1844), quotations from 134, 135, 137 and 141; *Second Annual Report*

*of the Board of Education, Together with the Second Annual Report of the Secretary of the Board* (Boston: Dutton and Wentworth, 1839), 37.

6. *Second Annual Report*; quotation at 45; *Ninth Annual Report of the Board of Education, Together with the Ninth Annual Report of the Secretary of the Board* (Boston: Dutton and Wentworth, 1846), 95–96; Caleb Crain, *American Sympathy: Men, Friendship, and Literature in the New Nation* (New Haven: Yale University Press, 2001), 4–5; *Eighth Annual Report of the Board of Education, Together with the Eighth Annual Report of the Secretary of the Board* (Boston: Dutton and Wentworth, 1845), 51.

7. *Remarks on the Seventh Annual Report*; quotations at 13, 47–48, 84, 104.

8. Jonathan Messerli, *Horace Mann: A Biography* (New York: Alfred A. Knopf, 1972), 19–23, 171–73; William Ellery Channing, *A Sermon, Delivered at the Ordination of the Rev. Jared Sparks, to the Pastoral Care of The First Independent Church of Baltimore, May 5, 1819*, 7th ed. (Boston: Cummings and Hilliard, 1821), 27; William E. Channing, "Remarks on Education," in *The Works of William E. Channing, D.D., First Complete American Edition, with an Introduction*, Vol. I (Boston: James Munroe, 1841); *Ninth Annual Report*, 87–88; see also R. C. Waterston, "Address at the Triennial Convention of the State Normal School at West Newton," *Monthly Religious Magazine*, Oct. 1848, 434. Mann's postmillennial faith—a belief that the world would advance to reach a thousand-year golden age before Christ's second coming—is indicated in *Twelfth Annual Report*, 96–97.

9. Kaestle, *Pillars of the Republic*, 75, 100; *Common School Controversy*, 10–13; Hogan, "Modes of Discipline," 2, 17, 20; *Eleventh Annual Report of the Board of Education, Together with the Eleventh Annual Report of the Secretary of the Board* (Boston: Dutton and Wentworth, 1848), 86–87; William E. Channing, "The Moral Argument Against Calvinism," in *The Works of William E. Channing*, 240.

10. *Twelfth Annual Report of the Board of Education, Together with the Twelfth Annual Report of the Secretary of the Board* (Boston: Dutton and Wentworth, 1849), 18; *Common School Controversy* (Boston: J. N. Bradley, 1844), esp. 3–6, 15–16, 22–23.

11. Kaestle, *Pillars of the Republic*, 13–15, 23, 114–15, 129.

12. Ibid., 130; Samuel J. May, *Memoir of Cyrus Peirce, First Principal of the First State Normal School in the United States* (Hartford: F. C. Brownell, [1857]), 6–12, 16–17, 25–26; *Fourth Annual Report of the Board of Education, Together with the Fourth Annual Report of the Secretary of the Board* (Boston: Dutton and Wentworth, 1841), 3–5, 45–46; *Third Annual Report of the Board of Education, Together with the Third Annual Report of the Secretary of the Board* (Boston: Dutton and Wentworth, 1840), 6; *Eighth Annual Report*, 76–77.

13. Mary A. Greene, *Nathaniel T. Allen: Teacher, Reformer, Philanthropist* (n.p.: 1906), 42, 45; Populus, "The West-Newton Normal School," *Boston Courier*,

Jan. 6, 1845; M. F. Sweetser, *King's Handbook of Newton, Massachusetts* (Boston: Moses King, 1889), 161.

14. Sweetser, *King's Handbook of Newton*, 170, 178; Messerli, *Horace Mann*, 407, 430, 435; Louise Hall Tharp, *Horace Mann and Mary Peabody* (Boston: Little, Brown, 1953), 211; Sharlene Voogd Cochrane, "Private Lives and Public Learning: Family Academy for the New Middle Class. The West Newton English and Classical School. 1850–1910,"(Boston College PhD dissertation, 1985), 38–41; transcription of Gilbert obituary from *The Newton Journal*, April 4, 1885, in Gilbert Family Papers, Historic Newton Archives; Smith, "Newton," 231, 238.

15. "Installation," *Boston Evening Transcript*, Oct. 19, 1846; "Horace Mann and Mr. Smith," *Boston Recorder*, May 6, 1847; [Matthew Hale Smith], "State Normal School at West Newton," *Boston Recorder*, June 3, 1847; "The Normal School at Newton," *Christian Register*, June 12, 1847; [Cyrus Peirce], "State Normal School at West Newton," *Christian Register*, July 8, 1848; "Normalty," *Boston Recorder*, July 28, 1848. Warren and Dicky attended the controversial tableaux too, but Warren did not think them worth remarking on in his journal (SEW I: 19 [7 Dec. 1846]).

16. SEW I: 28 (27 Jan. 1847); SEW I: 59 13 April 1848; *New England Historical and Genealogical Register*, lxiv; Mrs. P. A. Hanaford, *The Young Captain*, 41; letter by S. Edward Warren in "Our Lithographs of Horace Mann," *New England Journal of Education*, Dec. 25, 1875.

17. *New England Historical and Genealogical Register*, lxiv; SEW I: 18 (Nov. 25 1846); SEW I: 19 (7 & 8 Dec., 1846).

18. *New England Historical and Genealogical Register*, lxiv; Frederick S. Allis, *Youth from Every Quarter: A Bicentennial History of Phillips Academy, Andover* (Andover: Phillips Academy; Hanover, NH: University Press of New England, 1979), 119–22, 132, 147, 199; Claude M. Fuess, *An Old New England School: A History of Phillips Academy Andover* (Boston: Houghton Mifflin, 1917), 205–18, 252; SEW I: 3 (13 Sept. 1846); SEW I: 11 (23 Oct. 1846); SEW I: 31 (11–13 Feb. 1847); SEW I: 32 (16 Feb. 1847); *A Catalogue of the Trustees, Instructors, and Students of Phillips Academy, Andover, Mass., August, 1847* (Andover: William H. Wardwell, 1847), 18.

19. SEW I: 3 (17 Sept. 1846); SEW I: 11 (22 Oct. 1846); SEW I: 18 (20 Nov. 1846); Allis, *Youth from Every Quarter*, 188–90, 194; *A Memorial of Samuel Harvey Taylor, Compiled by His Last Class* (Andover, MA: Warren F. Draper, 1871), 113, 119; Fuess, *Old New England School*, 259, 302.

20. SEW I: 41 (17 May 1847); SEW I: 42 (21 May 1847).

21. John J. Currier, *History of Newburyport, Mass., 1764–1909*, vol. I (Newburyport, n.p.: 1906), 327; "Putnam Free School," *Daily Herald*, April 5, 1848; *Exercises at the Celebration of the Fiftieth Anniversary of the Putnam Free School, April 12, 1898* (Newburyport: News Publishing Co., 1899), 20–22.

22. *Exercises at the Celebration*, 21, 23, 31; SEW I: 81 (30 June 1848); SEW II: 19 (29 May 1849); SEW II: 35 (21 June 1849); SEW II: 56 (4 Sept. 1849).

23. *New England Historical and Genealogical Register*, lxiii; SEW I: 68 (12 May 1848); SEW I: 117 (18 Nov. 1848); SEW I: 121 (16 Dec. 1848); SEW I: 122 (19 Dec. 1848); SEW I: 123 (20 Dec. 1848); Greene, *Nathaniel T. Allen*, 26, 37, 46; "The Putnam School," *Newburyport Daily Herald*, April 13, 1848; Nason, *Biographical Record of the Officers and Graduates*, 138–39, 147, 592; SEW II: 100 (7 Dec. 1849).

24. SEW I: 145 (24 Feb. 1849); SEW I: 146 (27 Feb. 1849); SEW I: 148 (5 March 1849); SEW I: 150 (11 March 1849); SEW II: 40 (29 June 1849).

25. *Exercises at the Celebration*, 23; Hogan, "Modes of Discipline," 1–4; *New England Historical and Genealogical Register*, lxiv–lxv; SEW I: 69 (16 June 1848); SEW I: 97 (22 Sept. 1848); SEW I: 108 (21 Oct. 1848); SEW I: 109 (26 Oct. 1848).

26. SEW I: 100 (28 Sept. 1848); *The School and Schoolmaster: A Manual for the Use of Teachers, Employers, Trustees, Inspectors, &c., &c., of Common Schools. In Two Parts.* Part I, by Alonzo Potter, D.D., of New York (New York: Harper and Bros., 1842); quotations at 12 and 20; George B. Emerson, *Observations on a Pamphlet Entitled "Remarks on the Seventh Annual Report of the Hon. Horace Mann, Secretary of the Massachusetts Board of Education* (Boston: Samuel N. Dickinson, 1844); *The School and Schoolmaster. . . .* Part II, by George B. Emerson, AM, of Massachusetts; quotations at 274, 281; emphasis in the quotations appeared in the original.

27. SEW II: 56 (4 Sept. 1849); SEW II: 59 (10 Sept. 1849); SEW II: 63 (24 Sept. 1849); SEW II: 65 (27 Sept. 1849); SEW II: 69 (6 Oct. 1849). On high turnover, *Ninth Annual Report*, 40–41; Horace Mann reported that nearly half of all Massachusetts teachers had a year of experience or less; see also Kaestle, *Pillars of the Republic*, 131–32.

28. SEW I: 25 (7 Jan. 1847); SEW I: 32 (17 Feb 1847); SEW I: 38 (10 March 1847); SEW I: 142 (15 Feb. 1849); SEW II: 70 (8 Oct. 1849); SEW II: 71 (11 Oct. 1849); Address by H. Humphrey, *Tenth Annual Report of the Board of Education, Together with the Tenth Annual Report of the Secretary of the Board* (Boston: Dutton and Wentworth, 1847), 45; *Fourth Annual Report*, 87–88; *Ninth Annual Report*, 40.

29. *Twelfth Annual Report*, appendix p. x; *Annual Report of the School Committee of Charlton, for the Year 1848–49* (Worcester: Tyler and Hamilton, 1849), 3–6, 11. The schoolhouse remains standing to this day.

30. Rufus B. Dodge, "Charlton," in *History of Worcester County, Massachusetts, with Biographical Sketches of Many of the Pioneers and Prominent Men*, Vol. 1, ed. D. Hamilton Hurd (Philadelphia: J. W. Lewis, 1889), 757, 760; *Twelfth Annual Report*, appendix p. x; U.S. Census Schedules for 1850, Charlton, via ancestry.com; Donald H. Weinhardt, "Catalog of Early Building Construction in Charlton, Massachusetts, 1726–1899," Charlton Historical Society; William

O. Hultgren, *Rider Tavern: A Bicentennial History 1797–1997* (Charlton: Charlton Historical Society, 1997), 2, 19–20; Simeon Borden, *Map of Massachusetts* (Boston: S. Borden, 1844), via David Rumsey Map Collection, http://www.davidrumsey.com; accessed Oct. 20, 2014. The Charlton episode is recorded in SEW II: 71–108 (11 Oct to 24 Dec., 1849; the quotation is from SEW II: 71 (11 Oct. 1849).

31. SEW II: 71 (11 Oct. 1849); SEW II: 72 (12 Oct. 1849).

32. Myra C. Glenn, "School Discipline and Punishment in Antebellum America," *Journal of the Early Republic* 1, no. 4 (Winter 1981): 395–405.

33. SEW II: 74 (16 Oct. 1849); SEW II: 77 (22 Oct. 1849); SEW II: 80 (28 Oct. 1849); SEW II: 82 (29 Oct. 1849); Jo Anne Preston, "Domestic Ideology, School Reformers, and Female Teachers: Schoolteaching Becomes Women's Work in Nineteenth Century New England," *New England Quarterly* 6, no. 4 (Dec. 1993): 531–51; Anonymous, "Tales: Our School Teacher," *Literary Union*, July 28, 1849.

34. SEW II: 96–98 (5 Dec. 1849).

35. The quotation is from SEW II: 89 (10 Nov 1849).

36. SEW II: 88 (9 Nov. 1849); SEW II: 92 (16 Nov. 1849); SEW II: 95 (22 Nov. 1849); SEW II: 96 (5 Dec. 1849); C. M. Kirkland, "Thoughts on Education," *Sartain's Union Magazine* 5, no. 4 (Oct. 1849): 238; Julie A. Thomas, "Kirkland, Caroline Matilda," *American National Biography Online*; Stephen M. Frank, *Life with Father: Parenthood and Masculinity in the Nineteenth-Century American North* (Baltimore: Johns Hopkins University Press, 1998), 24–35.

37. SEW II: 96–98 (5 Dec. 1849); SEW II: 100–101 (6–9 Dec. 1849); SEW II: 103 (12 Dec. 1849); SEW II: 106 (19–20 Dec. 1849). On the turn against flogging in the early nineteenth century, see William Benemann, *Male-Male Intimacy in Early America: Beyond Romantic Friendships* (New York: Harrington Park Press, 2006), 65–68.

38. SEW II: 107–108 (24 Dec. 1849, and footnote dated 2 Oct. 1865); SEW II: 108 (1 Jan. 1850).

39. SEW II: 91 (14 Nov. 1849); SEW II: 100 (6 Dec. 1849).

40. Campbell Gibson, Population Division, U.S. Bureau of the Census, "Population of the 100 Largest Cities and Other Urban Places in the United States: 1790 to 1990," Population Division Working Paper No. 27 (June 1998): "Table 8. Population of 100 Largest Urban Places: 1850," https://www.census.gov/population/www/documentation/twps0027/tab08.txt; accessed March 23, 2015; D. O. Kellogg, *The City of Troy: Its Commerce, Manufactures, and Resources. By D.O. Kellogg, One of its Merchants* (Troy: Young and Hartt, 1847): quotation at 5; Edward Augustus Holyoke Allen, excerpts from letters dated May 16, 1847 and July 26, 1847, in Edward Augustus Holyoke Allen papers, Box I, Folder 2 "Extracts of Letters from the RPI, 1847–1854," RPI.

41. *C.L. MacArthur's Troy City Directory for the Years 1854–55* (Troy: C. L. MacArthur, 1854), n.p.; Susan Grigg, "Willard, Emma Hart," American

National Biography Online; Rutherford Hayner, *Troy and Rensselaer County New York: A History*, vol. 1 (New York: Lewis Historical Publishing, 1925), 276–78; Palmer C. Ricketts, *History of Rensselaer Polytechnic Institute, 1824–1914* (New York: John Wiley and Sons, 1914), 32, 44–45, 59–60, 82–83, 91, 93–96, 101, 104–105, 108 (the name change was unofficial until 1861); Samuel Rezneck, *Education for a Technological Society: A Sesquicentennial History of Rensselaer Polytechnic Institute* (Troy: Rensselaer Polytechnic Institute, 1968), 59, 78–84, 100; S. Edward Warren, *Notes on Polytechnic or Scientific Schools in the United States; Their Nature, Position, Aims and Wants* (New York: John Wiley and Son, 1866), 8; Terry S. Reynolds, "The Education of Engineers in America before the Morrill Act of 1862," *History of Education Quarterly* 32, no. 4 (Winter 1992): 459–82; E. A. H. Allen, excerpt from letter dated 23 Oct. 1851, in Edward Augustus Holyoke Allen papers, Box I, Folder 2.

    42. *New England Historical and Genealogical Register*, lxiii, lxv; Ricketts, *History of Rensselaer Polytechnic Institute*, 97–98; Nason, *Biographical Record of the Officers and Graduates*, 140.

    43. SEW VIII: 130 (1 Jan. 1857); Nason, *Biographical Record of the Officers and Graduates*, 286–87; SEW II: 11 (footnote dated 11 May 1856); "Obituary Notes," *New York Times*, Jan. 13, 1896.

    44. SEW VII: 8–9 (5 Feb. 1854); SEW VII: 149–152 (15 Nov. 1855). Richard Stott, *Jolly Fellows: Male Milieus in Nineteenth Century America* (Baltimore: Johns Hopkins University Press, 2009), 19–20, 113–24; Helen Lefkowitz Horowitz, *Campus Life: Undergraduate Cultures from the End of the Eighteenth Century to the Present* (New York: Knopf, 1987), 32–36.

    45. SEW VIII: 22 (11 Jan. 1856); SEW VIII: 23–25 (18 Jan. 1856); SEW VIII: 111 (31 Aug. 1856); SEW VIII: 130–31 (1 Jan. 1857); Nason, *Biographical Record of the Officers and Graduates*, 129, 291.

    46. SEW VIII: 73–74 (6 June 1856); SEW VIII: 89–90 (n.d., 15 June 1856, or any of the following four days). The missing pages are SEW VIII: 75–80 and 83–88. Two George Hunts attended RPI in the late 1850s. This is the George Hunt who entered in February 1856, not the George M. Hunt who later became an instructor; Nason, *Biographical Record of the Officers and Graduates*, 169–70, 314. The preparatory classes are referred to in Rezneck, *Education for a Technological Society*, 32, 96.

    47. SEW VIII: 114–16 (21 Sept. 1856); SEW VIII: 125 (30 Oct. 1856); SEW VIII: 203 (31 Jan. 1858).

    48. SEW VIII: 140–41 (11 March 1857); SEW VIII: 131–32 (1 Jan. 1857); SEW VIII: 121–22 (11 Oct. 1856); SEW VIII: 123–24 (30 Oct. 1856); SEW VIII: 160–64 (24 April 1857); SEW VIII: 204–205 (n.d., evidently February, March, or April 1858). Warren had originally written "sad" to describe his acceptance, but then crossed it out and wrote "sober." Students did complain that faculty seldom "take cognizance of the student, when outside of the recitation room"; *Transit*, vol. 1, no. 1 (Dec. 1865), 35.

49. James T. Gardner to Mother [Anne Terry Gardiner], Oct. 14, 1859 and March 24 1860, Folder 4, Box 12 A, James Terry Gardiner Collection, William Croswell Doane Papers, SC11835, New York State Library, Albany; Arthur W. Bower diary for Sept. 9, 1867–April 11, 1868, in Arthur W. Bower Papers [MC10], Box 1, Folder 10, RPI: entries dated Sept. 14, 1867, Oct. 9, 1867, and Nov. 8, 1867. Arthur W. Bower diary beginning July 1, 1869, in Bower papers, Box 1, entry dated Nov. 20, 1869.

50. *New England Historical and Genealogical Register*, lxiii; Warren, *Notes on Polytechnic or Scientific Schools in the United States; Their Nature, Position, Aims, and Wants* (New York: John Wiley and Son, 1866); quotations at 14, 15, 48; S. Edward Warren, "On the Future Development of Scientific Education in America" [part one], *Journal of the Franklin Institute* 55, no. 4 (April 1868): 279, 280, 282; Warren, "On the Future Development . . ." [part four], *Journal of the Franklin Institute* 56, no. 4 (Oct. 1868): 277–80; 278; Warren, "On the Future Development . . ." [part five], *Journal of the Franklin Institute* 57, no. 3 (March 1869): 211; Warren, "On the Future Development . . ." [part nine], *Journal of the Franklin Institute* 58, no. 1 (July 1869): 63.

51. SEW VII: 51 (23 July 1854); "Secretary's Book, Div. A. RPI, class of 1861," entry dated March 7, 1861, Rensselaer Class Collection, 1852–1886 (AC 26) Box 1 Folder labeled "Class of 1861 (2)," RPI; "Buril [*sic*] of 'Descriptive,'" May 12, 1865, in Samuel Fields scrapbook, RPI; "A Glance at Windy's Book," *The Surveyor*, Feb. 24, 1866; "Notice," *The Surveyor*, Feb. 24, 1866; "Professor Warren's Pamphlet," *Rod & Leveller*, March 24, 1866; "Editors of the Polytechnic," *The Polytechnic*, Dec. 18, 1869.

52. *The Transit* 2, no. 3 (March 1872), 20.

53. Warren, "On the Future Development . . ." [part three], *Journal of the Franklin Institute* 56, no. 3 (Sept. 1868), 212; Warren, "On the Future Development . . ." [part five], 211; Warren, "On the Future Development . . ." [part six], 283; Warren, "On the Future Development . . ." [part nine], 63; SEW II: 3 (18 April 1849); SEW II: 80 (28 Oct. 1849); SEW VIII: 82 (15 June 1856); Peter J. Wosh, "Sound Morals and Unsound Bodies: Massachusetts Schools and Mandatory Physical Training," *New England Quarterly* 55, no. 1 (March 1982): 39–60; "Physical Training," *Massachusetts Teacher and Journal of Home and School Education*, March 1861; "What They Are Doing in the Colleges," *Herald of Health*, Aug. 1869.

54. Rough draft of a letter to Henry Freeman Allen, on bluish-gray paper in pencil, tucked inside front cover of SEW I, probably written on or shortly before 16 July 1858; see SEW VIII: 185 (20 July 1858).

## Chapter 3. Evangelism

1. Transcription of article from *Newton Journal*, April 4, 1885, in folder labeled "Gilbert, Rev. Lyman and Family: Manuscript & Miscellany," Gilbert

Family Papers, Box 2, Archives at Historic Newton, Newton, Mass.; Lyman Gilbert, *The Genius of Christian Religion: A Sermon, Preached at the Dedication of the New House of Worship, Erected by the Second Congregational Society in Newton, Ms., March 29, 1848* (Boston: T. R. Marvin, 1848), 15, 28; Address of the Rev. Joseph B. Clark, in *Celebration of the One Hundredth Anniversary of the Organization of the Second Church, Newton, Mass., at West Newton* (n.p.: 1881), 133.

2. Lyman Gilbert, 1847 sermon on the text of Jonah 1:6, folder labeled "Gilbert, Rev. Lyman and Family: Manuscript & Miscellany," Gilbert Family Papers.

3. William Breitenbach, "The Consistent Calvinism of the New Divinity Movement," *William and Mary Quarterly* 41, no. 2 (April 1984): 243; *The Confession of Faith, the Larger and Shorter Catechisms, with the Scripture-Proofs at Large, Together with the Sum of Saving Knowledge (Contained in the Holy Scriptures, and Held Forth in the Said Confession and Catechisms) and Practical Use Thereof; Covenants, National and Solemn League; Acknowledgment of Sins, and Engagement to Duties; Directories for the Public and Family Worship; Form of Church Government, & c., of Public Authority in the Church of Scotland* (Philadelphia: William S. Young, 1842), 29–30, 59–65.

4. William R. Sutton, "Benevolent Calvinism and the Moral Government of God: The Influence of Nathaniel W. Taylor on Revivalism in the Second Great Awakening," *Religion and American Culture* 2, no. 1 (Winter 1992): 24–25; Mark A. Noll, *America's God: From Jonathan Edwards to Abraham Lincoln* (New York: Oxford University Press, 2002), 297–99, 315.

5. William E. Channing, "The Moral Argument Against Calvinism," (1820) in *The Works of William E. Channing, D.D.*, First Complete American Edition, with an Introduction, Vol. I (Boston: James Munroe, 1841), 218, 222; quotation at 238.

6. George E. Ellis, *A Half-Century of the Unitarian Controversy* (Boston: Crosby, Nichols, 1857), 7, 14–15, 39, 84; Daniel Walker Howe, *The Unitarian Conscience: Harvard Moral Philosophy, 1805–1861* (Cambridge: Harvard University Press, 1970), 7, 53, 56, 59–63; Channing, "The Moral Argument Against Calvinism," 240.

7. Thomas H. Skinner and Edward Beecher, *Hints, Designed to Aid Christians in the Efforts to Convert Men to God*, 7th ed. (New York: Anson D. F. Randolph, 1858), 13; Howe, *Unitarian Conscience*, 163–64; Joseph F. Kett, "Growing up in Rural New England, 1800–1840," in *Growing up in America: Historical Experiences*, ed. Harvey Graff (Detroit: Wayne State University Press, 1987), 181.

8. John F. Kasson, *Rudeness & Civility: Manners in Nineteenth-Century Urban America* (New York: Hill and Wang, 1990); Stuart M. Blumin, *The Emergence of the Middle Class: Social Experience in the American City, 1760–1900* (New York: Cambridge, 1989).

9. Howe, *Unitarian Conscience*, 64; "Unitarian and Episcopalian Affinities," *New Englander* 3, no. 4 (Oct. 1845): 556–61, at 558; Barbara M. Cross, *Horace Bushnell: Minister to a Changing America* (Chicago: University of Chicago Press, 1958), 42, 89; James Thayer Addison, *The Episcopal Church in the United States, 1789–1931* (1951; Hamden, CT: Archon Books, 1969), 138; William Stevens Perry, "The Organization and Progress of the American Church," in *The History of the American Episcopal Church*, ed. Perry (Boston: James R. Osgood, 1885), 381.

10. On catechism, SEW I: 6 (27 Sept 1846); SEW I: 24 (3 Jan. 1847). The revival was enthusiastic enough to prompt a warning sermon from principal Samuel H. Taylor; SEW I: 31 (14 Feb. 1847). On reform efforts, SEW I: 23 (27 Dec. 1847); SEW I: 25 (11 Jan. 1847); SEW I: 26 (14 Jan. 1847); SEW I: 36 (6 March 1847); SEW I: 47 (23 June 1847). Blake is identified in *A Catalogue of the Trustees, Instructors, and Students of Phillips Academy, Andover, Mass., August, 1847* (Andover: William H. Wardwell, 1847), 13. The perils of coffee are mentioned in B. R. Burg, *An American Seafarer in the Age of Sail: The Erotic Diaries of Philip C. Van Buskirk, 1851–1870* (New Haven: Yale University Press, 1994), 29.

11. Warren's comment about Medbery's kindness appears in *New England Historical and Genealogical Register*, 1910, Vol. 64 (Boston: New England Historic Genealogical Society, 1910), lxv. Warren describes Baptist services at SEW I: 57 (9 April 1848), SEW I: 70 (21 May 1848), SEW I: 117 (18 Nov. 1848), and SEW II: 62 (16 Sept. 1849); the "dirty dock" quotation is at SEW I: 73 (4 June 1848). His description of the shivering converts appears at SEW II: 2 (15 April 1849). The passage refers to a service at the First Christian Baptist Church, led by the Rev. Daniel P. Pike. Warren's reactions to Higginson's sermons appear in SEW I: 58 (9 April 1848) and especially SEW I: 82 (2 July 1848). The clergymen and their churches are fully identified in John J. Currier, *History of Newburyport, Mass., 1764–1905*, vol. 1 (Newburyport, n.p.: 1906), 256, 291, and 298–99, with additional details from John E. Tilton, *The Newburyport Directory Containing a New Map of the Town . . . January, 1851* (Newburyport: John E. Tilton, 1850), 106. Higginson, who lasted at the First Religious Society for only two years before being asked to leave by his more conservative congregation, went on to become a nationally prominent abolitionist and author; for a short overview of his life, see Tilden G. Edelstein, "Higginson, Thomas Wentworth," *American National Biography Online*.

12. On Universalists and Congregationalists, SEW II: 73 (14 Oct. 1849). On Episcopalians and Baptists, SEW II: 85 (4 Nov. 1849). On Universalist theology, E. Brooks Holifield, *Theology in America: Christian Thought from the Age of the Puritans to the Civil War* (New Haven: Yale University Press, 2003), 218–23.

13. Warren mentions attending Congregational services led by Rev. Luther F. Dimmick at North Church, in SEW I: 60, SEW I: 68, SEW I: 147, SEW II: 38, and SEW II: 113. He mentions attending Rev. Randolph Campbell's

Prospect Street Church in SEW I: 140, SEW II: 26 and SEW II: 44. He mentions attending Rev. John E. Emerson's Whitefield Church in SEW I: 140, SEW II: 26, and SEW II: 44. The Whitefield Church met for a while in the Town Hall instead of in its own meeting house. Among the numerous references to services at the Rev. Jonathan F. Stearns's First Presbyterian Church are SEW I: 62, SEW I: 94, SEW I: 122, and SEW II: 55. The pastors and their churches are identified in Currier, *History of Newburyport*, 270, 276, 283, 304, and 307, with additional details from Tilton, *Newburyport Directory, 1851*, 104–106.

14. SEW I: 77 (18 June 1848), SEW I: 87 (9 July 1848), SEW I: 98 (22 Sept. 1848); SEW II: 1 (11 April 1849); SEW II: 6 (22 April 1849); SEW II: 8 (29 April 1849); SEW II: 18 (26 May 1849).

15. SEW II: 8 (29 April 1849); SEW II: 18 (27 May 1849); SEW II: 13 (13 May 1849); SEW II: 58 (9 Sept. 1849).

16. SEW II: 73 (14 Oct. 1849); Rufus B. Dodge, "Charlton," in *History of Worcester County, Massachusetts, with Biographical Sketches of Many of the Pioneers and Prominent Men*, Vol. 1, ed. D. Hamilton Hurd (Philadelphia: J. W. Lewis, 1889), 751.

17. Ann Douglas, *The Feminization of American Culture* (New York: Knopf, 1977); Ann Taves, "Mothers and Children and the Legacy of Mid-Nineteenth-Century American Christianity," *Journal of Religion* 67, no. 2 (April 1987): 203–19. For an overview of the early scholarship on the separation of men and women into "separate spheres," see Linda K. Kerber, "Separate Spheres, Female Worlds, Woman's Place: The Rhetoric of Women's History," *Journal of American History* 75 (June 1988): 9–39. The concept of separate spheres has been employed less frequently since 2000, as scholars have pointed out that the metaphor exaggerates gender divisions both in American culture and in daily life. See, for example, Cathy N. Davidson, "Preface: No More Separate Spheres!" *American Literature* 70, no. 3 (Sept. 1998): 443–63; and Shawn Johansen, *Family Men: Middle-Class Fatherhood in Industrializing America* (New York: Routledge, 2001), 7–8. The term *separate spheres* is conspicuously absent from an overview of American gender historiography published in 2012: Cornelia H. Dayton and Lisa Levenstein, "The Big Tent of U.S. Gender and Women's History: A State of the Field," *Journal of American History* 99, no. 3 (Dec. 2012): 793–817. Still, it is important to note what nineteenth-century Americans identified as male and female qualities, and we can do so without recourse to this problematic term.

18. Richard Rabinowitz, *The Spiritual Self in Everyday Life: The Transformation of Personal Religious Experience in Nineteenth-Century New England* (Boston: Northeastern University Press, 1989), 157, 188; Bruce Dorsey, *Reforming Men and Women: Gender in the Antebellum City* (Ithaca: Cornell University Press, 2002), 83–85; Bret E. Carroll, "The Religious Construction of Masculinity in Victorian America: The Male Mediumship of John Shoebridge Williams," *Religion and American Culture* 7, no. 1 (Winter 1997): 27–60; 33.

19. Mullin, *The Puritan as Yankee*, 49; Barbara M. Cross, *Horace Bushnell: Minister to a Changing America* (Chicago: University of Chicago Press, 1958), 21–23; Horace Bushnell, *Views of Christian Nurture, and of Subjects Adjacent Thereto* (Hartford: Edwin Hunt, 1847), 37; Horace Bushnell, *Unconscious Influence: A Sermon* (London: Partridge and Oakey, 1852), 14; Horace Bushnell, "The Eternity of Love," in *Spirit in Man: Sermons and Selections* (New York: Charles Scribner's Sons, 1903), 245.

20. Howe, *Unitarian Conscience*, 113; William E. Channing, "Likeness to God: Discourse at the Ordination of the Rev. F. A. Faley, Providence, R.I., 1828," in *People's Edition of the Entire Works of W. E. Channing, Complete in Two Volumes, Vol. I* (Belfast: Simms and M'Intyre, 1843), 614–17, esp. 614.

21. William E. Channing, "The Imitableness of Christ's Character" in *The Works of William Ellery Channing*, vol. 1 (London: Chapman, Brothers, 1844), 149–60, at 158; Horace Bushnell, "The Personal Love and Lead of Christ," in *Sermons for the New Life* (New York: Charles Scribner, 1858), 130; Bushnell, "Christ the Form of the Soul," in *Spirit in Man: Sermons and Selections*, 39–43.

22. Rabinowitz, *The Spiritual Self in Everyday Life*, 208–209; Sigma, "Christ the Best of Friends: 'There Is a Friend that Sticketh Closer than Brother,' No. 1," *Christian Reflector*, May 20, 1840; Mrs. Ellis, "David and Jonathan," *New York Evangelist*, Aug. 10, 1843; Helen M. Arion, 'The Friendship of Jonathan," *Ladies Repository*, April 1847; Discipulis, "Jesus," *New York Evangelist*, April 29, 1847; W. H. Furness, "Jesus and His Disciples," in *Beauties of Sacred Literature*, ed. Thomas Wyatt (Boston: James Munroe, 1848); "The Friendship of David and Jonathan," *National Magazine*, March 1855. A British example of this genre is Amicus, *The Friendships of the Bible* (London: Partidge and Oakley, 1853), an excerpt from which was reprinted as "Friendship of Jesus and John," *Christian Advocate and Journal*, Aug. 10, 1854. Scriptural quotations from 2 Samuel 1:26 and John 13:23.

23. T., "Friendship," *Christian Register and Boston Observer*, July 8, 1843; A. M. C. F., "Friendship," *Christian Watchman*, June 7, 1844; J. Britton, "Friendship; Its Nature and Office," *Evangelical Magazine and Gospel Advocate*, Jan. 30, 1846; Mark Hopkins, "Sermon Occasioned by the Death of Prof. Ebenezer Kellogg, October 11, 1846," in Hopkins, *Miscellaneous Essays and Discourses* (Boston: T. R. Marvin, 1847), 313–14, 319; "Perpetuity of Virtuous Friendship," *Trumpet and Universalist Magazine*, Feb. 6, 1847; W. S. B., "Affection Universal," *Crystal Fount and Rechabite Recorder*, May 1, 1847; Eloise, "Friendship," *Evangelical Magazine and Gospel Advocate*, Nov. 10, 1848; Rev. Dr. Van Arsdale, "Christian Friendship, Addressed to Mrs. S. V. R.," *Sartain's Union Magazine of Literature and Art*, Aug. 1850; Hardric Yelad (pseud.), "True Friendship—What Is It?" *Watch Tower*, Aug. 5, 1854; "True Friendship," *Christian Reformer and Signs of the Times*, Feb. 13, 1855. On Christian friendship in a broader context and in an earlier era, see Janet Moore Lindman, "'This Union of the Soul': Spiritual

Friendship among Early American Protestants," *Journal of Social History* 50, no. 4 (Summer 2017): 680–700.

24. SEW II: 58 (9 Sept. 1849); Skinner and Beecher, *Hints, Designed to Aid Christians*, 7, 20, 26, 41, 47, 50, 55, 57.

25. Skinner and Beecher, *Hints, Designed to Aid Christians*, 10–11; SEW II: 29 (13 June 1849); SEW II: 32 (17 June 1849); SEW II: 36 (21 June 1849); SEW II: 56 (4 Sept. 1849); Philip Doddridge, *The Rise and Progress of Religion in the Soul* (1745; New York: American Tract Society, 1840?).

26. SEW I: 31 (14 Feb. 1847); SEW I: 95–96 (8 Sept. 1848); SEW I: 147 (4 March 1849); SEW II: 10–11 (6 May 1849); SEW II: 23 (5 June 1849); SEW II: 44–45 (8 July 1849); SEW II: 52 (22 July 1849); SEW II: 62 (16 Sept. 1849).

27. SEW I: 52 (25 July 1847); Shawn Johansen, *Family Men: Middle-Class Fatherhood in Early Industrializing America* (New York: Routledge, 2001), 87; Nathan O. Hatch, *The Democratization of American Christianity* (New Haven: Yale University Press, 1989), 9, 22, 37; Paula S. Fass, *The End of American Childhood: A History of Parenting From Life on the Frontier to the Managed Child* (Princeton: Princeton University Press, 2016), 16–19; Horace Bushnell, *Views of Christian Nurture, and of Subjects Adjacent Thereto* (Hartford: Edwin Hunt, 1847), 19–20.

28. SEW VII: 27–28 (17 May 1854); SEW VII: 56 (13 Aug. 1854); SEW VII: 90 (5 March 1855); SEW VII: 97 (23 April 1855); SEW VII: 99 (27 April 1855); SEW VII: 102 (15 ? May 1855). "Clem" may have been T. Clement Haddock, who would have been fourteen years old in 1854; he was the son of Mrs. H. C. Haddock of Troy's Second Ward (1850 U.S. Census Schedules for Troy, via ancestry.com); Warren mentions a New Year's Day social visit to "Mrs. Haddock" in SEW VII: 7 (3 Jan. 1855).

29. SEW VII: 27 (17 May 1854); SEW VIII: 219 (9 May 1858); SEW VIII: 229 (16 July 1858); F. W. Beers, "Section 34: Portion of Rensselaer County and City of Troy," in F. W. Beers, *Atlas of the Hudson River Valley from New York City to Troy* (New York: Watson, 1891); Edward Augustus Holyoke Allen, typescript copy of letters dated May 16, 1847, and July 26, 1847, Edward Augustus Holyoke Allen papers (MC 61), Box 1 Folder 2, RPI; James T. Gardner to Mother [Anne Terry Gardner], 7 April 1860, Folder 4, Box 12 A, James Terry Gardiner Collection, William Croswell Doane Papers, SC11835, New York State Library, Albany.

30. SEW VII: 56 (13 Aug. 1854); SEW VII: 64 (30 Nov. 1854); SEW VII: 90–93 (5 March 1855), with quotations at 93; SEW VII: 97 (23 April 1855); SEW VII:1 02 (15? May 1855); SEW VII: 133 (19 Aug. 1855); SEW VIII: Slip of paper tucked between pages 182 and 183, referring to page 15 of the missing SEW VI. "Love one another with a pure heart fervently," is a biblical quotation from 1 Peter 1:22.

31. SEW VII: 77 (3 Jan. 1855); SEW VII: 121–24 (24 July, 27 July, and 5 Aug., 1855).

32. The word *sweet* is readily apparent before Willie's name in the index entry for p. 23, which appears in SEW VII: 157. Sweet William is a garden flower, *Dianthus Barbatus*, with showy blossoms and a spicy scent. New York State Census for Troy, NY, third ward, 1855, via ancestry.com; *C. L. MacArthur's Troy City Directory for the Years 1854–5* (Troy: C. L. MacArthur, 1854), 88; *Troy*, vol. 1 (New York: Sanborn, 1885), sheet 20B; SEW VII: index entries on 157; Rutherford Hayner, *Troy and Rensselaer County, New York: A History*, vol. 3 (New York: Lewis, 1925), 443–47; Henry B. Nason, ed., *Biographical Record of the Officers and Graduates of the Rensselaer Polytechnic Institute, 1824–86* (Troy: William H. Young, 1887), 100; Arthur James Weise, *Troy's One Hundred Years, 1789–1889* (Troy: William H. Young, 1891), 168–69, 172, 273, 326. The Union Railroad Depot was located on the north side of Broadway, east of Union Street; RPI was located on the west side of Eighth Street, on the side of the hill overlooking Broadway.

33. SEW VII: 16 (9 April 1854); SEW VII: 17–18 (15 April 1854).

34. The description of the early evening appears in SEW VII: 22 (26 April 1854). The passage from II Corinthians 3:18 is as follows: "But we all, with open face beholding as in a glass the glory of the Lord, are changed into the same image from glory to glory, even as by the Spirit of the Lord." Warren's address at 161 First Street, and Willie's at 54 Fifth Street can be determined from SEW VII: 20 (15 April 1854); and *C. L. MacArthur's Troy City Directory for the Years 1854–5* (Troy: C. L. MacArthur, 1854), 26 and 88. Warren's remarks on urban and village life appear in SEW VII: 54 (5 Aug. 1854). On the 1848 inauguration of gas lighting in Troy, see Weise, *Troy's One Hundred Years*, 162. On the phase of the moon, Damrell and Moore and George Coolidge, *Boston Almanac for the Year 1854* (Boston: John P. Jewett, [1854?]), 11. The missing sheet of paper is SEW: 23–24. Warren's incompletely effaced comment about Eighth Street appears in SEW VII: 44 (7 July 1854). Locations of St. Paul's church, distances, and directions are derived from the map titled "City of Troy, New York," Weise, 375. The index entry appears on SEW VII: 157. Willie's birth date, Jan. 14, 1839, is given in Hayner, *Troy and Rensselaer County*, 446. As suggested by the minimally restrictive "age of consent" laws noted in the introduction, nineteenth-century Americans did not share the twenty-first-century legal and cultural fixation on the boundary between the potentially sexual sixteen-year-old and the forbidden fifteen-year-old.

35. "Felix Flinder's Night Latch," [Lowell, Mass.] *Vox Populi*, Jan. 14, 1848.

36. SEW VII: 25–26 (n.d., April or May, 1854); 27 (9 May and 17 May, 1854); SEW VII: 36 (12 June 1854); SEW VII: 38 (12? June 1854); SEW VII: 55–56 (5 Aug. 1854); SEW VII: 61 (17 Sept. and 24 Sept. 1854).

37. SEW VII: 64–65 (30 Nov. 1854).

38. SEW VII: 75 (22 Dec. 1854).

39. SEW VII: 76 (25 Dec. 1854); SEW VII: 99 (27 April 1855); SEW VII: 100 (15 May 1855); SEW VII: 113–16 (19 June 1855).

40. SEW VII: 132–33 (19 Aug. 1855).

41. SEW VIII: 128 (1 Jan. 1857).

42. If Warren was indeed referring to Romans I: 27, then it is possible that he meant not just manual caressing but sodomy. As noted in the introduction, the theologian Moses Stuart in 1832 had interpreted that verse as referring specifically to sodomy. On the other hand, a more recently published work by Abiel Livermore interpreted the passage as condemning licentiousness broadly as well as sodomy specifically: *The Epistle of Paul to the Romans* (Boston: Crosby, Nichols, 1854), 97.

43. See for example O. S. Fowler, *Love and Parentage Applied to the Improvement of Offspring* (New York: Fowler and Wells, 1846), and R. T. Trall, *Home Treatment for Sexual Abuses, A Practical Treatise* (New York: Fowler and Wells, 1853).

44. SEW VII: 76 (22 Dec. 1854); SEW VIII: 96 (n.d., early July 1856); *Proceedings of the Centennial Anniversary of the First Presbyterian Church, Troy, N.Y., December 30 and 31, 1891* (Troy: Troy Times, 1892), 19–21; Nason, *Biographical Record*, 30–34; SEW VII: 64 (30 Nov. 1854).

45. Beginning of his drift into Episcopalianism identified in SEW VIII: 72 (6 June 1856); previous view on Episcopalianism expressed in SEW II; 85 (4 Nov. 1849). *New England Historical and Genealogical Register*, lxv; Addison, *The Episcopal Church in the United States*, 126, 154–57; Diana Hochstedt Butler, *Standing Against the Whirlwind: Evangelical Episcopalians in Nineteenth-Century America* (New York: Oxford University Press, 1995), 31–34, 137, 139, quotation at 34; Phillips Brooks, "A Century of Church Growth in Boston," in Perry, ed. *The History of the American Episcopal Church*, 498.

46. SEW VII: 55 (5 Aug. 1854); SEW VII: 87 (23 Feb. 1855); SEW VII: 135 (19 Sept. 1855).

47. SEW VII: 88 (23 Feb. 1855); SEW VII: 94 (5 April 1855); SEW VII: 98 (27 April 1855); SEW VIII: 19–20 (11 Jan. 1856); letter on bluish-gray paper to Henry Freeman Allen, n.d., in pencil, tucked inside front cover of SEW I. In a later draft of the letter, Warren likened the Episcopal Church to "a living, breathing friend appealing both to our souls and our senses," SEW VIII: 185–86, copy of letter dated 16 July 1858.

48. Joseph Blenkinsopp, *Sexuality and the Christian Tradition* (Dayton, OH: Pflaum Press, 1969), 10, 76–78, For Warren's comments on Paul, see inscription dated Aug. 12, 1871, in Georgiana Allen, "Visitors Book," 1865–1883, HBSC. First Corinthians, ch. 5–7, quotations at 6: 19 and 7: 9; Romans 1, especially

1: 27. Abiel Abbot Livermore, *The Epistle of Paul to the Romans* (Boston: Crosby, Nichols, 1854), 97; "Wilton," *Vermont Chronicle*, Dec. 9, 1892.

49. Richard Godbeer, *Sexual Revolution in Early America* (Baltimore: John Hopkins University Press, 2001), 54–60, 72–82, 240–41; Jonathan Edwards, *Thoughts Concerning the Present Revival in New England* (1743), quoted in Ann-Janine Morey, *Religion and Sexuality in American Literature* (Cambridge: Cambridge University Press, 1992), 25.

50. SEW VIII: 164 (24 April 1857); Cross, *Horace Bushnell*, 28; Joseph S. Buckminster, "The Introduction of the Affections into Religion," in *Sermons by the Late Rev. Joseph S. Buckminster, with a Memoir of his Life and Character*, 3rd ed. (Boston: Wells and Lilly, 1821), 200, 211; Horace Bushnell, "The War of Our Desires," [1848] in *Spirit in Man: Sermons and Selections* (New York: Charles Scribner's Sons, 1903): 369–70; Bushnell, "The Motions of Sins,"[1853] in *Spirit in Man*, 252.

51. Patricia Cline Cohen, "Ministerial Misdeeds: The Onderdonk Trial and Sexual Harassment in the 1840s," *Journal of Women's History* 7, no. 3 (Fall 1995): 34–57; Bruce Dorsey, " 'Making Men What They Should Be': Male Same-Sex Intimacy and Evangelical Religion in Early Nineteenth-Century New England," *Journal of the History of Sexuality* 24, no. 3 (Sept. 2015): 345–77, quotations at 352 and 361; Ian C. Pilarczyk, "The Terrible Haystack Murder: The Moral Paradox of Hypocrisy, Prudery, and Piety in Antebellum America," *American Journal of Legal History* 41, no. 1 (Jan. 1997): 25–60.

52. Cohen, "Ministerial Misdeeds," Nathaniel P. Willis's cynical quote at 48; Gary Scharnhorst, *Horatio Alger, Jr.* (Boston: Twayne, 1980), 29; Altina Waller, *Reverend Beecher and Mrs. Tilton: Sex and Class in Victorian America* (Amherst: University of Massachusetts Press, 1982); Karin E. Gedge, *Without Benefit of Clergy: Women and the Pastoral Relationship in Nineteenth-Century American Culture* (New York: Oxford University Press, 2003), 149–53, 168, 173, 195.

53. SEW VIII: 49 (2 March 1856); SEW VII: 54 (5 Aug. 1854); SEW VIII: 47 (1 March 1856); SEW VIII: 55 (23 April 1856); Butler, *Standing Against the Whirlwind*, 140–41; N. S. S. Beman, *Episcopacy Exclusive: Two Series of Letters, Being a Review of Dr. Coit's Sermon and Pamphlet* (Troy: L. Willard, 1856). The biblical quotation is John 8: 15: "Ye judge after the flesh; I judge no man." The roughly analogous verse in Matthew is the better known "Judge not that ye be not judged," from the Sermon on the Mount (Matthew 7:1).

54. Weise, *Troy's One Hundred Years*, 173, 176–78; Nason, *Biographical Record*, 100; "Fugitive Slave Rescue in Troy," *Liberator*, May 4, 1860; SEW VII: 99 (27 April 1855). On Uri Gilbert's friendliness to Warren, SEW VII: 29 (21 May 1854).

55. SEW VII: 26 (4 May 1854); SEW VII: 42 (n.d., evidently June 1854); SEW VII: 55 (5 Aug. 1854); SEW VII: 119 (15 July 1855); SEW VIII: 72 (6

June 1856). Warren wrote in 1865 that Willie was later confirmed at St. John's church, but fell away from religion and ceased to attend services; SEW VII: 16 (footnote dated 2 Nov. 1865).

56. Brooks, "A Century of Church Growth in Boston," 498; SEW VII: 5 (5 Feb. 1854).

57. SEW VII: 5 (5 Feb. 1854); SEW VII: 41 (n.d., June 1854); SEW VII: 43 (7 July 1854); SEW VII: 49 (9 July 1854); SEW VII: 55 (5 Aug. 1854); SEW VII: 65 (30 Nov. 1854).

58. SEW VII: 125–31 (12 Aug. 1855); Mark Hopkins, *God's Provisions and Man's Perversions: A Discourse, Delivered before the Congregational Library Association in the Tremont Temple, Boston, May 29, 1855* (Boston: T. R. Marvin, 1855); SEW VII: 127 (explanatory note dated 19 Nov. 1865).

59. SEW VII: 128 (12 Aug. 1855).

## Chapter 4. Fatherhood

1. SEW VII: 131 (19 Aug. 1855); SEW VII: 127 (explanatory note dated 19 Nov. 1865).

2. SEW VIII: 1–2 (1 Jan. 1856).

3. SEW VII: 116–17 (28 June 1855).

4. *Catalogue of the Officers and Pupils of the Troy Female Seminary for the Academic Year, Commencing Sept. 13 1854, & Ending June 27 1855, Together with the Conditions of Admittance &c.* (Troy: A. W. Scribner, 1855), 33; SEW VII: 116–18 (28 June 1855); SEW VII: 118 (2 July 1855, and footnote dated 19 Nov. 1865).

5. SEW VII: 118 (28 June 1855); SEW VII: 118 (2 July 1855). Another example of a social call: Emma Willard diary for 1864, entry dated Dec. 22, 1864, Emma Hart Willard Family Papers, Box 5, Folder 9, Amherst College Archives and Special Collections, Amherst, Mass.

6. SEW VIII: 2 (footnote dated 19 Nov. 1865); Samuel Warren, "Jephtha's Vow," *Bibliotheca Sacra* 24 (April 1867): 238–48; 246; Judges 11:39.

7. Stephen M. Frank, *Life with Father: Parenthood and Masculinity in the Nineteenth-Century American North* (Baltimore: Johns Hopkins University Press, 1998), 36, 86; Smith quotation at 95. Frank's interpretation differs somewhat from the findings of John Gilbert McCurdy, who finds a major transition in the Revolutionary era when bachelors gained a new acknowledgment of their mature self-control, and a new acceptance of their full equality with other men; McCurdy, *Citizen Bachelors: Manhood and the Creation of the United States* (Ithaca: Cornell University Press, 2009). SEW VIII: 1 (1 Jan. 1856).

8. SEW VIII: 102–103 (15 Aug. 1856); SEW VIII: 171–74 (25 Aug. 1857); SEW VIII: 204 (31 Jan. 1858?). Stephen Frank notes that "the duty to

provide goes a long way toward explaining the close identification of marriage itself with middle-class manhood"; Frank, *Life with Father*, 86.

9. "Waltham: Lamentable Accident," *Boston Journal*, Oct. 17, 1867; "Sad Accident," *Newton Journal*, Oct. 19, 1867; Arthur Bower Diary, Sept. 9, 1867–April 11, 1868, entry dated Oct. 16, 1867, Arthur W. Bower Papers (MC10), Box 1, Folder 1, RPI; *The Newton Directory* (Newton: C. C. Drew and H. N. Hyde, and Boston: Sampson, Davenport, 1868), 107; U.S. Census Schedules for Troy, NY, 1870, via ancestry.com; *New England Historical and Genealogical Register* 1910, Vol. 64 (Boston: New England Historic Genealogical Society, 1910), lxv; Edward (S. Edward Warren) to Henry (Henry Freeman Allen), Oct. 1, 1870, in Henry Freeman Scrapbook, Harriet Beecher Stowe Center, Hartford, CT; SEW to J. D. Runkle, June 2, 1871, John D. Runkle Papers, box 1, folder titled "Correspondence, June 1871," MIT.

10. SEW VII: 17 (15 April 1854); SEW VII: 85 (23 Feb. 1855); SEW VII: 137–38 (3 Oct. 1855); SEW VII: 148–49 (4 Nov. 1855); SEW VIII: 152–53 (5 April 1857); SEW VIII: 207 (21 Feb. 1858). The verse is Revelation 3:2: "Be watchful, and strengthen the things which remain, that are ready to die: for I have not found thy works perfect before God."

11. Mrs. P. A. [Phebe Ann] Hanaford, *The Young Captain: A Memorial of Capt. Richard C. Derby* (Boston: Degen, Estes, 1865), 31–32, 37–40; Mary A. Greene, *Nathaniel T. Allen: Teacher, Reformer, Philanthropist* (n.p.: 1906), 21; Damrell & Moore and George Coolidge, *Boston Almanac for the Year 1854* (Boston: John P. Jewett, [1854?]), 124, 140; John Oakley, untitled article, *St. James's Magazine* 2 (May 1763): 173–179; "The Man-Milliner," *European Magazine and London review*, 1 (March 1782): 166–68; Don Herzog, *Poisoning the Minds of the Lower Orders* (Princeton: Princeton University Press, 1998), 338; Richard Hofstadter, *Anti-Intellectualism in American Life* (New York: Vintage Books, 1962), 188; Brian Luskey, *On the Make: Clerks and the Quest for Capital in Nineteenth Century America* (New York: New York University Press, 2010), 84–88, 101–102.

12. Hanaford, *The Young Captain*, 45–60, 66–67; manuscript schedules for Minneapolis, Hennepin County, Minnesota Territorial Census of 1857, Ancestry.com; Richard C. Derby, business card of Richard C. Derby of George Frost and Company, in *Allen-Johnson Family Papers, 1759–1992* (Alexandria, VA: Alexander Street Press, 2010).

13. U.S. Civil War Draft Registration Records, 1863–1865, ancestry.com; Hanaford, *The Young Captain*, 63, 156; quotations at 184 and 187 (at the time of his death, the papers had already been signed for Dickey's promotion to captain); *Massachusetts Soldiers Sailors, and Marines in the Civil War*, vol. 2 (Norwood, MA: Norwood Press, 1931), 184; image of Dicky from Terry Johnston, "Ball's Bluff Remembered," *Civil War Monitor*, Oct. 21, 2011; https://www.civilwarmonitor.com/blogs/balls-bluff-remembered; accessed March 27, 2019; Richard C. Derby Will, April 24, 1861, proved Oct. 27, 1862, Suffolk County

Massachusetts Probate Records, Vol. 160, part 2 (1862), 44237, Massachusetts State Library, Boston.

14. Luskey, *On the Make*, 2–4, 14, 18, 177–205; Thomas Augst, *The Clerk's Tale: Young Men and Moral Life in Nineteenth-Century America* (Chicago: University of Chicago Press, 2003), 41–47; Bret E. Carroll, "The Religious Construction of Masculinity in Victorian America: The Male Mediumship of John Shoebridge Williams," *Religion and American Culture* 7, no. 1 (Winter 1997), 34.

15. Loretta Cody and the Rev. Sarah Barber-Braun, *A Mighty Social Force: Phebe Ann Coffin Hanaford, 1829–1921* (n.p.: 2009), 76; Hanaford, *The Young Captain*, 11, 191–94, 220–22.

16. SEW VII: 57 (20 Aug. 1854 and footnote dated 12 Nov. 1865); SEW VII: 6 (1 Jan. 1858, and footnote dated 19 Nov. 1865).

17. SEW VIII: 91 (28 June 1856); SEW VIII: 198 (31 Jan. 1858); Thoughts I: 37 (5 Dec. 1858).

18. Henry D. Thoreau, *Walden* (New York: Harper and Brothers, 1950), 147; William E. Channing, *Self-Culture. An Address Introductory to the Franklin Lectures, Delivered at Boston, September, 1838* (Boston: J. Munroe, 1839); SEW VII: 72–74 (22 Dec. 1854). On Chapin's popular oration, "The Ideal and the Actual," see "Institute Lecture," *Hartford Courant*, Feb. 7, 1850, and "Rev. Dr. Chapin's Second Lecture before the Maryland Institute," *Baltimore Sun*, Jan. 6, 1853.

19. John Todd, *The Young Man. Hints Addressed to the Young Men of the United States*, 2nd ed. (Northampton [MA]: 1845), 139–41, 257; quotation at 141; Francis Wayland, *The Elements of Moral Science* (1835; Boston: Gould, Kendall, and Lincoln, 1845), 301–302; George W. Burnap, *Lectures to Young Men, on the Cultivation of the Mind, the Formation of Character, and the Conduct of Life: Delivered in Masonic Hall, Baltimore* (Baltimore: John Murphy, 1840), 110–11; Henry Ward Beecher, *Lectures to Young Men, on Various Important Subjects* (Salem, John P. Jewett, 1846), 207, 209, 212; Rev. Daniel Wise, *The Young Man's Counsellor: Or, Sketches and Illustrations of the Duties and Dangers of Young Men* (New York: Carlton and Porter, 1850), 204, 212; Thomas W. Laqueur, *Solitary Sex: A Cultural History of Masturbation* (New York: Zone Books, 2003), 220–21.

20. Daniel C. Eddy, *The Young Man's Friend* (Boston: Dayton and Wentworth, 1855), 113; Wise, *The Young Man's Counsellor*, 164–67; E. L. Magoon, "Scenery and Mind," in *The Home Book of the Picturesque: Or, American Scenery, Art and Literature* (New York: G. P. Putnam, 1852), 7; Thoughts I: 3 (8 Aug. 1858).

21. SEW VII: 56 (5 Aug. 1854); SEW VIII: 22 (11 Jan. 1856); SEW VIII: 200 (31 Jan. 1858); Thoughts I: 39–40 (7 Dec. 1858).

22. SEW VII: 75 (22 Dec. 1854); SEW VII: 135 (19 Sept. 1855).

23. SEW VIII: 2–4 (1 Jan. 1856). I am grateful to Jessica Linker for deciphering the concealed passage.

24. SEW VIII: 2–4 (1 Jan. 1856). The initials "D. R. B." appeared in SEW VII: 95 (15 April 1855), SEW VII: 102 (15 May 1855), and VII: 133 (19 Aug. 1855), in reference to a group of boys that Warren calls "our Brotherhood" in SEW VII: 19 (15 April 1854) and "the brotherhood" in SEW VII: 56 (13 Aug. 1854).

25. SEW VIII: 22 (11 Jan. 1856). Underlining in the original.

26. SEW VIII: 236 (18 July 1858); David B. Dearinger, "Palmer, Erastus Dow," *American National Biography Online*.

27. Thoughts I: 27 (3 Oct. 1858); Thoughts I: 53 (17 Jan. 1859); Thoughts I: 94 (23 Oct. 1859); Thoughts II: 25–26 (17 Feb. 1861); Thoughts II: 91 (6 July 1862). The first quotation is from Matthew 18:8. The second is from Romans 6:12.

28. Thoughts II: 1 (2 March 1860); Thoughts II: 13 (9 Aug. 1860). The supposedly emasculating effect of slavery was a frequent point of criticism at the time, though antislavery writers differed; some suggested, approvingly, that blacks were inherently "the feminine race of the world." Mia Bay, *The White Image in the Black Mind: African American Ideas about White People, 1830–1925* (New York: Oxford University Press, 2000), 14–15, 72; George M. Fredrickson, *The Black Image in the White Mind: The Debate on Afro-American Character and Destiny, 1817–1914* (1971; Middletown, CT: Wesleyan University Press, 1987), 114–15.

29. Heather Love, *Feeling Backward: Love and the Politics of Queer History* (Cambridge: Harvard University Press, 2007).

30. Thoughts II: 87 (21 Apr. 1862); Thoughts II: 19 (22 Oct. 1860).

31. SEW VII: 96 (15 April, 1855); S. Edward Warren entry dated May 28, 1868, Georgiana Allen "Visitors Book," 1865–1883, Harriet Beecher Stowe Center.

32. Thoughts I: 76 (n.d., possibly 10 May 1859).

33. Thoughts I: 80–82 (22 May 1859); Frank, *Life with Father*, 123–27. The Socrates anecdote appeared in "Artists' Excursion," *Harper's Monthly*, June 1859, 11. Bushnell's words on the subject appear in the 1861 edition of *Christian Nurture* but not the 1847 original; Horace Bushnell, *Christian Nurture* (New York: Charles Scribner, 1861), 341.

34. Thoughts I: 82 (22 May 1859); Thoughts I: 47 (19 Dec 1858); Thoughts I: 62 (25 March 1859); Thoughts II: 37–38 (6 April 1861).

35. SEW VIII: 217 (17 April 1858). The 1860 U.S. Census for Troy's Second Ward, dated June 30, 1860 (via ancestry.com), lists Walter Thompson as being nine years old, which would make him six or seven years at the time of the journal entry. The term *pet*, as defined in Webster's dictionary in 1857, meant "a babe or little thing" or "a fondling; any little animal fondled and indulged"; Noah Webster and Chauncey A. Goodrich, *An American Dictionary of the English Language* (Springfield, MA: George and Charles Merriam, 1857),

819. Katherine Grier observes that two key aspects of the pet were "proximity and the importance of touch"; Katherine C. Grier, *Pets in America: A History* (Chapel Hill: University of North Carolina Press, 2006), 6. An example of editing: SEW VII: 96 (15 April, 1855).

36. SEW VIII: 7 (1 Jan. 1856). Josephine Louise Gilbert ("Josie") was approaching her fifth birthday; Frances Adelaide Gilbert ("Addie") was fourteen; Rutherford Hayner, *Troy and Rensselaer County, New York: A History*, vol. 3 (New York: Lewis Historical Publishing, 1925), 446. Julia Adancourt is listed as being two years old when the New York State Census was taken in her part of Troy's First Ward on June 11, 1855; 1855 New York State Census for Troy, via ancestry.com. Warren's unguarded statements may lead some readers to wonder whether he was a pedophile. First, it is important to note, as does the twenty-first-century psychiatric profession, that there is a crucial distinction between those who have acted on sexual desire for prepubescent children and those who have merely thought about it. Second, it is debatable whether even Warren's thinking displays a tendency to pedophilia, as defined by the *Diagnostic and Statistical Manual of Mental Disorders*. No surviving journal passage describes an unambiguously sexual interest in a prepubescent child. Some researchers have defined adult sexual interest in pubertal teenagers as "hebephilia" and an interest in newly post-pubertal teenagers as "ephebophilia." (These terms are controversial and neither has been officially recognized as a category of mental disorder.) Warren's interests were overwhelmingly ephebophilic by these definitions. As an adult, he devoted far more space in the pages of his journals to desires and regrets concerning youths aged fifteen and up, whereas younger children were mentioned in passing and with less emotion. "Pedophilic Disorder," in American Psychiatric Association, ed., *Diagnostic and Statistical Manual of Mental Disorders, Fifth Edition* (Arlington, VA: American Psychiatric Association, 2013): 302.2 (F65.4); http://dx.doi.org/10.1176/appi.books.9780890425596; Patrick Singy, "Hebephilia: A Postmortem Dissection," *Archives of Sexual Behavior* 44, no. 5 (July 2015): 1109–16.

37. SEW VIII: 219 (9 May 1858); SEW VII: 140 (3 Oct. 1855); Sylvester Graham, *Graham's Lectures on Chastity* (Glasgow: Royalty Buildings, 1837), 33–34.

38. "Smoke-Outs," "The Pretty Girls of Troy," and "The Troy Female Seminary on Parade," *Rod and Leveller*, Nov. 18, 1865; "To the High School Ladies," *Rod and Leveller*, Dec. 2, 1865; "Two Faces at the Window," *Rod and Leveller*, Jan. 13, 1866; "The Students' Boarding Houses. Paper III.–Brewsterian," and "Drinking Song," *Rod and Leveller*, March 24, 1866; "An R.P.I. Flirtation," *Surveyor*, Dec. 23, 1865; "Ode to Lager," and "Seminary Struck," *Surveyor*, Feb. 24, 1866; Untitled item on Troy Female Seminary, *Surveyor*, March 17, 1866; Arthur W. Bower diary for 1869–70, 63–64 (entry dated Nov. 12, 1869), Arthur W. Bower Papers, RPI.

39. Undated slip of paper inside front cover of SEW VIII.

40. Undated slip of paper between pages 182 and 183 in SEW VIII.

41. Thoughts II: 55 (26 July 1861); Thoughts II: 59 (28 July 1861); Thoughts II: 73 (18 Aug. 1861); Thoughts II: 82–84 (1 Nov. 1861).

42. Copy of letter from Edward to Henry, dated July 16, 1858, in SEW VIII: 185–86; "Rev. Dr. H.F. Allen Dead," *Boston Daily Globe*, June 13, 1914; *Harvard University Quinquennial Catalogue of the Officers and Graduates 1636–1930* (Cambridge: Harvard University, 1930), 262; Andrew D. Mullen, "Stowe, Calvin Ellis," *American National Biography Online*; John Gatta, "The Anglican Aspect of Harriet Beecher Stowe," *New England Quarterly* 73, no. 3 (Sept. 2000): 423–24; Harriet Beecher Stowe to Hattie and Eliza Stowe, April 6, 1863, Beecher-Stowe Family Papers, folder 123, Arthur and Elizabeth Schlesinger Library on the History of Women in America, available online at http://pds.lib.harvard.edu/pds/view/43769689; Joan D. Hedrick, *Harriet Beecher Stowe: A Life* (New York: Oxford University Press), 322.

43. Untitled news item, *Pittsfield Sun*, March 30, 1865; Inscriptions by S. Edward Warren dated Sept. 9, 1865, Sept. 8, 1866, May 28, 1868, 25 Dec. 1868, and Aug. 12, 1871, Georgiana Allen "Visitors Book," Harriet Beecher Stowe Center, Hartford; S. Edward Warren to Henry Freeman Allen, Oct. 1, 1870, in Henry Freeman Allen Scrapbook, HBSC; Harriet Beecher Stowe to Hattie, Oct. 25, 1870, and Harriet Beecher Stowe to Hattie and Eliza, Oct. 30, 1870, Beecher-Stowe Family papers, folder 151, HBSC.

44. SEW VIII: 203 (n.d., possibly 31 Jan. 1858); SEW II: 2 (notation dated 11 May 1856); Thoughts II: 66 (7 Aug. 1861); SEW VII: 116 (notation dated 19 Nov. 1865).

45. Frank, *Life with Father*, 24–26, 31–34; Johansen, *Family Men*, 19, 88; Ann Taves, "Mothers and Children and the Legacy of Mid-Nineteenth-Century American Christianity," *Journal of Religion* 67, no. 2 (Apr. 1987): 211; Heman Humphrey, *Domestic Education* (Amherst: J. S. and C. Adams, 1840), 16, 23–24; A. B. Muzzey, *The Fireside: An Aid to Parents* (Boston: Crosby, Nichols, 1854) 9, 11; Horace Bushnell, *Christian Nurture* (New York: Charles Scribner, 1861), 341; Robert L. Griswold, *Fatherhood in America: A History* (New York: Basic Books, 1993), 11–13.

46. SEW VII: 87 (23 Feb. 1855); William Ellery Channing, "Discourse at the Ordination of the Rev. Jared Sparks, Baltimore, 1819," in *The Works of Wm. Ellery Channing, D.D.*, Vol. II (Glasgow: James Hedderwick and Son), 68, 69; Joseph Tuckerman, *The Principles and Results of the Ministry at Large in Boston* (Boston: James Munroe, 1838), 203.

47. E. Brooks Holifield, "Let the Children Come: The Religion of the Protestant Child in Early America," *Church History* 76, no. 4 (Dec. 2007): 771; Taves, "Mothers and Children," 205, 207. A stiff, formal tone prevailed in occasional pieces about God the Father that appeared in Episcopalian publications; for example, O. P. B., "Our Father," *Churchman*, Sept. 22, 1838; Yelverton Read,

"Our Father," *Churchman*, Dec. 17, 1842; "God Our Father," *Church Chronicle and Record*, Sept. 27, 1844; "The Child of God," *Churchman*, Feb. 24, 1855.

48. Richard Godbeer, *Sexual Revolution in Early America* (Baltimore: Johns Hopkins University Press, 2002), 52, 55, 79; Elizabeth Maddock Dillon, "Nursing Fathers and Brides of Christ: The Feminized Body of the Puritan Convert," in *The Centre of Wonders: The Body in Early America*, ed. Janet Moore Lindman and Michele Lise Tartar (Ithaca: Cornell University Press, 2001): 129–43; Frederick S. Roden, *Same-Sex Desire in Victorian Religious Culture* (Hounds Mills, UK, and New York: Palgrave Macmillan, 2002), 5, 14–20, 125. Martha Vicinus, writing about English lesbian relationships in the later nineteenth century, observes that in the life of her subject "the experience of erotic desire—and emotional support—became for Mary Benson a model of divine love." Benson, she writes, imagined Christ in feminized terms as a good mother. Vicinus, "'The Gift of Love': Nineteenth-century Religion and Lesbian Passion," *Nineteenth-Century Contexts* 23, no. 2 (2001): 241–64; 242.

49. Thoughts I: 68 (April 24 1859); Thoughts I: 82 (22 May 1859).

50. The eleven-line erasure appears in SEW VII: 59 (probably 20 Aug. 1854), preceding the following statement: "I was very much interested yesterday in looking over my first journal, some traits of my character are often shown there, which I did not recognize as fixed principles." The excised pages are 1–4, 23–24, and 39–40; the mutilated leaf is pp. 103–104. The index quotations come from p. 157, and refer to the entries in SEW VII: 23 (16 Apr. 1854), and SEW VII: 30 (probably 25 June 1854). The beginning of the 25 June entry is still in the volume, on p. 29, but is mostly effaced by scribbles and erasures. Willie's birthday, Jan. 14, 1839, is given in Rutherford Hayner, *Troy and Rensselaer County, New York: A History*, vol. III (New York: Lewis Publishing, 1925), 446.

51. SEW VIII: 198–99 (31 Jan. 1858).

52. SEW VIII: 203 (31 Jan. 1858). The missing pages, 75 through 80, deal with June 1856. There is no record of what they contained, though it is possible that at least the first of the missing pages continued to discuss the topic at the bottom of p. 74.

53. S. Edward Warren, *A Manual of Drafting Instruments and Operations* (New York: John Wiley and Sons, 1865), 31–32. He also discusses the blade erasure method in Thoughts I: 51–52 (16 Jan. 1859).

54. Several short passages in Volume II and the second Thoughts diary were photographed at the University of Connecticut's Thomas J. Dodd Research Center in January and May, 2014, by Mark R. Smith of Macroscopic Solutions, LLC, using a focus stacking technique that generates extremely high resolution images, thus allowing each letter to be examined at the microscopic level. Smith describes the process as follows: "Panoramic images are comprised of focus stacked frames, which have been stitched together to show individual lines of text. The focus stacked frames each contain approximately 30 individual focal planes

stitched together along the z-axis for unlimited depth-of-field viewing. Panoramic and focus stacked imagery were collected and processed with the Macropod imaging system by Macroscopic Solutions." (Emails to author from Mark R. Smith, January26 and 27, 2015). The composite images were then manipulated for further scrutiny by the author and Jessica Linker, using Adobe Photoshop software. Longer passages in the journals were merely scanned at high resolution with ordinary scanners by staff at the Dodd Center, the Winterthur Library, and RPI, and manipulated by the author and Jessica Linker using Adobe Photoshop. Most of the original wording could not be recovered with either method.

55. SEW VII: 60 (20 Aug. 1854?). The alterations to the bedroom scene with John, in SEW II: 25 (8 June 1849), are undated, though other changes in that volume were dated Oct. 1, Oct. 10 and Oct. 20, 1865; another revision to that same page is dated Oct. 10.

56. Description of the pretty boy is from SEW VII: 60 (17 Sept. 1854); Warren used the same word to describe another boy in SEW I: 90 (16 July 1848), but without any attempt at erasure. An example of thin cross-hatchings can be seen at SEW II: 1 (11 April 1849); "progress" quotation at SEW VIII: 1 (1 Jan. 1856); SEW VIII: 198 (31 Jan. 1858).

57. On the death of the elder Samuel Edward Warren in 1867, see "Died," *Boston Daily Advertiser*, Oct. 28, 1867.

58. SEW II: 9; SEW II: 20.

59. SEW II: 29 (13 June 1849 entry and 10 Oct. 1865 footnote); SEW II: inside front cover (20 Oct. 1865).

60. An insightful undergraduate student at the University of Connecticut, Danielle Toto, was the first to characterize the diary as having dual authorship. Given that Warren lived until 1909 (through the emergence of scientific writing about "homosexuality" in the late nineteenth century and the diminished latitude for sexual ambiguity that followed the Oscar Wilde trial of 1895), it is also possible that he decided near the end of his life that the surviving journals revealed behavior that had become unacceptable. A late purging of his papers might explain the absence of the remaining journal volumes. In this way, the emergence of modern concepts of homosexuality could have put its mark on a collection of documents produced a half-century earlier.

61. SEW VIII: 199 (31 Jan. 1858).

## Epilogue

1. Warren began preparing the manuscripts in 1856; *New England Historical and Genealogical Register*, 1910, Vol. 64 (Boston: New England Historic Genealogical Society, 1910), lxv. He ended up published thirteen distinct textbooks with John Wiley & Sons, with many revisions, multiple editions, occasional changes in

title, and some overlapping content. Warren wrote all but the last two of these textbooks during his years as a professor at the Rensselaer Polytechnic Institute and the Massachusetts Institute of Technology. The following list gives their dates of first publication: (1) *General Problems from the Orthographic Projections of Descriptive Geometry* (1860); (2) *A Manual of Elementary Geometrical Drawing* (1861); (3) *A Manual of Elementary Problems in the Linear Perspective of Form and Shadow* (1863); (4) *A Manual of Drafting Instruments and Operations* (1865); (5) *Plane Problems in Elementary Geometry* (1867); (6) *General Problems of Shades and Shadows* (1867); (7) *General Problems in the Linear Perspective of Form, Shadow, and Reflections* (1868); (8) *Elements of Machine Construction and Drawing* (1870); (9) *An Elementary Course in Free-Hand Geometrical Drawing* (1873; later reissued as *Elements of Plane & Solid Free Hand Geometrical Drawing*); (10) *Elements of Descriptive Geometry, in Three Parts* (1874; later reissued as *Problems, Theorems & Examples in Descriptive Geometry*); (11) *Stereotomy—Problems in Stonecutting* (1875); (12) *Elements of Descriptive Geometry, Shadows & Perspective* (1877); (13) *Primary Geometry: With Simple and Practical Examples in Plane and Projection Drawing* (1887). Some of these continued to be reprinted into the 1890s and even 1900s. Book #2 on the list went through at least thirteen editions. Books 11 and 12 in this list were reprinted as late as 1911, two years after Warren's death. Warren also wrote *Notes on Polytechnic or Scientific Schools in the United States* (New York: John Wiley & Sons, 1866), *The Sunday Question, or, The Lord's Day* (Boston: Earle, 1890), and several pamphlets and articles on matters of pedagogy and religion.

    2. Samuel Rezneck, *Education for a Technological Society: A Sesquicentennial History of Rensselaer Polytechnic Institute* (Troy: Rensselaer Polytechnic Institute, 1968), 143–63; Palmer C. Ricketts, *History of Rensselaer Polytechnic Institute, 1824–1914* (New York: John Wiley and Sons, 1914), 108–109.

    3. Rezneck, *Education for a Technological Society*, 137, 144–45, 163; SEW VIII: 102 (15 Aug. 1856) and 145 (footnote dated 10 Dec. 1865); SEW, "Memoranda of Items of Repair and Outfit Desired at Once . . .", March 11, 1865, RPI Board of Trustees Papers 1854–1901 (AC7), box 2, folder 1, RPI; SEW to Board of Trustees, Dec. 11, 1865, RPI Trustees Papers, box 2, folder 1; SEW to Board of Trustees, Sept. 21, 1868, RPI Trustees Papers, box 1, folder 11; SEW to James Forsyth and Board of Trustees, March 30, 1871, RPI Trustees Papers box 2, folder 1; Henry Morton to De Volson Wood, March 24, 1871, Presidents of Stevens Institute of Technology collection, 1870–2010 (Dr. Henry Morton's correspondence series), Special Collections, S. C. Williams Library, Stevens Institute of Technology, Hoboken, NJ; *New England Historical and Genealogical Register*, lxv.

    4. J. D. Runkle to W. B. Rodgers, Aug. 2, 1870, William B. Rogers Papers, folder 65, MIT; Philip N. Alexander, *A Widening Sphere: Evolving Cultures at MIT* (Cambridge: MIT Press, 2011), 68–69; SEW to J. D. Runkle, June

2, 1871, John D. Runkle Papers, box 1, folder titled "Correspondence, June 1871," MIT; Committee on the School of Industrial Science minutes for Dec. 29, 1871, MIT Corporation Executive Committee reel 1, volume 1: "Committee on the School of Industrial Science, Dec. 21 1871–Sept. 29, 1883," MIT; SEW to James Forsyth, June 15, 1872, RPI Trustees Papers, box 1, folder 11, RPI.

    5. Henry B. Nason, ed., *Biographical Record of the Officers and Graduates of the Rensselaer Polytechnic Institute, 1824–86* (Troy: William H. Young, 1887), 140 (Because of changes in the municipal boundaries, Warren recalled, the house on Washington Street was first in Brighton, then Boston, then finally in Newton.); Samuel C. Prescott, *When M.I.T. Was "Boston Tech," 1861–1916* (Cambridge: The Technology Press, 1954), 55, 90–91; *Massachusetts Institute of Technology, Reports of the President, Secretary and Departments. 1871–72* (Boston: A. A. Kingman, 1872), 3; *Massachusetts Institute of Technology, President's Report for the Year ending Sept. 30, 1874* (Boston: A. A. Kingman, 1875), vi; *Massachusetts Institute of Technology, Eighth Annual Catalogue of the Officers and Students with a Statement of the Courses of Instruction. 1872–73* (Boston: A. A. Kingman, 1872), 6–8; Rezneck, *Education for a Technological Society*, 483. Though the institute was not commonly called "MIT" until the twentieth century, I use the modern abbreviation here for simplicity; Alexander, *A Widening Sphere*, 23.

    6. *Massachusetts Institute of Technology, President's Report for the Year ending Sept. 30, 1873* (Boston: A. A. Kingman, 1873), xi; entries dated Oct. 10, 1872, Dec. 21, 1872, Jan. 11, 1873, Jan. 18, 1873, Feb. 4, 1873, May 10, 1873, and Sept. 30, 1873, "Records of the Faculty of the School of the Massachusetts Institute of Technology," MIT Faculty Collection, Series I, Minutes Vol. 1, MIT; XYZ, "A Suggestion," *Spectrum*, March 8, 1873, MIT; pamphlet titled *Class '74 Mass. Institute Technology* (Boston: Todd, printed for the class, 1875), in William E. Nickerson scrapbook, American Antiquarian Society, Worcester, MA; An Observer, "Words to the Point," *Spectrum*, Dec. 6, 1873, MIT; "Differences between the catalogue . . . and the tabular view as adopted on Jan. 30, 1874," inserted after p. 34 in "Volume II of the Records of the Faculty of the School of Industrial Science, of the Massachusetts Institute of Technology," Faculty Collection, Series I, Minutes Vol. 2, MIT. Warren admitted to difficulties maintaining classroom discipline at RPI in SEW II: 82–83 (footnote dated 2 Oct. 1865). Closing quotation, probably a paraphrase of Warren's own words, is from Nason, *Biographical Record*, 140.

    7. *Massachusetts Institute of Technology, President's Report for the Year ending Sept. 30, 1874* (Boston: A. A. Kingman, 1875), iii, vi; *Massachusetts Institute of Technology, President's Report for the Year ending Sept. 30, 1875* (Boston: A. A. Kingman, 1876), vii; *New England Historical and Genealogical Register*, lxiii; J. D. Runkle to William B. Rogers, Jan. 17, 1875, William B. Rogers Papers, Folder 70, MIT; Committee on the School of Industrial Science minutes for April 2 and June 8, 1875, MIT Corporation Executive Committee reel 1, volume 1, MIT.

8. *New England Historical and Genealogical Register*, lxiii; Charles Riborg Mann, *A Study of Engineering Education: Prepared for the Joint Committee on Engineering Education of the National Engineering Societies* (New York: National Engineering Societies, 1918), 6; *Thirty-Seventh Annual Report of the Board of Education, Together with the Thirty-Seventh Annual Report of the Secretary of the Board, 1872–73* (Boston: Wright and Potter, 1874), 41; Isaac Edwards Clark, *U.S. Department of the Interior, Bureau of Education, Art and Industry: Education in the Industrial and Fine Arts of the United States, Part I: Drawing in Public Schools* (Washington: Government Printing Office, 1885), 163; flyer titled *Lecture and Private Instruction*, tucked inside a pamphlet by S. Edward Warren, *Question and Suggestion [sic] Concerning Industrial Drawing as a Branch of Education*, American Antiquarian Society, Worcester, MA; Committee on the School of Industrial Science minutes for June 20, 1873, MIT Corporation Executive Committee reel 1, volume 1, MIT.

9. *New England Historical and Genealogical Register*, lxiii. The two textbooks first published after 1875 were *Elements of Descriptive Geometry, Shadows, & Perspective* (1877) and *Primary Geometry: With Simple and Practical Examples in Plane and Projection Drawing* (1887). The language about his connection to RPI but not MIT appears in the title pages of those books. It also appears in the 1883 edition of *Problems, Theorems, and Examples in Descriptive Geometry*, a revised version of his earlier *Elements of Descriptive Geometry, in Three Parts*, and in the 1895 edition of *Elements of Machine Construction and Drawing*. SEW, *Stereotomy: Problems in Stone Cutting* (New York: John Wiley and Son, 1875).

10. Will dated July 1861 and Executor's Inventory dated Jan. 2, 1868, in Middlesex County probate records for Samuel Warren, no. 44010, Massachusetts State Archives, Boston; Executor's Inventory filed Oct. 14, 1889, in Middlesex County probate records for Ann C. Warren, no. 26605, Middlesex County Probate and Family Court, Cambridge, Mass.; executor's account dated July 2, 1913, Middlesex County probate records for S. Edward Warren, no. 82704, Middlesex County Probate and Family Court; http://www.measuringworth.com; accessed March 25, 2019.

11. *The Newton Directory*, no. IX (Worcester: Drew Allis, and Boston: Sampson, Murdock, 1885), 316; *The Newton Directory*, no. XIV (Worcester: Drew Allis, and Boston: Sampson, Murdock, 1895), 513; *The Newton Directory*, no. XXI (Worcester: Drew Allis, and Boston: Sampson, Murdock, 1909), 617; *New England Historical and Genealogical Register*, lxiv–lxv; SEW, "Graphic Science in Text-Book and Teaching," *Papers Read before the Pi Eta Scientific Society, 1878–9, Rensselaer Polytechnic Institute, Troy, N.Y.* (Troy: Pi Eta Scientific Society, 1879), 5–11; SEW, *The Sunday Question or The Lord's Day: Its Sacredness, Permanence, and Value as Shown by its Origin, History, and Use* (Boston: James H. Earle, 1890); SEW, "Stoles and Color Laws," *Churchman*, Jan. 16, 1886; SEW, "Moral Instruction in Schools," *Canada Educational Monthly*, March 1895, 87–92; reader's

report and editorial decision on manuscript by S. Edward Warren, 1900, No. 8393, Houghton Mifflin Company reader reports on manuscripts submitted for publication, Houghton Library, Harvard University; Bruce L. MacDonald, *Grace Church Newton Corner, 1855–1906* (Newton: n.p., 1997), 62; emails to author from Don Kennedy, parish historian, Grace Episcopal Church, Sept. 8 and Sept. 14, 2013; Nason, *Biographical Record,* 146.

12. *New England Historical and Genealogical Register,* lxv; Nason, *Biographical Record,* 146; gravestone for Samuel Edward Warren and Margaret M. Warren, Newton Cemetery; U.S. Census manuscript population schedules for Newton, Mass., dated June 11, 1880 and April 21, 1910, ancestry.com; "Intentions of Marriage Entered in the City of Newton, Mass.," dated Nov. 2, 1884, in "Massachusetts, Town and Vital Records, 1620–1988," ancestry.com; SEW, will dated July 1, 1904, Middlesex County probate records for S. Edward Warren.

13. Toby L. Ditz, "The New Men's History and the Peculiar Absence of Gendered Power: Some Remedies from Early American Gender History," *Gender and History* 16, no. 1 (April 2004): 2, 3; SEW, will dated July 1, 1904; U.S. Census manuscript population schedule for Newton, Mass., dated June 1, 1900, ancestry.com.

14. Newton Cemetery, "History," https://www.newcemcorp.org/history; David Charles Sloane, *The Last Great Necessity: Cemeteries in American History* (Baltimore: Johns Hopkins University Press, 1991), 56.

15. Sloane, *Last Great Necessity,* xxii, 2, 15, 20–22, 44, 46–47, 72, quotation at 75; James J. Farrell, *Inventing the American Way of Death, 1830–1920* (Philadelphia: Temple University Press, 1980), 106–107.

16. This paragraph is based largely on discussions of the afterlife in works by two nineteenth-century Episcopal clergymen: the Rev. John Henry Hobart and the Rev. Benjamin Dorr. John Henry Hobart, *The State of the Departed: An Address Delivered at the Funeral of the Rt. Rev. Benjamin Moore* (1816; New York; H. B. Durand, 1864), esp. 5, 9–10; Benjamin Dorr, *The Recognition of Friends in Another World,* 3rd ed. (Philadelphia: R. S. H. George, 1840), 18–19, 47–51. Additional material comes from 1 Corinthians 15:52–53; and 1 Thessalonians 4:16.

# Index

Abbott, Jacob, 21, 28–29, 53
Adams School, Boston, 50–51
Allen, Edward A.H., 57, 86
Allen, Freeman, 119
Allen, Georgiana Stowe, 119
Allen, Henry Freeman, 33, 94, 106, 119
Allen, James T., 57
Allen, Joseph, 107
Allen, Nathaniel T., 25, 34, 57, 107
Alger, Horatio, Jr., 96
American Tract Society, 20–21
Andover, Mass., 20, 56
Andover Theological Seminary, 21, 27, 56, 78, 119
Andrews, Jenny, 44, 83, 126
Avery, Ephraim, 96

bachelorhood, 3, 104, 135
Bagley, John A., 34, 43–46, 58, 67, 70, 83–84, 124
Balch, Isaac Denny, 40, 41, 44
Barrett, Samuel, 51
Beckwith, George C., 50
bed sharing, American practices of, 33, 46, 47
Beecher, Edward, 77–78, 82–84, 90
Beecher, Catharine, 53
Beecher, Henry Ward, 30, 87, 96–97, 111

Beecher, Lyman, 92, 119
Beman, Nathan S.S., 92, 97, 98
Bigelow, Jacob, 39
Blake, Philip, 78
Blunt, John E., 40–41, 43, 79
body-soul dualism, 4, 14, 74, 92, 94–95, 113–14, 138
Boston Normal Art School, 133
Boston school controversy, 52, 59
Bower, Arthur, 71–72, 118
Buckminster, Joseph, 95
Bunyan, John, 25, 30, 90
Bushnell, Horace, 81–82, 84, 85, 94–96, 117, 121

Calvinism, 53, 54, 56, 76–77, 93, 102, 121
Channing, William Ellery, 52–53, 77, 81–82, 111, 121
Chapin, Edwin H., 111
Charlton, Mass., 60–61, 64, 80
childhood and youth, American ideas about, 13, 19–23, 85, 104–105
Christ, ideas about, 21, 52–53, 77–78, 81–84, 90, 93–94, 121–22
Clem, 86–87
Coit, Thomas W., 94, 97
Congregationalism, 27, 53, 55, 76–81, 93, 95, 96, 99

185

Conkling, Roscoe, 107

Damon and Pythias, friendship of, 22
David and Jonathan, friendship of, 82, 109
Davis, Seth, 50
daydreaming, 110–12
Derby, Elias Hasket (1766–1826), 26
Derby, Elias Hasket (1796–1840), 26, 34
Derby, Mary Ann Allen, 26, 38, 107–109
Derby, Richard C. ("Dicky"), 23, 26–27, 31, 33–35, 37–40, 43, 55, 70, 87, 106–109, 118
diary keeping, American practices of, 5, 7, 27–29, 31
Doddridge, Philip, 83
Drowne, Charles, 130
Dry River Brotherhood, 85–87, 113, 118

Edwards, Jonathan, 95
Emerson, George B., 58–59
Emerson, Ralph Waldo, 30, 111
emotions, American ideas about, 11, 16, 22–23, 32, 81, 83, 95–97, 111
Episcopal Church, 78, 93–94, 97, 99
evangelical friendships, 14

Fairbank, Josiah, 50
family size, 24
fatherhood and parental authority, 12, 81, 85, 117, 120
fellatio, 10
Finney, Charles G., 92
Fiske, Daniel T., 79
friendship, American ideas and practices, 11, 14, 19–23, 82–83
Fuller Academy, Newton, 50, 54

Fuller, Arthur B., 108, 109

Gale, Walter, 108
gender, American ideas about, 12–13, 22, 46, 62, 80, 97, 109
Gilbert, Addie
Gilbert, Lyman, 54–55, 76–77
Gilbert, Uri, 87, 97
Gilbert, William Eaton, 86–92, 98–102, 113, 123
Greene, Benjamin Franklin, 68

Hanaford, Phebe, 109
Hawthorne, Julian, 25
Hawthorne, Nathaniel, 25, 26, 96
heart religion, 12, 80–81, 100
Higginson, Thomas Wentworth, 79
Hobart, John Henry, 98
homosexuality, concepts of, 2, 8–9, 46
Hopkins, Mark, 99
Hunt, George, 68–70, 74, 162n46
Hunt, T. Sterry, 132

James, John Angell, 19–20
Jephthah, 104
journal keeping. *See* diary keeping.

Kalloch, Isaac, 96
Kirby, Katharine W., 102–104

Lamson, Samuel, 40
Lancaster, Joseph, 58
Lawrence Academy, Groton Mass., 38
letter writing, 32
Livermore, Abiel Abbot, 95
Locke, John, 51, 58
Loveland, George, 103
Lunt, Micajah (1796–1874), 45
Lunt, Micajah, Jr. (1832–1865), 43–47, 84

Magoon, Elias L., 111
Mann, Horace, 50–55, 59, 60, 62, 64
masculinity, American, 12–13, 22, 46, 107, 109, 135
Massachusetts Board of Education, 52–53
Massachusetts Institute of Technology (MIT), 7, 130–33
Massachusetts State Normal Schools, 53–54
  at Barre, 54
  at Bridgewater, 43, 57
  at Lexington, 54
  at West Newton, 25, 43, 54
masturbation, 9, 10, 46–47, 91
Medbery, Nicholas, 41, 46, 79
Medfield, Mass., 34
miniature portraits, 31
Muzzey, Artemas Bowers, 121

Nalle, Charles, 97
Newburyport, Mass., 35–36
Newman, John Henry, 98, 122
Newton Cemetery, 136–37
Newton, Mass., 24–25, 54

Onderdonk, Benjamin T., 93, 96, 97

Palmer, Erastus Dow, 113–14
parental authority. *See* fatherhood
Paul (Apostle), 91, 94, 95, 114
Peabody, Ephraim, 34
Peirce, Cyrus, 52, 54–55
Pestalozzi, Johann, 51, 58
Phillips Academy (Andover), 19, 21, 24, 27, 39–40, 55–57, 78
Potter, Alonzo, 58–59
Presbyterian Church, 79, 92–93, 99
Putnam Free School, 35, 36–37, 40, 57–58, 61, 72, 79
Putnam, Oliver, 36, 58

rape, forcible and statutory, 10
religious literature, 19–21, 80–83, 86, 111
Rensselaer Polytechnic Institute (RPI), 49, 57, 66, 102, 118, 129–30
Rice, Lewis F., 71
Romantic friendships, 2, 11, 39
Runkle, John D., 130–32

schools
  common, 59–60, 63, 64
  discipline, 41, 51–53, 56–64
  European, 41, 51
Shaw, Mary Ann, 58, 61, 62
Sherman, Eleazar, 96
Shinn, George W., 134
Skinner, Thomas, 77–78, 82–83, 90
Smith, Matthew Hale, 55
sodomy, 3, 9, 10, 46–47, 95
Stevens Institute of Technology, Hoboken N.J., 130
Stowe, Calvin E., 51, 53, 119–20
Stowe, Harriet Beecher, 119
Stuart, Moses, 9

Taylor, Samuel H., 56
Thoreau, Henry David, 110, 111
Thomson, Walter, 117
Todd, John, 111
Tractarian movement, 93, 97
Troy, N.Y., 1, 65–66, 87, 88, 129
Troy Female Seminary, 66, 102–103, 118
Tuckerman, Joseph, 121
Tweeddale, William, 103

Unitarianism, 11, 34, 39, 52–56, 77–78, 121
Universalism, 79

Van Buskirk, Philip, 46–47

Warren, Ann Catherine Reed, 6, 24, 99, 106, 131, 133–35
Warren, Margaret Miller, 134–35
Warren, Samuel Edward (1802–1867), 6, 24, 55–56, 98–100, 102, 104–106, 120, 133–34
Warren, Samuel Edward (1831–1909)
  antislavery views, 86, 93, 97, 115
  biographical outline, 6–7
  conversion to Episcopal Church, 75–76, 87, 92–94, 97–100
  education of, 50–51, 54–59, 66, 78
  employment as schoolteacher, 59–65
  employment at MIT, 7, 73, 130–33
  employment at RPI, 6, 67, 73, 105, 129–31
  fatherhood, ideas about, 15, 62, 101, 109, 116, 118–22
  friendship, ideas and practices, 13–15, 33–34, 37–47, 67–74, 83–91, 98, 106–107, 109–13, 115–17, 120, 126
  interactions with children, 1, 15, 40, 65, 85–87, 116–18, 127, 176n36
  journal keeping, 3–7, 15, 31, 44, 62–63, 65, 69, 88–89, 99, 109–13, 118, 122–27
  letter writing, 32–33, 42, 89, 106
  marriage to Margaret Miller, 7, 134–35
  masculinity, ideas and experiences of, 12–13, 46, 64, 68, 74, 86, 100, 101, 105–106, 115, 118
  published works, 72–74, 105, 124, 129, 134, 179–80n1
  reading, 30, 34, 58, 82, 83, 86, 116
  relationship with parents, 27, 98–101, 104–106, 126
  religious ideas and practices, 1–4, 13–15, 34–35, 37–39, 69–71, 75–76, 78–80, 82–95, 97–107, 111–22, 134
  sensuality, ideas about, 14, 89, 90, 93–94, 112–15, 120
  sexuality and physical affection, 11, 13–14, 33–34, 44–47, 84, 88–91, 112–15, 127
  teaching beliefs and practices, 49–50, 58–74, 131–34
  women and marriage, ideas about, 46, 102–104, 119, 123, 126, 135
Wells, William H., 37, 40, 56–57
West Newton, Mass. *See* Newton
West Newton Model School, 25, 38, 50, 54–56
Whipple, Jonathan Francis, 40–44, 73, 79, 102
Wood, Augusta E., 41–44, 47, 73, 102, 103, 126
Wood, Clarina, 41, 47

www.ingramcontent.com/pod-product-compliance
Lightning Source LLC
Chambersburg PA
CBHW031253230426
43670CB00005B/173